SLOW FOOD

Also Available from Bloomsbury:

Food Activism, Edited by Carole Counihan and Valeria Siniscalchi
Food Values in Europe, Edited by Valeria Siniscalchi and Krista Harper
Making Taste Public, Edited by Carole Counihan and Susanne Hojlund

SLOW FOOD

THE ECONOMY AND POLITICS
OF A GLOBAL MOVEMENT

Valeria Siniscalchi

BLOOMSBURY ACADEMIC
LONDON • NEW YORK • OXFORD • NEW DELHI • SYDNEY

BLOOMSBURY ACADEMIC
Bloomsbury Publishing Plc
50 Bedford Square, London, WC1B 3DP, UK
1385 Broadway, New York, NY 10018, USA
29 Earlsfort Terrace, Dublin 2, Ireland

BLOOMSBURY, BLOOMSBURY ACADEMIC and the Diana logo are trademarks of
Bloomsbury Publishing Plc

First published in Great Britain 2023

Copyright © Valeria Siniscalchi, 2023

Valeria Siniscalchi has asserted her right under the Copyright, Designs and Patents Act, 1988, to
be identified as Author of this work.

Cover design: Terry Woodley
Cover image © Franco Zecchin

All rights reserved. No part of this publication may be reproduced or transmitted in any form or by
any means, electronic or mechanical, including photocopying, recording, or any information
storage or retrieval system, without prior permission in writing from the publishers.

Bloomsbury Publishing Plc does not have any control over, or responsibility for, any third-party
websites referred to or in this book. All internet addresses given in this book were correct at the
time of going to press. The author and publisher regret any inconvenience caused if addresses
have changed or sites have ceased to exist, but can accept no responsibility for any such changes.

A catalogue record for this book is available from the British Library.

Library of Congress Control Number: 2022948381

ISBN: HB: 978-1-4742-8232-1
PB: 978-1-4742-8244-4
ePDF: 978-1-4742-8234-5
eBook: 978-1-4742-8233-8

Typeset by Deanta Global Publishing Services, Chennai, India
Printed and bound in Great Britain

To find out more about our authors and books visit www.bloomsbury.com and
sign up for our newsletters

In memory of my father, Massimo, whose curious, ironic and dreamy spirit continues to accompany me

CONTENTS

List of Illustrations		viii
Preface		ix
1	Negotiating Fieldwork: How to Study Food Activism?	1
2	From Politics to Gastronomy and Back: Where Did Slow Food Come From?	21
3	Power and Governance: How Is the World of Slow Food Governed?	43
4	Inside the Italian Association	59
5	Autonomy and Dependence: The Internationalization of Slow Food	83
6	The "Black Box.": How Does the Slow Food Machine Really Work?	101
7	Gastronomic Biodiversity: How Are the Environment and Food Connected?	123
8	Cheese Regulations: Political Battles and Economic Interests Inside the Presidia Project	143
9	Inclusion and Exclusion: The Political Taste of Slow Food	157
10	Politics at the Dinner Table and in the Vineyards	171
11	Real and Imagined Economies and Politics in Action: Terra Madre, Salone del Gusto, and Cheese	191
12	The Pragmatic Utopia of Food Activism: Coping with Ambiguity	211
Bibliography		227
Index		237

ILLUSTRATIONS

Figures

11.1	Terra Madre and the Salone del Gusto localization from 2004 to 2010 and the different places of the Presidia stands	207
11.2	The changing places and status of the makeshift market by small Terra Madre producers	208

Photos

1	Badges collected during the fieldwork	xiv
2	Lunch during one of the events organized by Slow Food: Slow Fish, Genoa (Italy), 2013	20
3	The president of Slow Food with a restaurateur and the director of the University of Gastronomic Sciences, after a political meeting, 2013	42
4	Slow Food's headquarters: The entry of the Italian association offices, Bra (Italy), 2012	58
5	A political meeting of a French convivium, Gap (France), 2012	82
6	Banner "Casa Slow Food" (Slow Food house), in Via Mendicità Istruita, the location of Slow Food's headquarters, Bra (Italy), 2017	100
7	Aromatic herbs' smell workshop, Cagliari (Italy), 2011	122
8	Roberto, a *Fiore Sardo* cheese producer, Ovodda (Italy), 2018	142
9	Tasting cheese and wine. A *laboratorio del gusto*. Cheese, Bra (Italy), 2017	156
10	Alessio inside his *osteria*, San Marco dei Cavoti (Italy), 2012	170
11	Visitors and Presidia exhibitors in the "Via dei Presidi," Cheese, Bra (Italy), 2017	190
12	Poster illustrating the Slow Food Network, the association's components, the key words of the movement, and the main projects. Bra (Italy), 2013	210

Table

4.1	Members and leaders	62

PREFACE

In the year 2000, after spending much of the previous decade in the Campania region of southern Italy where I was doing ethnographic research in economic anthropology, I decided to embark on a new project in the Hautes-Alpes department in France. At the time, I was still living in Rome (where I was born) while teaching at La Sapienza University, so the road trip to the French town of Gap took me up the Italian peninsula and through the Langhe, a part of northern Italy with which I was not very familiar. I stopped for a few days to visit the towns of Alba, Cherasco, Barolo, and Barbaresco: names I knew primarily because of the wines produced there. During the visit, I bought a couple of food and wine guides and some of Slow Food's publications. As an Italian, I was of course aware of the association. Slow Food's media presence was already strong in Italy even if it had not yet achieved the notoriety it developed in the following years. As I read through the books I had picked up, I was intrigued by the passages about producers, intellectuals, the local economy, food policy, and events organized by Slow Food. Even then I began to think that perhaps I had taken a wrong turn, and instead of going to France I should be starting an ethnographic research there in northern Italy. But the French fieldwork was already in place, so I placed my curiosity on a back burner, telling myself that a project involving Slow Food could wait. Nevertheless, I continued to cultivate an interest in it while I continued my planned fieldwork on the French side of the Alps.

A dear and now deceased friend in France, André Pitte, knew about my interests and often talked to me about Slow Food. In those years he had started a local Slow Food group in the Drôme department, and in 2003 he went to Bra—which is the location of Slow Food's headquarters—to participate in Cheese, one of the events that Slow Food organizes. He returned with brochures, documents, and everything else that he thought might interest me. Along with my Langhe guidebooks, the literature he brought from the event in Bra constituted my initial literary introduction to the Slow Food world. At this point I had left Italy and was living in Marseille while teaching anthropology at the neighboring campus in Aix-en-Provence before obtaining a position in the École des hautes études en sciences sociales (EHESS). Another friend and research colleague from Aix-en-Provence, Dionigi Albera, was born in the Langhe region and was able to put me in touch with the organizers of Terra Madre, a biennial event organized by Slow Food that takes place in tandem with the association's Salone del Gusto in Turin. This was during the preparation for the second edition of the event which would take place in 2006. The event attracted about five thousand delegates: small producers, farmers, ranchers, and fishermen from all over the world. Among the objectives that year was a commitment to extend the association's network to academics and university teachers whose research

Preface

interests were linked to food and other related themes which had become part of the movement's focus: the environment, local economies, sustainability, biodiversity. It was in this capacity as the French academic delegate, together with other members of the French association, that I had my first experience with Terra Madre and the Salone del Gusto (events organized by Slow Food).

When I returned to Marseille, the leader of the local Slow Food convivium and member of the French national board, Lucien Biolatto, knowing that I had participated in Terra Madre, invited me to participate in the meetings and events that he organized in the area. Another friend and previous national board member, Mike Tommasi, had been involved in setting up national meetings and then worked with Lucien in the organization of local events. These two men were among my first guides within the French association, but gradually I met others who were, or had been, active or had political roles in the movement. There was Eugenio Mailler who had had several years of work experience in Bra, in the international office; then Jean Lhéritier, Gilbert Della Rosa, Philippe Rostain, Didier Chabrol, Michel Chauvet, and numerous others. Between 2007 and 2008 I followed the activities of the Marseille convivium and then the Gap convivium; I participate as an observer in the meetings of the French Ark of Taste (committee to select products for protection), a second Salone del Gusto and Terra Madre in 2008, and (between 2009 and 2011) Slow Food France's national board meetings (*conseil d'administration*). During this period, I interviewed members, leaders, and the administrative staff of the French association. In 2009, I finally started my fieldwork in the association's headquarters in Bra (Italy) which also houses the Slow Food Foundation for Biodiversity, the offices of the International association and the Italian national association. This had been my goal from the beginning, but the anticipated long periods of fieldwork in Bra were delayed by family and work obligations.

As it happened, the "local" fieldwork in France turned out to be much more than just a way to make contacts and prepare for the more intense research at the heart of the movement. Although closely linked to the Italian structure from a symbolic, historical, and economic point of view, Slow Food in France functioned differently than in Italy and in some ways dramatically so. First observing Slow Food through the activities of two French convivia, one in an urban setting, the other in the mountains, and analyzing the function of a national structure allowed me to understand many of the dynamics in the international Slow Food movement that I would not have grasped in the same way had I started directly at the association's headquarters. Being a bilingual Italian who has continued to navigate between Italy and France from a private and professional point of view, I have certainly benefited from this advantageous position for understanding the French context as well as the Italian society and culture.

From 2009 to 2014 I stayed for extended periods in Bra at Via Mendicità Istruita, where Slow Food's historic headquarters is located, accumulating around twenty-four months in the field. I followed the daily lives of the people who construct and coordinate this polymorphous and, in some ways, opaque phenomenon that is Slow Food. I spent time with employees and leaders in the offices, attended the frequent meetings that characterized those years, and traveled with the staff to national and international meetings. Benefiting from the advantage of "participant observation"—as anthropologists call this specific type of fieldwork—I followed the different political entities governing the various parts and levels of the association, and finally, I was backstage, observing the preparation and execution of the events that I had initially attended as a "foreign" delegate. I could make a list of the hundreds of formal interviews and the important number of official and unofficial meetings I attended, but what counts even more was the sharing of daily life, the informal exchanges, the fact of living with the people who were the subject of my research. Thirteen of my articles and book chapters on Slow Food, published from 2010 to the present, formed the first foundation of this book.[1]

In 2011, three months as a visiting professor at the University of Cagliari allowed me to expand my understanding of the Slow Food world from the point of view of a single region, Sardinia, in a different part of Italy. The months spent in Sardinia allowed me to interview local leaders and provided an opportunity to gather firsthand knowledge from producers linked to the movement, particularly those involved in the six Sardinian *presidia* (products labeled by Slow Food): the *Fiore Sardo* cheese, the *Pecorino di Osilo* cheese, the *Casizzolu* cheese, the *Pompia* (a candied citrus fruit), the San Gavino's Safron, and the *Bue rosso* (the red ox of the Sardinian-Modican breed). Some of these Slow Food producers and members became travel friends and "guides" for research in subsequent years, Anna Sulis, Roberto Logias, and Salvatore Bussu, among others.[2]

An important element in this research process was meeting Carole Counihan, a dear friend and colleague, who had been working on the subject of Slow Food at the same time. When two anthropologists meet in the field or find they are not the only one working on some topic, problems can sometimes arise. But Carole and I have made our research complementary and have profited from frequent cooperation and fruitful exchanges. In Sardinia, Carole did research with local *condotte* leaders, and then on forms of food activism that included Slow Food but have developed well beyond the movement (Counihan 2019). Our meeting was the beginning of a long collaboration and sharing of ideas that led to our organization of panels at the annual meeting of the American Anthropological Association (AAA) in 2010 and 2011. Following those meetings and thanks to the network of researchers working on mobilizations in the field of food production and consumption, we edited a book, *Food Activism. Agency, Democracy and Economy*, published in 2014. It constitutes, in some respects, the starting point of the reflections that I develop in these pages. I would like to thank Carole for supporting with affection the long stages of this work from the beginning and for her rigorous and careful re-reading of this manuscript.

Other panels and meetings at the AAA and the European Association of Social Anthropologists (EASA) and invitations for conferences or through the visiting professors' program at US universities—from Carole Counihan, Krista Harper, Richard Wilk, Susans Terrio, Jaqueline Urla—and in Italy—from Filippo Zerilli, Franco Lai, Cristina Papa—were all valuable opportunities to share and enhance reflections on Slow Food. My seminars at EHESS, where I teach Anthropology of Economies and Anthropology of Mobilization (and until a few years ago, Anthropology of Economic Spaces), and discussions with graduate and PhD students have been rich spaces in which

Preface

to test several ideas that I cover in this monograph. The seminar on the Anthropology of Economic Regulations that Birgit Müller and I spent two years coordinating and the workshop on the values related to food that Susana Narotzky and I organized have allowed me to refine my reflections on the research. The invitation of Krista Harper for three consecutive years through the EHESS visiting professor program and the intellectual exchange that her presence in Marseille allowed us to develop were important elements in the elaboration of this volume. The book that Krista Harper and I edited, *Food Values in Europe*, presents still other perspectives on consumer and producer movements, perspectives which nourished those developed in these pages. I would like to warmly thank all of these colleagues and companions in research, and Krista more particularly.

A warm thank you goes to my friends in Slow Food who accepted me within the walls of the movement's headquarters and tolerated my presence with patience and affection, who often expressed interest and curiosity about my work, and with whom I had many valuable intellectual exchanges. The time I spent among them was always a rich experience, from both a personal and intellectual point of view. The list is too long to name them all here, but they will recognize their contribution in the pages of this book. I must offer a special thanks to Silvio Barbero, Laura Bonino, Gino Bortoletto, Roberto Burdese, Salvatore Ciociola, Valeria Cometti, Fabrizio Della Piana, Paolo Di Croce, Alberto Fabbri, Barbara Forno, Fabiana Graglia, John Irving, Maria Mancuso, Michèle Meisman, Serena Milano, Paola Nano, Fabio Palladino, Carlo Petrini, Mauro Pizzato, Raffaella Ponzio, Serena Rinaldi, Piero Sardo, and Cinzia Scaffidi: they are among the people I spoke with the most. The majority of these companions, all in their own way, thought that my work was useful. With some of them, the experience represented a road traveled together which left traces of affection and friendship far more important than this book. Over the years, I am sure a number of them thought this book would never be finished. I have to thank Piero Sardo also for the nickname, *Spia* (Spy), that I gladly carried during the years of research.

A special thought goes to two dear people with whom I shared points of view and journeys within the Slow Food world and who have passed away: Antonello del Vecchio, for years Slow Food leader of one of the South Italian regions, an attentive, clever, and generous person. And Ursula Hudson, a dear friend, met in a food line during my first participation in Terra Madre, years before she became the president of a national Slow Food association. Exchanges with her were always intellectually rich and joyful.

The B&B "L'ombra della Collina" and the family of Giovanni Chiesa were my home and adopted family for several years: their hospitality, their affection, our long discussions, and our humorous disputes about vegetables and frozen foods have been more important than they may realize.

A special thanks to Ben Boswell who helped me with my English skills during the writing. He helped translate or revise much of the text that finally made its way into this book. His intervention did not only allow this book to be published in English: he helped me to clarify the three languages in which it was conceived, English, Italian, and French, and his advice as an attentive reader was invaluable in clarifying what I say in these pages.

I would like to thank the anonymous reviewers for their advice and encouragement, and Geneviève Marotel for our long discussions about food and activism.

Last but not least, I would like to thank my husband, Franco Zecchin, and my son, Adriano Zecchin, who have supported and sustained this multiyear project from the beginning to the end: a project made of long absences at first and then long periods of writing. Without their affective, material, and intellectual contributions, this book would never have seen the light of the day. When I was working on my previous book, *Food Activism*, my son said to me "mom, what an idea you had to write a book, having a son of my age to take care of! You should have waited until I was fifteen. At that age I would need my mom less." I can't say that the time spent between the years of research and the publication of this book was a direct response to his request, but I can add it among the credible reasons.

The cover photo depicting a Sicilian food festival and the images at the beginning of each chapter are by Franco Zecchin. Choosing an image for the cover that synthesizes the varied aspects of Slow Food was not easy. Unlike the chapter photos which were taken in the field, the cover photo is not directly related to Slow Food, but for me, it reflects the essence of the Slow Food saga. This volume is an analysis of Slow Food life from behind the stage, far from the glossy image that the movement uses in its communication tools. In this metaphorical image I can see the diversity in the world of Slow Food, the individuals that live it, the cheerful and ironic dimensions, the competition and power dynamics, and, of course, the food.

Notes

1. The fieldwork was funded in large part by a first research grant from the EHESS and two subsequent projects supported by the French Provence-Alpes-Côte-d'Azur Region. The translation of parts of this text was funded by the LabexMed project.

2. The research on the political and economic life of Sardinia PDO cheeses (from 2017 to 2020) was part of the project Vipomar, *La vie politique des marchandises*, funded by the French National Agency for research (ANR).

Photo 1 Badges collected during the fieldwork. ©Franco Zecchin.

CHAPTER 1
NEGOTIATING FIELDWORK
HOW TO STUDY FOOD ACTIVISM?

"Slow Food is a political movement," "Slow Food is an association of gourmets," "Slow Food is a global network," "it is an NGO," "Slow Food moves large amounts of money": in one sense or another, these statements are all true, but none really describes what Slow Food is. I have long been intrigued by the opacity of this object, by its visible contradictions, and by the passionate commitment of members, employees, and leaders, many for whom Slow Food is "their life." For this reason, I spent several years immersed in its daily life, attempting to understand its frictions, tensions, and fracture lines.

These introductory pages are not intended, nor the book itself, to define once and for all what Slow Food is. Here, I attempt to situate Slow Food in the broader context of contemporary producer and consumer movements, dialoguing with some of the rich literature that exists on Slow Food. I then introduce the specifics of my fieldwork inside this particular object of study. The following chapters explore the practices and visions of the protagonists and the various dimensions of Slow Food from an anthropological perspective. I analyze the mechanisms, the logics, and the dynamics at work within the complex machine that is Slow Food at particular moments in its recent history (corresponding to the years of my fieldwork, between 2006 and 2014). Exploring the tensions that characterize its inner functioning, my analysis also helps to explain some of the transformations that have occurred over time and what Slow Food has become today. Hopefully, this also provides keys to the analysis of other experiments in the field of food activism.

What Slow Food is, and what it is not?

In the larger landscape of food activism, peasant movements, and alternative consumer movements, Slow Food is a difficult phenomenon to grasp. First and foremost, it is an international association with dues-paying members and statutes that regulate its functioning. Slow Food members and leaders present it as a widely supported social and political movement, and this is how Slow Food is perceived on the political scene in some countries and in international arenas. It also corresponds to certain aspects of its development and the mechanisms used to diffuse its actions and ideas. As a political movement, it is possible to adhere to its philosophy beyond membership, and many claim to share the same ideals without being a member.

Slow Food

Today Slow Food is an organization capable of putting on big events and negotiating with a large spectrum of widely divergent political powers and economic actors. Some of its components function as a private enterprise, others as a nonprofit organization that acts in the Global South. It has elements—some of his actions or aspects of his philosophy—in common with other social movements that have emerged over the last thirty years, but it also has unique characteristics and history that differentiate it in the field of food activism. Some of its characteristics offer an alternative, almost revolutionary image during certain periods of the movement's history and have inspired other "slow" movements; still other elements suggest an economic perspective more aligned with the dominant food and economic system. What is certain is that it escapes any monolithic definition.

Slow Food is well established in Italy, where it originated, and has spread to about 160 other countries. The association has nearly 100,000 members worldwide. It is composed of a number of national associations, the oldest being Slow Food Italia (30,000 members), created well before the international structure in which it is now a part. When I began my research, there were eight national structures outside of Italy: Slow Food Germany, Slow Food Australia, Slow Food USA, Slow Food France, Slow Food Switzerland, Slow Food Japan, Slow Food UK, and Slow Food Netherlands. Over the years, France, UK, Japan, and Australia have closed their national offices or changed their structure, while still maintaining members and local groups. Members are organized into local groups (*condotta* in Italy and *convivium* in the rest of the world)[1] through which they carry out local actions or pursue international campaigns on a voluntary basis. In countries that do not have a national association (the majority) members and convivia are directly linked to the international membership structure. For all of them, the offices dealing with membership management and the coordination of actions at the international level are located in Bra, where the Italian association and other components of the complex Slow Food world are also based. The Italian association has become increasingly complex over the years with components that actually operate as private enterprises even as they serve the association. One particular example is Slow Food Promozione, which handles the organization of large events, fairs, and the publishing house, Slow Food Editore.

Since the end of the 1990s a large number of the projects and activities of the international structure have concentrated on the Global South. In the early 2000s, the association created a Foundation for Biodiversity to conduct projects through a nonprofit structure. During the same period, it launched a network of small producers located throughout the world, the Terra Madre network, which coexists with the more structured operations of the association in a mixture of compromise and cooperation. Finally, in 2004, Slow Food founded a private university, the University of Gastronomic Sciences located in Pollenzo, a few kilometers from its historical seat of Bra where students, mainly from the United States, Latin America, Asia, and Europe, study the Gastronomic Sciences.[2] This complicated structure that includes the Italian and the International offices—illustrated in images, diagrams, and brochures by Slow Food itself—is very hierarchical and slow to change. It involves between 130 and 170 employees, depending on the time period, working mostly in Bra and nearby Pollenzo, a few other employees located in the offices of countries that have a national association, and a large base of volunteers worldwide.

Slow Food philosophy has also shifted over time: from an initial advocate of gastronomy with a focus on taste and local products, Slow Food has become environmentally conscious with an "eco-gastronomy." This interest in the environment (from the standpoint of production) has been joined over time by an interest in small producers around the world and their living and working conditions, all of which has been condensed into the formula "good, clean, and fair." Defending responsible consumption and quality production that is respectful of the environment and the rights of small producers around the world, Slow Food has become a legitimate actor not only in simple debates concerning food issues, ecology, and local economies but also in the spaces of active political and social contestation about food. The fight against intensive production, homogenization of taste and food, GMOs, nuclear power and nonrenewable energy, non-traceability of products, and the privatization of water were some of the battles in which leadership and members engaged during the years of my research.

Today, the association continues to be a visible, well-known entity that has provoked both strong criticism and unconditional adhesion. It produces abundant literature about itself and has become highly mediatized in Italy and other countries such as Germany, the United States, and Switzerland where it has a strong presence. But this heavy media coverage also produces an optical illusion of familiarity, when, in fact, its internal workings are not at all transparent to outsiders, and not even to its own members.

Although the private university and its wonderful location[3] contribute to the impression of wealth and privilege, as do many of the magazines or books the association has published over the years, Slow Food can be characterized as a militant organization in several respects. Not only do its employees and directors have relatively modest salaries in comparison to the private sector, but most of the leaders, employees, and members devote themselves to the cause full-time. This commitment can be seen from the top at the headquarters offices down to local groups that function on a volunteer basis.

The Slow Food "machine" is a singular combination of multiple aspects and components. All of these dimensions coexist in Slow Food, and they should be considered together as an ensemble in order to understand the inner workings of this "militant" machine, whose specificity resides in these multiple, often obscure, and sometimes contradictory facets. In this book, looking at how all these elements cohabit and contribute to the social reproduction of Slow Food over time and from the point of view of its members (leaders, employees, volunteers, producers), I examine the tensions and the inner workings of an association that was born in a small Italian province but has become a global movement whose influence, at certain points in its history, has reached as far as Brussels or the White House.

Slow Food

Food Activism

The literature on social movements is extremely rich. First a topic of a branch of sociology (see Buechler 2000, 2011; Cefaï 2007), social movements became an object of study for anthropologists later on (Edelman 2001; Pratt 2003; Nash 2005; Graeber 2009; Koensler and Rossi 2012; Juris and Khasnabish 2013). Social movements change over time, as do the people who act within them: some movements become institutionalized or professionalized, others are diluted to the point of dissolution, old initiatives fade, and new mobilizations appear. The objectives shift—some are added, others are replaced. Any attempt to fix and define a movement by its position on a particular political front or its composition in a given social class risks losing the nuances of the changing complexity that characterizes most movements. For these reasons, I believe that the best way to study activism and movements like Slow Food is to analyze them from a processual perspective while being attentive to transformations and the agency of social actors. Looking at processes helps us avoid constructing fixed and stereotypical images— particularly in terms of goals, functioning, or social configuration—of mobilizations or activism.

Carole Counihan and I used the notion of "food activism" to indicate different forms of mobilization that share the objective of gaining some degree of democratic control over the contemporary food system and changing it, at least in part. Food becomes the catalyst for mobilizations that take different forms—from buying groups and campaigns for critical, fair, and solidarity-based consumption, to urban agriculture initiatives, to more structured movements such as Slow Food or federations of multiple organizations such as La Via Campesina.[4] The goals of these mobilizations are often aimed at economic and social justice in terms of food or a general opposition to large-scale agribusiness and the capitalist system that supports it. Pratt and Luetchford (2014: 3) have shown that "contesting food" can mean contesting agricultural methods, producer remuneration, and prices. Moreover, we could say that by contesting "through" food, the space of resistance becomes a space of action (Counihan and Siniscalchi 2014; Siniscalchi 2015). The phenomena that lie within this analytical range are expressed through different practices, such as the defense of small-scale peasant agriculture and local economies or efforts to create fair remuneration for producers by eliminating the middlemen and promoting direct sales of local agriculture.

As Richard Wilk reminds us, food allows abstract political issues to be transformed into a visceral and material reality (2006b: 21–2). When food becomes the central focus of movements and mobilizations, it makes it possible to reconnect parts of the food system that the agroindustry has separated and distanced, namely producers and consumers. Krista Harper and I (Siniscalchi and Harper 2019) analyzed this set of practices as "food projects": experiences and experiments of food production and consumption that allow people to redefine the values of exchange. Food projects often constitute spaces which also include social and political experimentation. Movements which oppose the dominant economic system through actions and new imaginaries of the economy are, in some respects, an integral part of the capitalist system (Narotzky 2012a). Nevertheless, and without creating fictive dichotomies, their analysis is crucial to understanding contemporary political and economic reconfigurations. To study them, it is necessary to consider their internal functioning, their transformations (in terms of professionalization, institutionalization, or even political positioning), the interactions they establish with institutions, and their forms of funding. Some of them operate in the main arenas where the future of food is discussed; others are rather situated in the interstices of the economic system. Slow Food combines these two aspects, a structured international association whose existence is also made possible by a myriad of local micro-actions.

How to study Slow Food?

When I started working on Slow Food, the opinions of colleagues towards it were divergent. Some saw it as being similar to a large company that could move money and expressed doubts about the critical scope of the movement's messages and actions. Others, especially in Italy or the United States who were directly involved in some cog in the Slow Food machine—a local chapter or initiative, one of the magazines, or even a course at one of the movement's university campuses—viewed it favorably. At the time, Slow Food was little known to most of my French colleagues.

Existing anthropological research on Slow Food emerged from various perspectives and was no less divided in those years. I had the impression that I was moving through a field split between pro-Slow Food and anti-Slow Food partisans, between strong criticism and unswerving allegiance. Among the articles published in the early 2000s, only two or three were highly cited and dealt seriously with some aspects of the movement. They provided an in-depth examination of the philosophy of Slow Food, even though they didn't delve into the inner workings of the association. One such work was that of Alison Leitch (2003), an anthropologist who conducted research on pork fat from Colonnata (*lardo di Colonnata*, Tuscany), a Slow Food Presidium.[5] Her text provides an interesting analysis of the political positioning of the association at the time of her investigations. Mara Miele and Jonathan Murdoch (Miele and Murdoch 2002; Murdoch and Miele 2004), geographers, wrote about Slow Food's network of restaurants in Tuscany, emphasizing the aesthetic dimension of Slow Food philosophy and ways to apply it in the field. Finally, I should mention a dense essay on the movement's philosophy, based on the analysis of documents and interviews with certain Slow Food leaders written by sociologists, Roberta Sassatelli and Federica Davolio (2010), during the same period as my own research. Their analysis captures important aspects of the philosophy of the movement and its transformations; however, the predominating attention to rhetoric and data from Slow Food–produced documents and a few interviews with Slow Food leaders and officers (confirming what is said in the official documents) does not allow the authors to avoid some over-interpretation.

Other texts have described Slow Food either from an internal viewpoint or from its periphery. The former are generally the work of authors who largely share Slow Food thinking (such as Andrews 2008; Parkins and Craig 2006; or Kummer 2002) or authors from institutions who collaborated with some segment of the movement (university, publishing house), giving them some degree of access to the internal structure (such as Corti 2011, 2016; Fontefrancesco and Corvo 2019; Migliorini et al. 2010; Parasecoli 2003; Perullo 2010). Those from the exterior point of view have tended to examine a local group, a project, or an event with the intention of analyzing Slow Food's perspectives and limits, often by highlighting its weaknesses (Assmann 2010; Chrzan 2004; Deléage 2014; Friedmann and McNair 2008; Gaytan 2004; Green 2018; Littaye 2015; Lotti 2010; Meneley 2004; Paxson 2005; Peace 2006, 2008; West and Domingos 2012). These publications reveal only a small, often misleading part of Slow Food's inner workings. While in many cases the criticisms are based on field observations and the way some of the projects are implemented, in other cases the attacks seem to be largely superficial and ideological criticisms. As Sassatelli and Davolio also point out, many contributions are purely descriptive and others acerbic and vindictive, "As a result SF is often portrayed as a disembedded cultural identity unchanging across time and space, rather than a diverse and disperse organization which continuously adjust to its circumstances. The result is often that SF rhetorical claims are not properly contextualized in institutional terms" (2010: 208). Indeed, a large number of articles published in the English-speaking literature and written from different disciplinary perspectives (from geography to sociology, from food history to economics) analyze Slow Food only through the texts produced by the association itself as if they were a mirror of what Slow Food is (Hsu 2014; Myers 2012; Pietrykowski 2004; Pratt 2007; Schneider 2008; van Bommel and Spicer 2011). Some of the authors whose positions are the most critical of Slow Food have had direct experience with the movement. They appear as members or participants in the implementation of a project that has left them disappointed, and personal experience is mixed with scientific posture. Nevertheless, some of these texts, such as Chrzan (2004), have elements of interest. Although her observations result in erroneous generalizations that tend to use criticism to produce a definitive description of what Slow Food is, they do provide a picture of how Slow Food was being peripherally interpreted in the early 2000s. Later, I will return to the related problem of foreign translations of Slow Food messages.

The main problem with this literature is that it reproduces some common biases. First of all, these texts take seriously, in a very literal sense, what Slow Food says about itself. They base their description completely on the communication tools used by the association, and from that singular viewpoint, they imagine a unique thought and a functioning consistent with that thought, leading them to criticize Slow Food for not doing or not being what it says it does or is. Interviews, if the authors have conducted any, serve to corroborate official Slow Food communication. More importantly, they interact with Slow Food as if it were a "scientific" actor, putting its written production (especially textes signed by Carlo Petrini) on the same level as scientific analyses, and thereby confusing political actions and statements with scientific assertions, as we will see later. When later studies use Slow Food as an example (even if it is not the main object of analysis) they draw on the static image of the movement produced by this literature and in doing so perpetuate misleading ideas such as the one that portrays Slow Food as being mainly concerned with typical products.

Leaving aside these criticisms, the number of publications confirms that Slow Food is a good, if slippery, object to contemplate and one which can be analyzed from many angles. Moreover, in spite of the notoriety that the movement had in Italy and in other parts of the world, no work had provided an in-depth look at its inner workings and dynamics. Above all, the association's headquarters had remained largely unexplored, beyond a few interviews with certain leaders or office and project managers. What interested me most was to observe inside the headquarters, as with any other fieldwork, how the daily life of the leaders and staff unfolded, what went on behind the scenes of this object that was decidedly opaque, in spite of its "glossy" appearance. I wanted to grasp the inner workings of the whole organization, and the only way to achieve this was to position myself in the heart of the association, in its headquarters and governing groups, spending extended periods of time with the people I would study in order to analyze what really happened inside the machine rather than the ideal statements produced by Slow Food itself.

The anthropological "spy"

Communication is one of Slow Food's main activities—one reason for the prolific research interest in its publications—and is undoubtedly an instrument of power. It is used to publicize the movement's actions, which are conducted around the world through the efforts of the associations' members and employees. Communication also spreads the movement's philosophy, helps to recruit new members, and raises funds that support Slow Food actions. It is not difficult to imagine that the control of communication is a strategic element in this type of structure. What kinds of tools are needed to analyze a global movement that already communicates extensively about itself and also keeps track of what is being said? How can the simple repetition of what the movement already says be avoided?

Like any other fieldwork, working on Slow Food has been a learning process, fine-tuning the best ways of interacting, of recognizing and understanding relationships and internal genealogies. At the beginning, I knew very little about the history of Slow Food, and I was not very familiar with the Italian Piedmont region, where that history began, nor with its particular dialect. But years later, several of the movement's leaders, including Carlo Petrini (the president of Slow Food), told me that they felt I was the only one who has an overview of Slow Food, who knows all its mechanisms in the different offices and services. What does this mean from an ethnographic point of view? For certain individuals in the organization's internal hierarchy, my cross-sectional perspective gave me a critical voice from which the movement's leadership might benefit in the search for solutions to what they perceived as structural problems in the Slow Food "machine." For others, the fact that I had accumulated a layered knowledge of the way Slow Food works could have been a danger (in terms of an image I might present to the outside world, in contradiction to the official one) or a source of disappointment (in terms of the image held within the movement itself). These concerns were dispelled thanks to the multiple years of ethnographic writing and publication. But recognizing that an anthropologist can sometimes know the object of study more fully than someone inside it—with the caveat that ethnography only allows us to capture part of the social reality, albeit over a long period of time and in depth —means recognizing the "power" of the external gaze that is capable of revealing what lurks behind the self-produced image. In the case of Slow Food, it meant admitting that the machine had elements that were obscure to the members themselves, whether those protagonists were salaried or volunteers, office workers or leaders in the movement. The reality was much more complex and contested than what the tools of communication portrayed.

My first contacts in the offices of Slow Food's headquarters were suggested by people I had met during my first years of research in France. The association had a *Centro Studi* (Research and Documentation Center) whose functions included "sorting" requests for information and contacts from students or researchers interested in understanding Slow Food: As standard procedure, the *Centro Studi* sent documents and data taken from official publications, thus keeping away those who wanted to look inside the black box. One of my first meetings in those headquarters was a brief interview with Piero, president of the Slow Food Foundation for Biodiversity (*Fondazione Slow Food per la biodiversità onlus*), historical leader, and one of the founders of Slow Food. The meeting was programmed for only half an hour by a dutiful employee of the *Centro Studi*. But Piero, who was at first gruff and unwilling to engage in unnecessary chitchat, was more interested in my research than he had anticipated, and the meeting ended with an agreement to meet again and take more time to continue the discussion. I had broken the first barrier of the fieldwork, the short meeting, fixed according to the scheme in use for journalistic interviews.

Sometime later, the same person coined my nickname, "Spy," which I carried during the years of my fieldwork in Bra, a sort of affectionate vocative used in our daily conversations and exchanges. "Hello Spy, how are you? Spy, are you coming to the meeting too? When are you coming back to Bra, Spy?" One day, Claudia, who was in charge of the coordination and organization of the events, smilingly told me: "You don't have to be offended if we call you Spy; it means that you have been accepted. If you hadn't been, we would still have called you Spy, but behind your back, without telling you." Many people referred to me—half humorously, half seriously—as Spy, but only within the intimate spaces in the life of the movement. And I have to admit that I was quite proud of my nickname, which seemed to confirm that my presence had not only been accepted but had also become part of the routine. I remember a preparatory meeting for an international gathering: attendees included the Slow Food presidents of Germany, the United States, and Italy (the countries with the most influential association and the largest Slow Food membership) and the general secretary of Slow Food International. The latter, before starting the meeting in which strategic elements were to be discussed, asked the American president if it bothered him that an outside person was watching their exchange of views. The American president looked at him, somewhat puzzled, and then asked him with a smile, "Are you referring to the Spy? No problem." Not only did he already knew who I was, using my nickname, but my presence was seen as normal.

The photo of badges that opens this chapter illustrates the evolution in status that characterized my presence as a researcher within Slow Food: French delegate, Italian delegate, organizer, staff. Hardly any of those roles corresponded to reality, but they reflected the progression of my integration. There was only one which told the absolute truth, a badge I am very attached to that Serena from the Italian association office prepared for me before a meeting with the *fiduciari* (*condotte* leaders). She showed it to me with a big smile, waiting for my reaction. The badge said, "The observer." By itself, the word "observer" was always used on the badges of external, nonaffiliated people during big events. But adding the definite article suggested a completely different meaning. "The observer, there is only one," Serena told me. "But why didn't you just write Spy?" I asked her. "Because you can't write Spy," she said, "we call you Spy [in the offices at headquarters], and only we know what it means. You can't write Spy on the badge for a meeting with *fiduciari* who don't know you; it could be misinterpreted." I agreed with her, but there was something more. Serena's word game was a confirmation: the term "Spy" identified me and my place in an intimate social space, while "The observer" (with the definite article) officially confirmed my position to the members of the association outside of the headquarters.

With my one-of-a-kind badge, another level of leaders in the association were made aware of the fact that I had a legitimate role within the machine. As researchers, how do we succeed to this degree? Probably by speaking honestly about what we are doing, by showing that we have no intention of demolishing a movement or discrediting it, nor inversely, of spreading propaganda for the benefit of a movement. The first element was key to convincing the leaders of my impartiality; the second was key to convincing members of the staff that they needn't feel threatened. It reassured them that they were free to reveal their point of view, sometimes in disagreement with that of the leadership, confident that I would listen to them, take account of their words and feelings, and safeguard their secrets. Some of the leaders also may have felt that my research could actually be useful to them; for the first time someone from the outside was going behind the scenes of the movement with the goal of observing everything that could be observed. Perhaps, thanks to all of those elements combined, they opened the doors of political meetings to me, and gradually those of the internal and informal meetings as well, where the association's strategies were prepared.

Positioning

Looking back at the many episodes of my fieldwork, I recall what happened when I attended the first meeting of the board of directors of Slow Food France in 2009. The eight members were getting ready to sit around a table in the living room of Louis, a board member who was hosting the meeting in his house in Marseille. At that point some of them, seeing that I was approaching one of the chairs to sit with them, raised the issue of my position: "She can't sit around the table with us; she is an observer; she is not part of the board." Other members were divided on the question; some tried to come up with an alternative solution, and one of them suggested that perhaps I could sit on a chair in the corner of the room, outside the circle of people around the table. I waited for them to discuss among themselves, showing my openness to whatever arrangement they felt would be acceptable, but letting it be known, between the lines, that in the political meetings I attended inside Slow Food in Italy, I occupied a chair around the table like the other participants. Someone began to point out the absurdity of the situation where everyone is around the table, while I scrutinized them from a distance, almost behind them. Finally, they all agreed that it would be less uncomfortable for everyone if I sat with them, and I promised not to talk and to let them discuss, uninterrupted.

That episode reminds me of a satirical situation in the Norwegian film *Kitchen Stories* (by Bent Hamer 2003). Set in the 1950s, the film follows a group of Swedish sociologists who are sent to study the behavior of unmarried men in a Norwegian village. Each sociologist goes to the home of a person who had agreed to be observed and sets himself up in a high chair in a corner of the kitchen. He is tasked with recording the subject's behavior and specifically prohibited from talking with him (or drinking or eating). After a series of comical episodes in which the subject tries to escape the gaze of the observer, the sociologist finally agrees to get down from the high chair and have a coffee with his host. As they subversively drink their coffee, the subject asks him, "How can you pretend to study people without talking to them?"

Putting aside the irony with which an anthropologist might read this caricature of a sociologist's work, the film depicts the attempt to escape the rigid classifications of a behavioral study that purports to qualify as objective, where the researcher is positioned "at the proper distance" from his or her subject. The failure of such a position becomes evident when the two begin to actually talk with each other.

The problem of the "right" position of the researcher is present in any study, but working on movements and social mobilizations requires the anthropologist to make precise choices in terms of posture and positioning—probably more than when working on other issues. How does one avoid opposing, dichotomous positions: an uncritical partisan of the movement or an infiltrator aiming to unmask secrets, the voice of the movement or a judge of its relevance and effectiveness, a friend of the study's object or a hasty researcher who slips away in the night? How does one find the right position that doesn't lead to the criticism of principle (not a motivation for my research), or conversely, slide into uncritical ideological adherence (an error I sometimes recognize in other scholars' publications and did not want to emulate)?

Just as the political colors of different mobilizations range from the far left to the far right (Wilk 2006a: 22), researchers' choices range from direct involvement and partisanship to uninvolved observation (Edelman 2001: 301–3; Graeber 2009; Mahmud 2014). The question of the degree of implication has produced numerous debates and dichotomous opinions. Researchers in the field of social movements are often thought to have a certain sympathy for the object they decide to analyze. But this is not always true. Martina Avanza's work on the Italian far-right party, Lega Nord, provides a good example of research on an object far removed from the researcher's own political views and for which the anthropologist had no sympathy (2008). Despite the ideological and political distance between the researcher's views and the position of the activists of the Northern League, a xenophobic party, the researcher took seriously the views of the people she was studying, who were often described by the press of the time and scholars as political buffoons. At the same time, she had to use a number of stratagems to limit her involvement and to protect her private life.

My own work on the Slow Food movement falls somewhere in-between. Even if I agree with many of the association's positions on food and local economies—positions that I discovered during my years of research and had little to do with the choice of Slow Food as an object of study—my goal was not to measure the effectiveness and relevance of the movement's philosophy and actions, nor their coherence. I wanted to understand its workings, tensions, and contradictions from the perspective of those who make the association what it is on a daily basis; I wanted to uncover the power dynamics and strategies and understand how this complex machine was thought out, rethought, and orchestrated from within. In terms of my personal positions, it is true that I sometimes needed to set them aside or nuance them because they were frequently more radical than those of my contacts. It is not surprising for individual positions to be more radical than those of an entire association that has to maintain a collectively acceptable vision. Naturally, I might have had a different perspective on strategic choices or political positions, personally disagreed about how something should be done, or felt compelled to distance myself from emerging power conflicts inside the headquarters. These personal feelings were controlled but not always concealed, and they remained a part of the involvement and a moderate level of complicity which I decided to allow myself during the fieldwork.

I define the posture that I assumed as a negotiated posture. One usually thinks of the early stages in fieldwork as a period of negotiation in which the researcher must gain acceptance, convince his interlocutors of his good faith, and establish trust. Then, as if by magic, the research begins and unfolds as if it were a long quiet river. Of course, in reality, things are much more complicated. The American deconstructionist turn of the 1980s radically questioned the position of the anthropologists in the field, the power relation, and, consequently, the author's position in writing a classic monograph. It is no longer possible to think of fieldwork as it was practiced by early anthropologists. Today, anthropologists who take fieldwork seriously, as the constitutive and fundamental element of anthropological knowledge, know, even if they do not always manage to make it fully explicit, that the fieldwork is a process in which the anthropologist will always be involved. Involvement is among the main characteristics of fieldwork. It does not mean becoming part of the object of study, partisan or defender (although in some cases anthropologists assume these roles as well). Nor does it mean taking on the role of one of them by leading a double life like that of a character in Jack London's, *South of the Slot* (1909). He was a sociologist divided between the life of an academic, solitary and somewhat reactionary, and the role of a combative worker and then union leader, which he undertook during fieldwork, hiding his true identity from the people

Slow Food

he studied. Involvement does mean, however, being aware of being part of the field, not only because the anthropologist with his research choices makes the field exist as such, but because the anthropologist is "inside" the field, living with the people whose social world he or she tries to understand.

What I would like to emphasize here, looking back over the years of research on Slow Food, is the fact that in a long-term research project, the researcher goes through different phases.[6] I'm not referring to the linear succession of phases outlined in the ethnographer's manuals (ranging from the preparation of the fieldwork, to the first surveys, to the actual research period that ends when the back-and-forth becomes rare), but to the steps of progressive involvement in the social "game" of familiarization, of gaining an understanding and then questioning what we thought we had understood, of negotiating our presence and the very possibility of analyzing what we observe. Letting oneself get caught up in the game means allowing oneself to be involved in long discussions about what is best to do or not to do, about what strategy should be adopted, about who or what could produce what effects. In my work on Slow Food it also meant eating, tasting, drinking, experiencing the research mentally and physically, the fatigue or the lack of sleep from meetings that ended too late or seemingly endless evening discussions, even the seasickness or car sickness during the many trips accompanying staff to meetings in other Italian cities or foreign countries.

We may shape the fieldwork, but in a way, it shapes us as well. At the end of my first year of research in Bra, I was having lunch in the garden of Milena, a friend and director of one of the Slow Food departments. My husband, who had come to visit me, was there as well and watched as I swirled my glass to let the contents breath—a gesture repeated thousands of times during the previous months of fieldwork. At first perplexed and then smiling, he said to me, "it is really time for you to take a break." I was making what had become an automatic gesture of letting the wine in my glass breath, without realizing that the glass was filled with water rather than wine. In the midst of fieldwork, we tend to be involved, mind and body. "Living with" means taking it seriously, letting oneself be involved, without losing one's critical, external gaze. It means moving cautiously along the faults and internal disagreements, paying attention to dissonances and contradictions, because through them social dynamics emerge that allow one to understand a part of reality and its stakes. "Living with" means sharing spaces of intimacy, confidences, laughter, quarrels; it means accepting to get involved (cf. also Okely 2012: 14). In the case of Slow Food, this also meant sharing a lot of irony.

Ethnographic trust

In the 1970s, before the deconstructionist turn in anthropology, Clifford Geertz posed the question, "What does the ethnographer do?" and answered, "He writes" (1973: 19). Geertz was referring to our work of inscribing social discourse, noting fleeting events and turning them into accounts that are dense interpretations of a small part of what we have come to understand about the social meanings "acted out" by those we observe. In the hundreds of interviews done and Slow Food meetings that I attended over the years, my time was spent writing down from A to Z what took place and what was said. Much of my time in the field was spent discussing, asking questions, and listening while I was in the offices, at dinners, at events or traveling, but even then, I was constantly writing field notes. When someone new arrived at a meeting I attended, they would ask what I did and someone would immediately reply, "Nothing, nothing, she writes." But what can we legitimately write, and what will never find a place in our final texts?

During the years of my research, the directors and leaders of Slow Food were particularly attentive to the external image of "their" movement, carefully guarding the intimate and daily life within the association's headquarters as if they were defending a "family secret." "Spy, remember! This is *omissis!*" *Omissis* is Latin for something censured, a deliberate omission, and the admonition was repeated over and over again in the first months of my fieldwork. Naturally, by Piero, who had coined my nickname, but also by others whenever there were intimate discussions about internal issues, or conflicts over officially defended positions, or snippy gossip. After one instance of someone "reminding" me that something I had heard should be with the *omissis*, the then president of the Italian association, Riccardo, smiled and told me, "You know, if you had decided to study the KGB, you could have written about many more things. Here everything is censured!" The phrase "Spy, omissis!" had almost become a joke, but it served to remind me that I could not write about, or reveal, everything that was going on in the daily life of Slow Food.

What kind of secrets were they protecting? And why? In the beginning, I didn't have a clear grasp of the aspects that they needed or wanted to hide, or why. There seemed to be a strong need to protect the sometimes incoherent internal logics and operations of the organization, especially from the prying eyes of the outside world. This need, or its perception, has become stronger with the passage of time and the increasing internal complexity. It is, in fact, at the origin of the controversial public image of Slow Food. The core of the movement fears external gazes which could unmask lingering contradictions. But how can an anthropologist study an organization that jealously defends its public image? Moreover, what are the implications for ethnographic writing? Can different kinds of writing coexist?

Only a small part of what we see, hear, and note will find its way into our published writings. The challenge was not so much my presence in the field, but the constant micro-negotiations required by the research itself, the access to some piece of the Slow Food machine, to every office, in every political instance, and in every historical moment (e.g., after some election or congress, all the occasions that could mark a change, a transition, or a rupture). My collection of badges in the opening photograph summarizes this aspect of fieldwork. But the negotiation of an intimate and critical relationship also means the construction of ethnographic trust. This is also something that must be constantly discussed and reaffirmed during the fieldwork, perhaps particularly with an object of study like Slow Food, where, at least in the early stages, almost nothing seemed to be able to be said about the internal life of the association.

Slow Food

One day, I had been granted my first access to the private rooms of the Salone del Gusto, where piles of cash from the large event were being sorted and counted. A new staff member of the administration, who did not know me, was astonished and worried that a "stranger" had passed a security door, even if I was accompanied by other people from his own office. I tried to reassure him by explaining the anthropological work I did. After my initial attempts to reassure him seemed to fall flat, I brought up my research on a textile district in southern Italy. The relationship of trust that I had developed with the workers and entrepreneurs—who really did have something to hide since they were working at the limits of legality—had not been betrayed. After asking me exactly where my fieldwork had taken place and letting me explain, the administrator in charge told me that his mother was originally from a village near the one where I had done my research. She had even been a worker in one of the factories featured in my investigation. For an anxious moment I mentally reviewed what I had said and whether I had revealed anything that might suggest that I couldn't be trusted. Happily, my example was even more effective than I had hoped, but at the same time, the experience was a warning to me: the respect on which the (ethnographic) relationship of trust is based does not stop at the spatio-temporal limits of a specific fieldwork but extends far beyond it. Over time, respect becomes familiarity; in many cases esteem and affection are added to it, in others dissent or annoyance, but it continues to be an essential key to the ethnographic relationship.

The issue of anonymity is an old problem in anthropology, which recent regulations concerning informed consent and data protection have made more complicated. When researching a well-known phenomenon such as Slow Food, the problem takes on a particular form. How can one claim relevance and empirical validity of his or her work without putting the people observed or spoken with at risk? How does one report others' speech and point of view without revealing their names and violating their confidentiality, especially when most of them have visible, sometimes highly mediatized roles? How do we respect and acknowledge the role each person played in the research without putting them at risk?

The choices I have made in this volume are as follows: for all the people who appear, I have used only a first name, including for the well-known international president Carlo Petrini, known internally as Carlin, and Piero Sardo, the president of the Foundation for Biodiversity during my fieldwork. For all the other people, I have used pseudonyms along with a few descriptors to situate them within the Slow Food structure when they first appear in the book. When I report on dialogues that took place within meetings or points of view on specific issues, I identify people through their more or less recognizable role depending on the case. For example, I have referred to "the national president," "the regional president," or "the president of the foundation for biodiversity" when a precise identification is necessary for the understanding of the text. When full anonymity is important, I refer to someone less precisely as "a regional president," "a *fiduciario*," "a staff member," or "a staff leader." The internal politics of an organization like Slow Food are extremely delicate. The purpose of this book is to analyze them and make them understandable, not to harm those who work there or who volunteer there with energy and passion. The contradictions that I address in the book are part of understanding how movements like Slow Food work, while at the same time highlighting its specificities. But during the months I spent with them, many people encouraged me with comments like "Talk about this," or "I hope you'll tell about that," expressing their thoughts that an external perspective could also improve understanding among those who work inside the machine and support improvements in its internal functioning as well. I hope that this book will contribute to those ends while preserving the confidentiality of the many people who entrusted me with their stories.

How did this book come about, and how is it organized?

The economic and political dimensions of social phenomena have been the central axis of my research for more than thirty years. During the years of fieldwork in southern Italy (from 1990), in the French Alps (from 2000), in Sardinia, in the Marseille area, and within Slow Food itself (from 2006), the thread that binds all my research is drawn from a political anthropology of the economy. It has taken me from agrarian contracts and exchange circuits in the countryside of Benevento (Campania region) to the textile factories of an industrial district, from the construction of spaces and places in the Hautes-Alpes to the practices of employees in the Parc National des Ecrins, from the distribution systems of vegetable baskets in the city of Marseille to the heart of the Slow Food movement. In all this research, I have sought to understand the ways in which individuals situated in specific social and cultural contexts act, think, and practice activities that have to do with production, exchange, and consumption, and how they relate to the construction of power and political dynamics (Wolf 1990, 2001; Wilk and Cliggett 2007; Gudeman 2001).

Food has been another common thread in my research, as seen through the lens of economic and political anthropology. The circuits of flour and wheat, and the construction of typical products, first in southern Italy and then in the French Alps, have long been themes in my research while simultaneously acting as entry points to the understanding of political relationships, the organization of work, and the circulation of money. Money, debt, exchanges and the values expressed in them, the modes of production and commercialization, and the forms of regulation are all topics in my research on food supply systems in the region of Marseille. A more recent project in Sardinia on the artisanal and industrial production of cheese also explores the subject of food from the perspective of political and economic anthropology. The analysis of food activism, forms of mobilization, and economic experimentation are common to these recent research projects as well as to the fieldwork on Slow Food.

This book uses long-term fieldwork inside Slow Food's international headquarters in Bra, Italy, as well as in some of its political hubs and local, regional, and national implantations, to reach into the "black box" and explore its intimate workings. These pages synthesize research conducted over a ten-year period that began in 2006 and covered various locations: extensive fieldwork in the city of Bra (between 2009 and 2014);

fieldwork inside Slow Food France (between 2007 and 2012), particularly with two French *convivia* and French producers linked to Slow Food; and fieldwork in the Sardinia region among producers, local politicians, experts, and local Slow Food leaders (between 2011 and 2019). While organizing the book, I decided to give priority to ethnography, keep footnotes to a minimum, and use in-text references to make reading easier.

The next chapter looks at the history of Slow Food while analyzing the intellectual genealogy of the movement and following its political evolution. These elements are linked to specific moments of Italian history and to the specific regional context of the Piedmont. The link between the political and economic dimensions of Slow Food, which is often hidden behind the more visible dimension of gastronomy, will be exposed, and some of the tensions that characterize the Slow Food phenomenon begin to appear: the tension between association and movement, between center and periphery, and between horizontality and hierarchy.

Chapter 3 explores the process of "democratization" and changes in the leadership of the association. New modes of operation continue to coexist with structural logics of the past and produce new tensions. The official political bodies (the national and international boards and councils), as well as "non-visible" ones, constitute the heart of this chapter.

Chapter 4 uses the Italian association case study to explore the complex relations between the center and the base in order to analyze the ambiguous links between power and production of commitment, those between autonomy and fidelity, and the reconfiguration of volunteering.

Chapter 5 analyzes the association's expansion through the example of the French national association. Slow Food leaders have always considered France as the country of gastronomy, an element of high symbolic value since the early years of the association, and one that was exemplified by the signing of the international manifesto in Paris. At the same time, France is one of the countries where the movement has never grown. The relationship between two associative structures (the French national and the Italian-based International), linked to each other in political, economic, and symbolic terms, is the core of this chapter which addresses the issue of autonomy and dependence at the level of international relations of Slow Food. Part of the analyses in this chapter have been published in different articles (Siniscalchi 2017, 2020).

Chapter 6 looks inside Slow Food "black box" to lay out its internal logics and contradictions through the practices and visions of people working inside the headquarters. Gender and generational relations among personnel delineate an extremely conflictual social space.

Chapter 7 illustrates Slow Food's political and economic involvement with environmental questions and the evolution of Slow Food philosophy through certain projects and actions. The adoption of the triad, "good, clean, and fair," as the movement's slogan and key words marks the integration of farmers and small producers inside Slow Food.

Chapter 8 examines the role and contradictions of the Presidia project in particular. Several case studies are explored: the "Fiore Sardo" pecorino cheese (Sardinia) and the

"Brusse du Rove" (Provence) cheese are analyzed from the point of view of producers. Explicitly or implicitly "against" the norms established by the State or by Europe, Slow Food proposes new normative models to replace those considered inadequate by small producers. These issues and parts of Chapters 7 and 8 have been published in Siniscalchi (2013a, b).

Chapter 9 focuses on the role of taste, one of the pillars of the association. It is revealed as a double-edged tool that can be used to include or exclude at the same time. This chapter incorporates, with some modifications, a chapter from the volume *Making Taste Public* edited by Counihan and Højlund (Siniscalchi 2018a).

Chapter 10 analyzes the relationship linking restaurateurs and small winemakers to Slow Food. An earlier piece reflecting on the role of restaurateurs in the association was published in Siniscalchi (2014b).

Chapter 11 looks at certain large events organized by Slow Food (Salone del Gusto and Terra Madre in particular) and their role as economic and political spaces where Slow Food philosophy is updated and performed and political battles are waged. Sponsoring and promotion activities cohabit with the economic aims of producers, while the economic imaginations and moral dimensions provoke tensions between Slow Food's political goals and its need for economic survival.

Chapter 12 questions the ways in which food activism rethinks economic and (social) values while maintaining different kinds of relationships with the market economy. Taking account of the different economic registers elaborated and practiced by Slow Food, I analyze its capacity to participate in diverse and sometimes divergent battles in order to establish strategic alliances with economic actors and cope with the ambiguities that appear in these economic and political fields. At the same time, these economic alliances and political battles allow the movement to reproduce itself over time. But what about its reproduction in the long term? What is going to happen? Without resorting to a crystal ball, I try to address those questions by analyzing the contradictions and tensions which appear throughout the earlier chapters of this book and can be said to characterize Slow Food and food activism in general.

Notes

1. The term used in Italy to name a local Slow Food group is *condotta*. In Italian, the term is used to refer to a medical or veterinary practice (*condotta medica, condotta veterinaria*): the doctors or veterinarians employed by a municipality or a consortium of municipalities, with the obligation to treat and assist the sick free of charge. By extension, the term indicates the territory or office where the doctor or veterinarian practices. The term *convivium* was chosen by the leaders of Slow Food to "translate" the meaning of the word *condotta*, putting the emphasis on the dimension of conviviality (in Latin *convivium* means banquet and by extension the guests). In the United States, the term *convivium* has been replaced by the term *chapter*. In this book, I will use the term *convivium* to refer generally to a local Slow Food group and *condotta* when referring to local groups located in Italy.

2. At the time of the university's creation, there were two campuses, one in Pollenzo and one in Colorno, in the province of Parma (Emilia Romagna region), which was later closed.

Slow Food

During the years of my research, the University of Gastronomic Sciences did not (yet) receive public funding. Although accredited by the Italian Ministry of Higher Education, it operated exclusively through private donations.

3. The royal estate of Pollenzo is a group of buildings commissioned by Carlo Alberto di Savoia in the early nineteenth century, which later fell into neglect. Carlo Alberto di Savoia was king of Sardinia from 1831 to 1849; his son Vittorio Emanuele II was the first king of Italy.

4. On alternative and ethic consumption, see Dubuisson-Quellier (2009), and Carrier and Luetchford (2012); on food movements, see Alkon and Guthman (2017), Borras, Edelman and Kay (2008), and Holt-Giménez and Patel (2009); on social movements against agribusiness, see Juris (2008), Fitting (2011), Heller (2013), Schurman and Munro (2010), Thivet (2014, 2019).

5. A Slow Food Presidium is a label and a project intended to defend and valorize quality products considered "in danger." See Chapters 7 and 8.

6. See, among others, Kilani (1992), Palumbo (2021). In another text (Siniscalchi 2018b), I retrace the ways in which the fieldwork I have done over the last thirty years has changed my way of doing research—from the south of Italy to the French Alps to Slow Food—because the objects and perspectives, and the scientific contexts of my subsequent ethnographies, were no longer the same.

Photo 2 Lunch during one of the events organized by Slow Food: Slow Fish, Genoa (Italy), 2013. ©Franco Zecchin.

CHAPTER 2
FROM POLITICS TO GASTRONOMY AND BACK
WHERE DID SLOW FOOD COME FROM?

When I started my research on Slow Food, I decided to take less interest in the past of the association than in its present dynamics. There were already many stories about the birth and history of Slow Food, and I wasn't interested in writing another one. Above all, I didn't want to be mistaken for yet another journalist or scholar interested simply in the history of Slow Food. The Slow Food "chronology" has been repeated and reproduced thousands of times in brochures, websites, reviews, books, films, political events, and public occasions. It has always maintained a fixed structure, but it has constantly been readapted to the context. At certain times in the movement's history, some of these narratives have been presented and considered by Slow Food leaders in Bra as the "true" story or the "official" story. The different versions of these stories and their utility to the movement are interesting as an object of study, but what really intrigued me at the time was more how this extremely mysterious machine worked on the inside. Nevertheless, it was and is important to understand the main elements of the past. They create a common foundation which supports the association, like a family history that is recalled on certain occasions. The interviews and conversations which help to elaborate this historical context were also instrumental in creating a necessary degree of cultural intimacy with the people I was observing and studying.

Arcigola

Slow Food was founded in Bra, a city in the Langhe wine-growing area of northwestern Italy. But to examine its roots, we need to start with another association, the ARCI, or Associazione Ricreativa e Culturale Italiana. Created in 1957, the ARCI was a national organization that grouped together leftist and antifascist clubs and defended values such as solidarity, mutuality, and cultural promotion and experimentation.[1] At the end of the 1970s and the beginning of the 1980s, the organization encouraged the creation of several thematic, branch associations which became autonomous structures known as Legambiente, Arcidonna, Arciragazzi, Arcigay, and Arcigola-Lega eno-gastronomica. The last one in this list—known simply as Arcigola—was the first step in the evolution of Slow Food as an association and, later, a movement. The first part of the name Arcigola, "arci," is both a reference to the mother organization and an Italian prefix that reinforces adjectives in a superlative manner. The second part, "gola," literally means gullet, but is also used to refer to gluttony, and members of Arcigola were called *arcigolosi* (literally, very gluttonous). In fact, at the beginning, Arcigola appeared to be an association of gourmets devoted to good wine and food, and to local culinary traditions.

Arcigola's founders and leaders came from the Italian *circoli*[2] that included left-wing political parties, militants, and intellectuals who in the 1970s had been involved in local politics, the trade union movement, or cultural associations. Some of them were ARCI executives at the provincial level, while others came from the ranks of the Communist Party itself. But the attention of Arcigola's founders was focused on the rural world of local products and peasants (*contadini*). At the time, small- and medium-scale agriculture continued to be important in some parts of Italy. They distanced themselves from the preoccupations of the Communist Party and political left which were more closely linked to the proletariat and urban working class. In this respect, their position was considered marginal within the Italian left, but the founders readily claimed this marginality for themselves.

Antonio, one of Slow Food's "historical" leaders (*leaders storici*) who had been in the Communist Party, told me, "We were the 'remnants' of 1968. . . . Bringing experience with the '68 movement and hailing from the galaxy of the left, . . . we carried a bundle of disillusion and exhaustion with the traditional manner of doing politics." They were looking for new means and spaces of engagement in Italy of the 1980s, a period characterized with the word *riflusso* (disenchantment),[3] when the ideals and causes that had led large numbers to commit and mobilize collectively in the 1970s seemed to have vanished and ceded to individualism. It is important to remember that the end of the 1960s and all of the 1970s represent a period of struggle in Italy: first among workers, then the student movement, and finally the so-called *anni di piombo* (years of lead) in which terrorism from the right, and from some on the extreme left, bloodied Italian social and political life (see, among others, Orsini 2009; Ventura 2010). These events were linked to the geopolitical position of Italy in the Mediterranean and in a Europe divided into two large blocs, one under the influence of the United States and the other the USSR. At the end of these particularly violent years, the Italian political world seemed to have abandoned the great ideologies, and the populace seemed to have put aside social struggles and the values that animated them in order to pursue consumerism.

The group of friends who founded Slow Food did not abandon their political ideals, but they did try to translate them into innovative forms that acknowledged the end of earlier political struggles while maintaining a political awareness. Silvano, another historical leader, said to me, "Everything starts from our political sharing, [Carlo Petrini and I] had experience in the late sixties and seventies with this group of the extreme left that had strong popular roots in Bra." Some of these activists, those who were originally from Bra and the surrounding area in particular, had already transferred their experiences of political leadership to local associations of various kinds. Some of these associations were focused on wine and local traditions, such as the Libera e Benemerita Associazione Amici del Barolo which literally translates as Free and Well-deserved Association Friends of Barolo (a local and renowned red wine). Created in the early 1980s, it published a mail-order catalogue of wines that was based on direct knowledge of local wine-producing cellars. The activists involved saw it as a working space, almost an experiment to create youth employment, and in some ways, the association provided inspiration for Arcigola. Silvano was one of the founders; he had previously been involved in the organization of ARCI Langhe, the provincial branch of the ARCI. Professionally, he had first been a trade union representative, then the provincial secretary of one of the most important left-wing trade unions, and finally an employee in an engineering factory. When the factory went bankrupt, he found himself without a job and participated in the creation of the association. He then worked in a related cooperative, the Cooperativa I Tarocchi. Silvano said,

> Taking advantage of ARCI's policy, but applying it to wine, we thought that we could create some work activity, so we organized "green weeks" where we brought young people from other cities, like Rome, to the Langhe to visit, to get to know the territory. We also took them to visit wine producers. The territory had many good qualities, it was beautiful, and tourism could be developed. We did it with a logic linked to educational and recreational activities.

Food occupied an important place in the association, whose members shared the pleasure of eating and drinking together: "Our organizational experience, which was very local, converged in an association like Arcigola, and even from a goliardic[4] point of view, food was important. This territory offered opportunities like the Barolo wine or the truffle, and the attention to food was a strong substrate. In our private life food and drink were important," explained Silvano. For example, one moment of celebration filled with food and conviviality was the *Cante i'euve* (literally, egg singing), a local tradition of groups touring country farmsteads during Lent, singing and asking for food and wine. This group of friends from Bra revitalized the tradition. The event become a folk music festival and allowed the group to consolidate ties with local and international intellectuals and musicians, who were later among the first supporters of Arcigola and the emerging Slow Food association.

As some historical members noted, the public food world in those years was mostly linked to professional structures (associations of cooks, or sommeliers) or to small groups like confraternities, linked to a product and to a geographical and cultural area; it was elitist and not shared. Silvano opined, "These aspects were in conflict with our experience in the trade unions and in the ARCI, which was oriented more towards the masses. At the time we were thinking that we could develop a large association around the theme of food, something that has not been done before."[5] Through politics, wine, food, and the *goliardia*, this group of friends and people coming from the same intellectual and political background reintroduced notions such as "pleasure" that had been rejected during years of social tensions and political battles in the 1970s. The pleasure of eating and drinking well among friends became one of the pillars of Arcigola and then Slow Food's philosophy. It is important to note that they refer to a collective, shared pleasure and not one that is simply experienced by the individual. This pleasure is linked with the idea of conviviality and is not lacking in political significance.

Slow Food

Politics and economy appear closely linked from the beginning of Arcigola and this relationship continues with the evolution of Slow Food, not only because of the leaders and early followers' origins but also because of the association's actions and public positions. In March 1986, the Langhe region suffered a major scandal of "methanol wines" (wine to which methanol had been added to increase the alcohol content) that killed more than twenty people in Italy and caused serious lesions in many others. Arcigola's founders took a public position against the adulteration of wine, the root of the human tragedy and its economic consequences, especially the collapse of the Langhe wine market. They began conducting information campaigns defending the need to focus on wine quality in order to overcome the crisis.

During the same spring of 1986, the first McDonald's opened in the Piazza di Spagna in Rome. I still remember the voices on the pages of the newspapers shouting, "Scandal." The symbol of fast food and American imperialism was installed in the heart of the capital, threatening the small artisan trade and the *trattorie* that animated the streets of central Rome. This event was one of those that prompted the Bra group and their supporters to take a stand, and today its importance is extolled in the official versions of their story. It is interesting to note that, especially in the English-speaking literature on Slow Food, this episode is considered the association's founding event par excellence. Many articles, while declaring an analytical posture, start with that assumption and in doing so trade on the same mythology of the origins constructed through the association's communications. In my opinion this is but one example among many of the activities and stances taken by the founders of Slow Food in that period. Arcigola was officially created some months later, in July 1986. The association started operations immediately and, among other actions, began publishing a newsletter, *Rosmarino* (rosemary), whose name would later become *Prezzemolo* (parsley), and a wine guide, which in a few years would become a reference publication in the field of wine.

Manifesto

In 1987, the *Manifesto dello Slow Food. Movimento per il diritto al piacere* (Manifesto of Slow Food. Movement for the defense of the right to pleasure) (Portinari 1987) was published in the *Gambero Rosso. Il mensile dei consumatori curiosi e golosi*, the monthly cultural and oeno-gastronomic supplement of the communist independent newspaper, *Il Manifesto*. The supplement was edited by the wine and gastronomy journalist, Stefano Bonilli. The original Slow Food Manifesto was written in ironic prose full of double entendres (although some of that irony may be lost in translation). This irony is characteristic of the publications and actions of Slow Food, expressed in a very articulate vocabulary. The Manifesto declared that the contemporary epoch was born of an industrial civilization dedicated to speed, where human beings have elevated the machine as the ideal model for life, reducing humankind to a species on a path to extinction in a monstrous sort of autophagy—"*ingestione e digestione di sé*" (ingestion and digestion of itself). The manifesto was not explicitly directed at climate change, but these expressions can be read as one of the early warnings of the environmental movements. Reading between the lines, the Slow Food Manifesto evokes and opposes the manifesto of futurism written by Filippo Tommaso Marinetti and published in *Le Figaro* in 1909, which glorified "aggressive movement" and the "beauty of speed." By contrast, the Slow Food Manifesto underlines the importance of taking time as a reaction to the frenzy of the "fast life" and the standardization of food and taste incarnated by fast food and rapidity in general. It warns against the virus of *fast* and all its collateral effects and suggests that suitable doses of sensual pleasure and slow, lasting enjoyment may preserve us from the contagion of the multitude mistaking frenzy for efficiency. It contends that taste and the pleasure of the *gourmandise* must be returned to the table, and with expressions like "slow mastication," "recuperation of time," and "organization of pleasure," it conveys the concept of "slow" as taking time to enjoy the pleasure of conviviality and dining.[6] At the end, the Manifesto presents the snail as a symbol of the project. Folco Portinari (literary historian and critic, and author of the text), Carlo Petrini, Stefano Bonilli, and ten others well-known personalities from the world of art and culture signed the Manifesto.[7]

In its elaborated philosophy and textual style, the Manifesto is firmly situated in the Italian culture of the time, particularly in the intellectual and critical left-wing politics, which were able to take advantage of the cultural space left unoccupied by the governing center and center-right parties. Along with the influence of Arcigola, the Manifesto marks the advent of food as an increasingly important cultural and political element. We can say of Arcigola and Slow Food what we can say more generally of other forms of food activism: they are contesting "through" food (Counihan and Siniscalchi 2014; Siniscalchi 2015; Pratt and Luetchford 2014). The space of resistance becomes a space of experimentation on several levels: political, economic, social, and cultural. "Inside the left, the theme of pleasure was not there," recalls Giuliano, another historical leader and for several years vice president of Slow Food, who had been elected within a left-wing group in the municipality of his own town in the narrow Lombardia region. Pleasure becomes a way to rethink politics. However, some of Slow Food's critics on the left claim that adding the notion of pleasure actually detracts from its political meaning. And in fact, Slow Food has always seemed to walk a fine line between traditional left-wing ideology and a new way of approaching politics from the left.

Over time, this Manifesto—the first in a long series published by Slow Food[8]—has been rewritten, adapted, simplified, and translated in order to be exported internationally. But minor variations aside, the following current version from the Slow Food USA website clearly emphasizes the wealth of taste and "material" pleasures of the table: "A firm defense of quiet material pleasure is the only way to oppose the universal folly of Fast Life. . . . Our defense should begin at the table with Slow Food. Let us rediscover the flavors and savors of regional cooking and banish the degrading effects of Fast Food" (Slow Food Manifesto, cf. www.slowfoodusa.org/manifesto).

In December of 1989, two years after its first publication (and one year after the first congress of the association, held in Siena), the Manifesto was publicly signed by several personalities from the world of gastronomy, cinema and theater, intellectuals, chefs, and food critics. The official signing took place at the Opéra-Comique in Paris

Slow Food

because France, considered by the movement's founders as the country of gastronomy, was symbolically important for the movement's visibility. This event formally marked the birth of Slow Food International. In reality, however, at this point Slow Food was still neither international nor even well established in Italy.

Genealogies

The history of Slow Food is sometimes represented as a sort of "genealogy" with ancestors, founding fathers, and internal groups.[9] This approach is useful in the current efforts to build and extend the association while at the same time helping maintain its roots in the city of Bra and in the circles of the Italian left. But the people portrayed in the various versions of the story are not always the same, or they are not presented in the same way. Take, for example, two volumes written by the same author, the journalist Gigi Padovani, who recounts conversations with Carlo Petrini. The first one, published in 2005 by Rizzoli, was rarely mentioned during the time I spent in Bra, between 2009 and 2014, and then only by a couple of the historical leaders when the conversation veered into the association's past. No one from the new generation spoke to me about it. And in fact, the pages of the book seem to have been intended for an inner circle of people who knew each other well and were familiar with the intellectual milieu of the left in those years. These are probably the very reasons the book was not in phase with the changes that the leadership of the movement was trying to promote (an international movement involved in environmental issues). The second was published in 2017 by Slow Food Editore, the publishing house of the association. In the introduction, the author says that it was meant to be an updated version of the first, but then the transformations of the movement forced him to change and rewrite large parts of the project. The publisher's note indicates that the work can be considered as "the official 'biography' of the Slow Food movement." Within the association, the choice of which text is the official version of the moment is not anodyne. The internal voices within the leadership of Slow Food are often discordant, and the choice of how to promote the story is not always the result of an agreement. But it is still possible to interpret the reasons for the choice as directly related to the internal dynamics of the association. Instead of starting with anecdotes and people of the first generation, the text of 2017 takes on a more journalistic style. The first pages evoke the most recent changes at the time (the creation of the Terra Madre network and event, for example)[10] and give voice to younger members who had had more recent political roles within the movement. Other volumes had either undertaken the objective of reconstructing the official genealogy of the movement—such as Carlo Petrini's book, *Slow Food, le ragioni del gusto*, published in 2001—or had been invested with this role after their publication.[11]

Internal genealogies, intended for staff and local leaders or officers are another case where names and key moments are edited, valorizing some and excluding others, such as certain internal conflicts. A document elaborated by the Italian association's headquarters and disseminated to incoming *fiduciari* (*condotta* leaders) after the congress in Abano

Terme (in 2010) refers to particular conferences and historical figures and gives considerable space to the publications of the association. Using certain key events, it weaves together the most recent developments in Slow Food's position on gastronomy and politics. On another level, this genealogy portrays and reaffirms the central role of Slow Food Italia, the first national association. But it hides other characteristics of the association and internal tensions, such as gender issues, which I gradually came to understand during the months I spent inside the national headquarters. Apart from one or two artists (as the singer Ornella Vanoni), the names usually mentioned in these narratives are all men. This becomes even more evident when the genealogy recalls the names of the president, vice president, and the ten *governatori* (governors)—a number that will remain important within the political structure of the association—elected at the founding congress of Arcigola on July 26, 1986.

At the beginning of Slow Food, women were practically absent or at least hardly visible. As Antonio, another historical founder and leader, kept explaining to me,

> Slow Food was conceived by men—in the masculine sense of the word . . . we made gastronomy a mass heritage. . . . Before us, haute cuisine was elitist and gastronomy was a mannerism. . . .There was an enthusiasm for breaking the norms, also for the joy, the excitement of the game. . . . We wanted to experience pleasure, enjoy life. . . . There was, yes, some misogyny among us.

In fact, women are generally absent in the stories of this first generation of Slow Food activists, sometimes explicitly, sometimes more subtly. Antonio's explanation continued:

> We didn't practice democracy, but we were democratic. One can't say the same thing with respect to women. It was a misogynous association. The leading groups consisted of men. Sometimes women were sought to be included. But there were very few. One of the reasons was that we came from the galaxy of the left: there too, there were very misogynous attitudes. This continues today, a little less, but this continues. For years, leaders were men but not because there were no women to recruit. There were also those among us who said, 'I don't give a damn; on the contrary, if there are no women, it's even better!' From the point of view of diversion, it was better to be among men. In our dinners, we didn't talk about women, never. Even in the membership, even today, the member is often first a man and the woman comes later, like an addendum.

Although Slow Food started as a predominantly male association, this characteristic must be analyzed with respect to the play of continuity and changes in the association. "The concept of pleasure [in Slow Food] has always been the pleasure of wine, food, comradeship (*cameratismo*), conviviality, a mischievous spirit (*goliardia*), and flirting with revolution, but on the sexual field no, sexual pleasure has never been a part of it, it has always been banished," said Antonio. In some ways, this seems to be linked to the character of Carlo Petrini, who is not married and has dedicated most of his life

Slow Food

to the Slow Food movement. Oddly enough this aspect has in my opinion affected the development of the association and, in particular, its headquarters. I will come back to gender tensions in Chapter 6.

Making members

In the early stories of those who later occupied leadership positions, they appear above all as a group of friends who liked to joke and eat. All of them were initially swept away by Carlo Petrini's enthusiasm, some in Bra, others in other Italian regions. "Obviously when you were friends with Carlin you liked to go around eating and drinking," said Andrea, who was for many years the head of one of the departments at the headquarters. Carlo, nicknamed Carlin by people close to him, has unquestionably held the central role among Slow Food's historical leaders and founders since the beginning, and he has continued in this role, holding the position of the President of the International Slow Food Association since its creation.[12] I suspect that in the early years he was already one of the most talented communicators of the group. He was certainly the most charismatic, with a natural political instinct, and capable of producing brilliant ideas for the development of the association. Many of these men seem to have been involved almost by chance; some of them spent years with the association, finally abandoning other activities to make Slow Food not only their passion but also their work. Some recall their involvement in the activities of the association beginning with a simple "Come with us" from Carlin. They scoured the countryside for local producers and small restaurateurs. "We also liked to go to restaurants with a little bit of prestige sometimes," Andrea told me. They mixed gastronomic criticism with promotion of the association and its philosophy advocating the valorization of the "territory," its traditions and local characteristics.

Contrary to the way Slow Food has evolved in other countries,[13] the national structure in Italy was consolidated before the local network developed, and the headquarters remains the heart of the association, its driving force, and the place where the ideas and actions of the movement are developed. From very localized beginnings, this oeno-gastronomic association gradually developed and extended its reach to every Italian region. The 1990 creation of its publishing house, Slow Food Editore, helped spread the Slow Food messages and philosophy among its membership and outside of the association, as many of them claimed, in a "transversal" way. As Andrea described it, "The reality was very different than today. I went around setting up agreements with producers and I had to explain to everyone who I was because nobody knew about us. I left the offices with Slow Food books to sell and the materials to make membership cards. It was pioneering, it was all land to conquer."

A friend, who worked for a few years within Slow Food, told me with affection and irony, "they are salesmen, Piedmontese and salesmen." In fact, many of them had backgrounds in associative commitments with management roles or had worked in commerce, some in the wine trade, others in other sectors not necessarily related to gastronomy. For those who came from other realms of work, as in Silvano's case, the association made it possible to change professions, offering work inside the headquarters. Others, like Giovanni, used their experience at the regional level of the association as an introduction into other activities linked to food and wine. "I am part of the old generation, one of the historical figures . . . I was at the ARCI, I worked there. In 1986 we created Arcigola, Carlo Petrini in Bra and I in Mantova. When ARCI was dissolved, I found myself without a job. Carlo told me, 'Come here, [to the offices] in Bra,' but I didn't want to, I liked to cook," said Giovanni, who decided to open a restaurant in Mantova that would remain linked to Slow Food through the association's activities. Giuliano noted, "Many [of the early leaders] came from experience in political organizations, bringing the ability to organize conferences and assemblies which are very useful for expansion. We applied those same methodologies and for this reason the expansion went quickly in those years." Food and wine events (called *conventions*), together with Slow Food publications, were and continue to be an important means of diffusion of the association and an effective means to increase its visibility and legitimacy. The related commercial skills, alongside political commitment and the pleasure of wine and good food, are characteristic features of this first generation. These skills have consolidated over time through the organization of several kinds of events and projects and have been used as a lever and support for the development and maintenance of the association.

Up until 2004, Andrea was in charge of the events and organization of the Salone del Gusto, the fair of high-quality food, organized by Slow Food in Turin every two years. He said,

> We started with the marketing of wine: select the wine, select the cellars. It was the circle of people on the left. We'd gone to a friend's for dinner, and Carlin had just got back from New York. He had been visiting a big wine event, and he arrived enthusiastically, it was 1989. I didn't know what a *convention* was, but soon enough I found myself having to organize a convention on Piedmont wines! In 1990, we organized the first wine convention in Alba. It was a great event. We invented everything: lunches, tastings, dinners, more or less large groups, people who were from different countries but spoke a common language. The following year we organized it in Tuscany, then in Friuli. In 1994, we created *Milano golosa*.[14] Automatically I became responsible for the events office, but only because I had organized the first event, not because I had special skills.

From this time on, we can discern specific operating modes in terms of the organization and its internal hierarchies. Until recently, the principal leaders and representatives of the association were chosen from the top, a schema that assumes a head and a base. This not only included the President, but also the *fiduciari*, and the *governatori* (governors), who represent the association within a "territory." Carlo appointed the *fiduciari* during his meetings and his travels in the different regions. The *fiduciari* were often described as "those who have the trust or confidence" of the President and head of the association, and their devotion and loyalty to Slow Food would eventually allow them to have "the greatest freedom in their territory." Trust was therefore seen as a key element in the

Slow Food

relationship between the top leadership and the local actors. As one of the "historical" *fiduciari*, Giovanni described the process:

> Carlo would arrive in a place where a *condotta* could be or was being created, and it was enough for him to look around to find the most appropriate person to be the *fiduciario*. I myself came from this mode of operation. I wasn't appointed by the members; I was appointed by Carlo. His idea was that you do what you want at home [in your territory], just do it in the name of Slow Food and for Slow Food.

Carlo himself said to me, "I have always told them, 'Do what you want to do, enjoy yourself.'"

These local leaders were chosen on the basis of their networks and their social and sometimes political involvement in the area, which they would then place at the service of Slow Food. Their ability to promote the association (through dinners, meetings, wine, or product presentations), to gather and motivate new members, and, above all, to maintain the trust placed in them over time were necessary characteristics for being a *fiduciario*. Giovanni again said:

> Arcigola's birth and development were directly related to the earlier, public roles played by its leaders. For many Slow Food personalities, their participation became an opportunity to find an identity, but for many others it was just the opposite, it was their public role that helped develop Slow Food. I, for example, when I was interviewed, it wasn't so much the fact that I was a member of Arcigola; it was because I was someone well known, who had been political and was now involved in Arcigola.

The first explosion

According to the memories of staff who were active in the early years, there were about twenty people working in the Bra headquarters in the late 1980s. In the beginning, without any particular skills, everyone played several roles. "Everyone did everything," communication, recruiting members, organizing events, even if individuals concentrated on one specific task or field, they and the work they did continued to be interchangeable.

Although Slow Food International was officially born in 1989, when the Manifesto was signed in Paris, the expansion of the association into other countries was a slow process. It began to accelerate in 1998 following the organization of what is considered today as the first Salone del Gusto. Actually, there had been a previous edition, two years earlier, in a single pavilion at the Lingotto Fiere (the original site of the Fiat car factory). On the occasion of that previous edition, the President of the Piedmont Region had even provided important funding. But it was the 1998 edition—occupying all the four pavilions—that gave Slow Food a significant boost in visibility on a national and international level. In some ways it represents a bridge or turning point between the small association that was Arcigola in the early years and the internationally known movement that it later became. Furthermore, from this moment on, the Salone del Gusto became the most important public and political platform of Slow Food, evolving with each edition in relation to the changes that took place in the movement. At the same time, adding to its significance, the event became one of the sources of funding for the association's headquarters, mainly through the sale of stand space and admission tickets, thus heralding an explosion in the size and functions of its governing structure, as seen in the number of employees and projects undertaken.

The Salone brought a significant amount of money into the coffers of the association and the offices in Bra, and typical of significant events, it is well remembered among the first staff members and historical leaders, who give the early edition almost "mythical" status. Beatrice, the director of personnel, told me,

> This fair was a wreck from all points of view, physical, psychological; we weren't ready; we weren't prepared to deal with the dimensions of the fair and the masses of public. For example, the cash boxes didn't have enough change to give back. We had to get the banks to open on Saturday morning.

Andrea, describing the same event, recalled,

> Slow Food in reality was born in 1998. In 1986 it was not known, it hardly existed. The 1998 Salone del Gusto kicked off Slow Food. It was something, I can tell you, we weren't expecting. We didn't think we'd make any money. Instead, we sold hundreds of thousands of 2,000 *lire* [roughly 1 euro] tasting tickets, and in the end, we didn't know how to manage it. I called someone at Fiat, an executive who sent us a strongbox to put the money in. It was the tastings that we managed directly, and there we saw extraordinary things happen, people pushing the cash boxes when they bought tickets, overturning them and spilling all the cash among the workers behind them.

And Beatrice again recalled,

> The [entry] ticket was cheap, [fifteen thousand lire, roughly seven euros], which had attracted the cautious visitor, but also the one who only wanted to eat bread and ham. . . . This fair was a giant leap from all points of view, economic as well. An incredible number of visitors came, and this was the only time when everyone received a bonus at the end of the year.

This sudden influx of money was totally unexpected, and as a consequence there was a redistribution at the end of that year, probably the sign of a system with a weak hierarchy and a militant heritage. From that time on, the headquarters structure began to become more and more articulated and hierarchical (see Chapters 4 and 6). The dozens of militants and lovers of wine and food threw themselves into more and more activities in communication, promotion of products, education, publishing, and fundraising. Projects followed one after the other and the Salone del Gusto established itself as an important biennial exhibition of high-quality food products, especially Italian, but also from other countries around the world. Capturing the attention of the members of the association and also the national political authorities, it became the showcase of Slow Food projects: the prix of biodiversity, the Presidia project, the school gardens, the farmers' markets, and the network of food communities. With its hundreds of thousands of visitors, the Salone is one of the places that continues to give the association the opportunity to talk about itself and display new themes at the heart of its philosophy; but it is also an important source of money that enables the association's offices to function.

After the success of the Salon del Gusto, in 1998, recruitment in the headquarters increased progressively and exponentially, and the first generation was joined by younger arrivals. Around thirty or thirty-five years old, almost all of them came from the same circle of friends in Bra. Some were children or relatives of members of the first generation; others became "spiritual" children of some of the historical leaders. In the meantime, the name of the association had begun to change, more slowly than one might imagine, but at every quadrennial congress. During the third congress held in Terrasini, Sicily, in 1994, Slow Food was added to the original name (Arcigola Slow Food). Four years later, during the Orvieto congress, the two terms were inverted (Slow Food Arcigola). Finally, the term "Arcigola" disappeared in the early 2000s, and the name of Slow Food alone was definitively adopted during the fifth congress held in Riva del Garda, in 2002. Silvano recalled these changes:

> We have only included the symbol Slow Food in our logo since the 1994 congress of Terrasini in Sicily where we decided to remove the name Arcigola from Arcigola Slow Food. . . . Abroad they mispronounce the name. In Italy there was the Arcigola, and we were the Arcigolosi, but this was illegible in other countries. . . . It was a long journey that also met with internal opposition. In Tuscany for example there was a resistance group, they didn't want to change the name. Along with the name, we also had to separate ourselves from the perception that we were the transmission belt of the left, that we were the *cambusieri* [galley workers] of the left that called on us to slice the salami.

The gradual change of the name marks the association's emancipation from the ARCI, and the desire to distance it from the Italian political context and make it more comprehensible internationally.

> The Slow Food project was born in Italy in opposition to the fast food that landed in our shores and tried to take over, so the awareness that the issue was international was there from the start. The name we chose for our project, and the irony behind it, have caught on. Its force and its bite come from the choice of an English-language name conveying a stance that people all over the world immediately understand. In taking a stand against McDonald's and Pizza Hut,

multinationals that flatten out flavors like steamrollers, we know that we have to fight our battle on their ground, using their weapons: globalization and worldwide reach. (Petrini 2003: 17)

In the original Italian version of that quotation—*Slow Food, le ragioni del gusto* (2001: 19)—this last sentence doesn't stop there. Petrini concludes it with a precision, "appropriating them and reversing their meaning," which was omitted by the translator but expresses a strategy that pervades many of the movement's choices from the beginning and into the following years. The problem of translation is constant within Slow Food, as we will see in the next chapters.

Complexification

The number of members increased, certainly in Italy, but also at the international level. In the early 2000s, Slow Food encouraged or supported the creation of national structures in other countries: Germany, Switzerland, the United States, Japan, France, and the United Kingdom. Like other forms of mobilizations in the field of "food activism" (Counihan and Siniscalchi 2014), Slow Food evolved and changed during its existence, expanding its actions and becoming a legitimate actor in the political arenas of food production and consumption as well as other food-related issues such as climate change and the menace to common goods like resources, energy, and biodiversity. A Foundation for Biodiversity and the Terra Madre network were created and projects focusing on environment, production, or local economies multiplied. In 2004 a private university started by Slow Food, the University of Gastronomic Sciences, opened in a complex of historical buildings, in Pollenzo, 4 kilometers from Bra.

Beginning in the late 1990s, the association set about expanding the repertoire of food-related events. Besides the Salone del Gusto, it launched other international events: Cheese in 1997 (in Bra), Slow Food on film in 2008 (in Bologna), Slow Fish in 2004 (in Genoa), and Terra Madre in 2004 (in Turin). The national and international structures became more and more complex. Even though the headquarters and center of decision remained in Bra, it grew in proportion to new offices created as new projects were developed: the press office, the events office, the communication office, the presidium office, and the wine office, as well as the expanding the international offices. The statutes of the association were constantly modified, and new internal political bodies and roles were created. The political structure of the Italian association also became more complex.

Along with the expansion and internationalization of Slow Food, the philosophy of the early days continued to evolve and be enriched with new elements; its vocabulary also began to change. The repertoire of intellectual references of Slow Food leaders has been a part of this process, beginning with *Physiologie du goût* (*Physiology of Taste*)[15] (1825) by Jean Anthelme Brillat-Savarin and *Tools for Conviviality* (1973) by Ivan Illich, and continuing with works from Edgard Morin, Massimo Montanari, Serge Latouche, and many other intellectual critics. Some of them are even seen as "travelling companions" of the movement. Leitch notes how "an explicit organizational strategy has been the cultivation of an international network of journalists and writers" (2003: 440). Sassatelli and Davolio (2010) perform a relevant analysis of texts and narratives from some of the movement's leaders during this period of rapid growth. Here I simply want to bring attention to the main elements, which help us understand the internal political changes in the movement and the transmission and evolution of its philosophy. The intellectuals from whom the philosophy of the movement is inspired do not all have the same perspective, and there is no unanimity as to which theoretical contribution is the most pertinent. They coexist in a mélange that is not particularly coherent, but which allows everyone to find references that are "good to think about" (to use Levi-Strauss's well-known expression about food).

From the beginning, the notion of pleasure has been one of the pillars of the association. *Il Dizionario di Slow Food* (The Slow Food Dictionary), published in 2002, fifteen years after the Manifesto, defines pleasure by evoking the face of the nineteenth-century gastronome and complaining that his characteristic smile is now lost.

> Gastronomy should be a joyous science, a branch full of epicurean fruit. . . . In contrast to political activism, that has always considered it a succumbing to the worst bourgeois vices, in contrast to a gastronomic criticism that describes food as objects and does not involve those who taste it, the presence [of pleasure] in conversation at the table sounds like a call to concreteness. . . . The pleasure expressed, therefore, the contagious pleasure, returns all its vitality to the body sitting at the table [my translation]. (Ruffa and Monchiero 2002: 125–6)

The authors expanded the "liberating claim of the right to pleasure" found in the Manifesto with the notion of responsibility "towards the environment and the world of agricultural production" (Ruffa and Monchiero 2002: 136). In the 2000s, the term "eco-gastronomy" began to replace that of eno-gastronomy, signifying the attempt to reconcile interests of gastronomy and ecology, often perceived as antagonistic. Consumers started to be defined as "co-producers,"[16] placing the consumer in a symbiotic relationship, alongside the producer. The "co-producer" is a performative term in the sense that it encourages Slow Food members to see their engagement as being concomitant with the producers, who are recognized and considered as increasingly central to the movement's interests.

Many of the actions, projects, and visions of the future that developed during the various phases of the association's life have been promoted or described in Carlo Petrini's books. These books were either ghostwritten or cowritten with another Carlo (Bogliotti), a staff member at Slow Food's offices, and represent the fruit of their exchanges, conversations, and shared ideas. Since the publication of *Buono, pulito e giusto* (2005, translated in English two years later as *Slow Food Nation*), the triad "Good, Clean and Fair" has become the movement's slogan and rallying cry. It signals the evolution of the philosophy along with its formalization: "'Good' is what one likes, and what one likes should be related to the sensorial sphere, which is strongly influenced by personal, cultural, historical, socioeconomic, and contingent factors" (Petrini 2007: 96). "Clean" directs attention to the place and manner of production and hence to the environment, indicating products that respect the environment, or techniques of production and forms of distribution that reduce or eliminate chemicals and environmental damage. Finally, the notion "fair" refers to social justice for producers and to the fair remuneration of peasants,[17] farmers, and food artisans. But Carlo's books are not the only ones advocating Slow Food principles. I am thinking, for example, of a book by Cinzia Scaffidi, who spent several years as the head of one of Slow Food offices; *Mangia come parli* (Eat like you speak) was published by Slow Food Editore in 2014, the year in which the author took on an important political role in the association. Her book is written like a dictionary, and the idea of pleasure is presented as something more complex than what the authors of the Slow Food dictionary wrote ten years before:

> There is no pleasure without knowledge, or rather, the pleasure that is based on knowledge and relationship is a deeper, longer lasting and more solid pleasure. We can say that we like an apple. But if we know that apple is organic, that it was produced by people who do not exploit the work of anyone, that we have it in our hands because someone has recovered an ancient variety that was in danger of disappearing, if we know all these things, we will like that apple much more [my translation]. (Scaffidi 2014: 128)

The more elaborate concept of pleasure in Scaffidi's book reflects another step in the transformations of the movement's thinking, an evolution in the philosophy that has produced changes in style and posture. In the early years, the published guides primarily contributed to the public awareness of Arcigola and then Slow Food and the recruiting of new members. Now they follow and alert members about the transformations in the philosophical views proposed by the association. Moreover, the vast repertoire of collections, books, and guides now published by Slow Food Editore contributes to the development of new themes and new approaches. It is no coincidence that one of the aforementioned "true" narratives treats the dates of Slow Food publications like those of conventions and other events, qualifying them as key moments in its history. These types of references to Slow Food's evolution provide insights into the changes in philosophy and image. Also, the presence of Slow Food in the media has become increasingly widespread in recent years, even if in some cases there has been less variety in the type of voices heard. This expanding coverage reflects the evolution of Slow Food's stronger presence in public platforms, actively advancing its opinion and taking positions for or against a vast range of subjects with the common denominator of food.

The (International) President

Carlo received a Catholic education, was involved in Catholic and left-wing associations from a young age, and became a political activist from the extreme left. He was trained as a sociologist, worked as a journalist, and in the 1970s was elected to the administrative

Slow Food

body of his native city as a member of the PDUP, *Partito di unità proletaria* (Party of Proletarian Unity, situated on the left of the Communist Party[18]). Although he was not the only founder of Slow Food, he became and remains the most visible leader, and his biography is described in most of the documents and narratives produced by the association.

Above and beyond his public notoriety, or his official role, Carlo Petrini spreads charisma and arouses affection and respect from many of the people he meets, even if there have been a few cases of instinctive antipathy. Endearing and unpredictable, with the occasional spike of nerves—visible only to those who work with him and know him very well—but with a political flair and visionary ideas, Petrini is a bright and clever "politician" able to rub shoulders with national (Italian) ministers from the left as well as those from the right and able to collaborate with the highest representative of the Catholic Church. Active on the world political scene and close to the European agriculture commissioner, he might be seen dialoguing with Prince Charles, Barack Obama, Pierre Rabhi, or Pope Francis, or negotiating with other planetary celebrities about the future of food. Today he is considered to be the personification, almost an icon, of Slow Food, even if personally, he seems annoyed and even angry when journalists identify him as such. I often heard him say, "I hate when they call me the guru of the movement."

In 2004, *Time Magazine* dubbed Carlo Petrini an "Innovator," including him in their list of European heroes. A few years later, *The Guardian* named him as one of the "50 people who could save the planet." That evaluation came from a *Guardian* panel which took nominations from key environmental figures and compiled a list of their "ultimate green heroes." They called him a "Food activist." This article appeared at a time when he had become almost unique as a leader in this arena, and his international notoriety was at its peak (although in more recent years the fame seems to have faded).

> Carlo Petrini . . . is the only anti-McDonald's activist who has been welcomed to the offices of David Cameron, David Miliband, Prince Charles, Al Gore and Barack Obama. The founder of the international Slow Food movement, nominated here by Vandana Shiva, is idolised by rich and leisured foodies for promoting high-quality, small-scale farming and organising a relaxed life around long lunches. But Petrini, an Italian leftist of the old school, has a far more serious purpose than saving the pilchard or Parma ham. The Slow Food movement has now expanded across 100 countries and is throwing poisoned darts at the whole fast food culture and the multinational food producers that between them have wrecked so much of the environment. (*The Guardian*, January 5, 2008)

In June of 2009, when I started my research work at Slow Food headquarters in Bra, I began my interviews with leaders from various parts of the association. I met Carlin a couple of months later, after my presence had already been accepted. It was beginning to be considered normal to see me in meetings or the offices, or just circulating from one building to another in the complicated Braidese world of Slow Food where I would meet people, do interviews, or work together. I remember the stress that preceded this first meeting: other directors had already spoken to him about my presence and their interest in what I was doing. I was the first researcher accepted inside the "black box" and I had carefully prepared—even more than usual—the topics I wanted to discuss with Carlo. During the meeting we discussed several topics, but it was only a formal exchange compared to the observations and deep conversations I gathered in other situations over the years I followed the movement. On these various occasions, he was the same as he appeared in everyone's stories: ironic, severe but goliardic at the same time, always ready to pull pranks.

During my fieldwork, Carlo Petrini moved from the headquarters of Slow Food International to offices he occupied as head of the University of Gastronomic Sciences in Pollenzo. This move reflected the importance he placed on the University structure in the future of Slow Food, but it was also the result of internal dynamics within the association which I will address later. His day planner was always full of appointments at the four corners of the planet, and there were only a few days each month when he could be found in his office. During this time, he was invited to the Center for Disease Control (CDC) in Atlanta to address the center's 280 physicians on the prevention of obesity and the relationship between health and food. A few days earlier, he had also given a talk at the Georgia Organics Conference, devoted to sustainable agriculture. Petrini has not only been invited all around the world, he has also received visits from important international personalities, such as Prince Charles during the Salone del Gusto in 2004. Dacian Ciolos, European commissioner for agriculture and rural development from 2010 to 2014, whose defense of small agriculture is close to that of his "friend" Carlo Petrini, was one of the guests of honor during Slow Food International Congress in October 2012.

The progressive Italian newspaper *La Repubblica* has a collaborative relationship with Petrini and regularly publishes his writings. In October 2013, a piece appeared titled *La mia telefonata con il Papa* (My telephone conversation with the Pope). In it the author recounts the call he received from Pope Francis and the points that these men, both from the Piedmont, discovered they shared. These included a family history, but above all, they included important viewpoints on the economy, small farmers, and the defense of common goods. Over the years the exchanges between these men have intensified, and Petrini was asked to write the reading guide for one of the editions of the papal encyclical "Laudato sii" published by Edizioni San Paolo in 2015. A new book titled *Terrafutura: Dialoghi con Papa Francesco sull'ecologia integrale*, and based on his exchanges with the pope on integral ecology, was published in 2020. This reflects the connection between the consolidation of the moral dimension in Slow Food's messages and the intellectual ties that Carlo Petrini has woven in recent years with the pontiff.

Examining the complicated career of this man, who has become a leader of opinion and now the only visible leader of the movement, one might wonder if he is an activist or a "flexian", to use Janine Wedel's term. "Flexians", according to Wedel (2010), are particular social actors who are proficient in the "flexibility" required by current society and capable of exercising power while playing several roles at the same time. But actually, that reflection misses the mark: he is probably both, an activist who copes

Slow Food

with ambiguity, and one whose trajectory embodies some of the characteristics and the transformations the movement has undergone over the years, many of which he initiated. The ability to maneuver among contradictions and ambiguities as well as the capacity to be present simultaneously in very different political fields are essential qualities of Petrini's leadership and probably of this movement in particular. In a way Slow Food is a creature of his making, whose notoriety and diffusion are in large part a result of his actions and visions, even though he has had the support of many others. His personal and emotional involvement is extremely strong, and this emotional dimension is mirrored in the association, in the movement as a whole, and in those involved in it, regardless of their position. "Carlo's intelligence was to know how to gather important ideas from other people; he is not jealous. If you have a strong identity, you become enriched, you don't lose [that identity]. With every exchange, Carlo brings home a new flavor, like food, this is intelligence and originality," recalled Giuliano. Andrea, another historical leader provided a similar view:

> Carlin is not only honest; he is very honest. He lives in another world; he is still a driving force. It's not a problem that he is a dictator; he makes you agree. Today [in 2011] although he is 62 years old, he manages to engage an 18-year-old. It has always been that way; he has the ability to dialogue with an 18-year-old now, just as he could when he was 20 years old. He [also] manages to establish a dialogue with older people. When Carlo was in all the governing bodies, in the end, you already knew who commanded but in a good sense of the word. . . . It was difficult for someone to contradict him. I think he saw far ahead of the others.

Some of the terms in these descriptions (e.g., dictator, commanded) evoke the central and driving role of Carlo. In some ways, the movement has fashioned itself around his personality. These types of terms also hint at the relationships of power within the political and administrative structure of the movement. Fracture lines, friction, and ambiguities developed inside the headquarters between the people with leadership roles (staff leaders) and the salaried "workers" (staff) and outside the headquarters between the seat itself and the local territories. In the following pages I am going to analyze these fractures and frictions and power dynamics in order to expose the ambiguous links between power and production of commitment, between autonomy and fidelity, and between inclusion and exclusion from the point of view of the individuals who make up the association.

Notes

1. The "Opera Nazionale Dopolavoro" was created by the fascist regime in 1925 to promote and support "free time" for workers (through canteens, vacation colonies, parties, etc.). After the Second World War it was transformed into the "Ente nazionale d'Assistenza Lavoratori." In 1948, the Catholic and Republican political forces created their leisure and after-work organization (ACLI, ENDAS). The ARCI was created some time later, as a

national organization of *circoli* (groups as explained in the following footnote) linked to the Italian struggle for liberation from fascism and to antifascist values. In 1986, ARCI became a confederation of associations.

2. In Italy, the word *circoli* refers either to groups of individuals with shared interests and ideas or to the places where these groups gather or meet. *Circoli* are usually organized around themes such as sports, politics, culture, or trades.

3. The word *riflusso* (the medical term for "reflux") is used to refer to an attitude and behavior characterized by a withdrawal into the private sphere that is associated with political and social disengagement in a climate of diminished expectations and falling political and social activism, ultimately returning to a legacy of the past and values deemed as outdated (https://www.treccani.it/vocabolario/riflusso).

4. *Goliardico* refers to the Latin poems written and sung between the tenth and thirteenth centuries by goliards (clerics and monks who had attended renowned schools and then made a career in the courts), whose main motives were the exaltation of love, youth, wine, and social criticism directed especially against the ecclesiastical world—pushed to the point of parody. *Goliardata* is defined as an "Action, enterprise, speech or affirmation that has the character of improvisation, lightness, bluster, and at the same time audacity, daring, and non-conformist boldness." (http://www.treccani.it/vocabolario/goliardata/). By extension, the term *goliardia* means carefree and irreverent (https://www.treccani.it/vocabolario/goliardia).

5. For an analysis of the existing links between instances of assembly, food, and the militant sense of community at the core of the Italian Communist Party, see Tonelli (2012).

6. For a semiological analysis of the Manifesto and the snail symbol, see Marrone (2016). He analyzes and breaks down the various parts of the manifesto into semiotic components. Some aspects of his analysis intersect with my own.

7. Other signatories were the editor of the newspaper *Il Manifesto* Valentino Parlato; the theater actor Dario Fo; the singer and songwriter Francesco Guccini; the writers Gina Lagorio, Enrico Meduni, and Antonio Porta; the *Legambiente* president Ermete Realacci; the art director Gianni Sassi; and the cartoonist and illustrator Sergio Staino.

8. Manifesto del latte crudo, Manifesto dell'educazione secondo Slow Food, Manifesto dei Vignerons, Manifesto delle Isole Slow, Manifesto del Buono Pulito e Giusto, Manifesto Slow Medicine. The manifesto became the favored way to express and diffuse the principles of the movement in the various fields in which it has been active.

9. "Slow Food Story" is also the title of a film, realized by the son of one of the historical leaders and founders of the movement (Stefano Sardo, *Slow Food Story*, 2013).

10. *Terra Madre* is both the biennial event where producers from all over the world gather, and the name for the network that these meetings enable. The participants represent small producers from Asia, Africa, Oceania, and the Americas, but also the European countries in which Slow Food is active (see Chapter 11).

11. An example is the book *The Slow Food story*, by the journalist Geoff Andrews (2008) which proposes a description, with some imprecision, and an analysis of the movement's history, associating some aspects of the Slow Food philosophy with Gramsci's thought. The book concludes with a list of *osterie* and restaurants, which is somewhat disorienting to the reader because it imitates one of the guides published by Slow Food. When it was translated in Italian, errors were corrected with the intervention of some staff members, and a preface signed by Carlo Petrini was added suggesting the reading of the volume by the students of the University of Gastronomic Science.

Slow Food

12. He was also President of Slow Food Italia until 2006, when he decided to relinquish the leadership of the Italian association to one of his designated successors. Other changes occurred at the last international congress in 2022, during the last revision of this book (see Chapter 12).

13. In France or in the United States, for example, the establishment of Slow Food began with the creation of local units and the dissemination of Slow Food principles. The national associative structure was created later, when the international association began encouraging the creation of national units in other countries (see Chapter 5).

14. In a way, *Milano golosa* was the event that preceded the *Salone del Gusto*.

15. The entire title—*Physiologie du goût ou Méditations de gastronomie transcendante, ouvrage théorique, historique et à l'ordre du jour, dédié aux gastronomes parisiens, par un professeur, membres de plusieurs sociétés savantes*—evokes the world of Parisian gastronomy and learned societies.

16. This term is similar in its intentions to "consumer actor" (*consom'acteur*) used in *Association pour le Maintien de l'Agriculture Paysanne* (AMAP) networks in France. Similar to Community-Supported Agriculture, AMAPs were established in the early 2000s. They link consumers and producers with the aim of supporting small-scale community-based agriculture (see Lamine 2008; Siniscalchi 2019b). However, the term "co-producer" emphasizes the rapprochement of the consumer to the producer and his needs (see Chapter 11), while *consom'acteur* emphasizes the consumer himself as an actor able to make responsible and supportive choices in his consumption.

17. The use of the term "peasant" to refer to small farmers goes in the direction taken by other political movements to reevaluate (from an economic and political point of view) a term long used with a negative connotation and an equally demeaning image of those who work the land.

18. In Italy, the small parties or movements of the extreme left, which are not represented in parliament because they are numerically insufficient or because they are opposed to the rules of parliamentary democracy, were referred to as the extra-parliamentary left (*sinistra extraparlamentare*).

Photo 3 The president of Slow Food with a restaurateur and the director of the University of Gastronomic Sciences, after a political meeting, 2013. ©Franco Zecchin.

CHAPTER 3
POWER AND GOVERNANCE
HOW IS THE WORLD OF SLOW FOOD GOVERNED?

Notes by a congress

Friday, May 14, 2010. What is about to begin is the seventh national congress of Slow Food Italy, the first congress in which I am participating. In the lobby of the Alexander Hotel in Abano Terme, the tables prepared for the sponsors are full of documents; there are many of us filling out folders, some are preparing the stand for the publications [of Slow Food Editore], others are moving chairs into the large hall where the congress will soon begin. Delegates continue to arrive from all regions of Italy. The details have been defined, the speaking times, the order of presence on the stage of the current "governors," who will soon be designated, without nostalgia, as "national councilors." In a small room next to the one that is about to fill with over six hundred delegates, the committee that will discuss and file the new statutes will meet. The congress begins. Marco, the new president of Slow Food Veneto, opens, and then leaves the floor to Gino, the ex-president who will preside over the congress. Roberto's speech summarizes the axes along which the association has moved in the last four years of presidency and begins to draw the future lines. Then, one after the other, dozens of delegates and guests take the floor. The seven minutes available for each speech is barely enough, many would like to say more about their experiences, their *condotta*, their region, their new role as leaders within the association.

A few politicians take turns on stage, the newly elected president of the Veneto Region [Luca Zaia, *Lega Nord*, Northern League, an extreme right party], and the mayor of Rome [Gianni Alemanno, *Alleanza Nazionale*, National Alliance, an extreme right party], both former ministers of agriculture. A deputy of the Democratic Party and the former president of the virtuous and rebellious Tuscany region are not enough to remove the impression, amplified by the press in those days, that the left is not there. In reality, contrary to the concerns of some newspapers, this is not a congress that sanctions Slow Food's siding with the right or the left. It is not even the congress of the change of presidency, like the one in San Remo in 2006. It is a congress to renew some of the executive bodies, but above all to validate what has happened in recent months within the association. The internal functioning of the association is not discussed here because it has

Slow Food

already been discussed during the last year, in the meetings of the *segreteria nazionale* and within the regions. The congress sanctions the structural changes of the *condotta*, and the end of the single *fiduciario*, the active role on several levels in the local contexts. "We have made people take on governing responsibilities . . . we have expanded the leadership base," says the president in his opening speech. The congress is a ritual moment in the politics and life of the association and one of its institutional tools. In a discreetly subversive fashion—the congress reconfirms the key elements of the internal organization and legitimizes the redistribution of roles. It allows the members to renew the reasons why it makes sense to continue to invest time and energy in the activities of the association, to share new projects and transform them into challenges. Carlo steers [members] toward the challenges of a "holistic" vision, strengthening "reciprocity," and defending local cultures and languages. "Communicate, communicate, and organize campaigns," insists Silvio.

The congress, with its timing and its ceremonial form, allows the movement, which Slow Food now is, to think about the ways in which it can reproduce itself and to project itself into the future, a future that goes beyond the next congressional deadline, scheduled for four years from now.

What does it mean to do politics and what kind of politics are they doing? With whom to make alliances? How can a real involvement of producers be achieved? And which producers are they talking about? How to take responsibility, collectively? In what happens during the three days in Abano, it is possible to read several levels and several rhetorical registers. A rhetoric of political action that is declared and assumed, one of social and economic utopia, stands in contrast to an organizational one, more juridical and formal. But actually, they are necessary to each other, and they alternate in the interventions of the leaders. Rhetoric and poetics, as linguistic acts, have a performative value; they shape and modify reality, just as practices express meanings.

The unanimity in voting on (almost) all the points submitted to the evaluation of the delegates does not mean uniformity of intent, or absence of conflicts and divergences. This congress is too public for divergences to be revealed. Some discontent emerges, but only like a faint watermark on paper. When it appears on the stage, it is immediately reabsorbed into a movement that seems natural because this is a public moment in which one exposes oneself to the gaze of journalists, politicians, and all those who look at the association from the outside. Here is being woven the web that will hold together old and new leaders, the minds and hearts that have led Slow Food to imagine and be what it is today and proposes to be—a politically involved movement—and bind them with those who have recently joined the association, who have accepted new responsibilities and positions, but who have not experienced the transitions and changes with suffering, as has been the case for many of the historical leaders. It is a web that will have to hold together those who are interested in food and those who talk about food and politics, those who organize dinners and those who feel invested with other responsibilities along with the dinners, the nostalgic and the more militant, those who continue to create spaces of local power through the association and those who instead seek to build other forms of distribution of power and commitment, the producers and co-producers whose prefix is not enough to ensure that the objectives and modes of action are based on and proceed in common agreement. And finally, [this web must bind together] the national leaders and all the others, staff officers, councilors, fiduciari, trainers, and volunteers who at different times and in different ways shape the association. (Siniscalchi 2010b: 176–9, my translation)

I wrote this short text, somewhat reluctantly, for the magazine *Slowfood*, one of Slow Food Editore's publications for the association's members. Silvana, then head of the magazine, had asked me to write it, but behind her request came the request of other Slow Food leaders who, after more than a year, wanted me to start writing for them as well, to put some of what I had understood at the service of the association, and perhaps even to lay my cards on the table. I couldn't refuse, but the exercise wasn't easy. Even more than I had imagined at the beginning of the fieldwork in Bra, I was trying to follow the thread of the power dynamics within the offices and more generally within the Braidese structure. All things I didn't feel like I could (yet) talk about. A year of fieldwork didn't seem to me to be enough time to look at that complex world with the necessary analytical distance. An article of a couple of pages was too short and from the beginning of my work on Slow Food I had decided not to deal with these issues in articles but to wait for the writing of this book so that I could develop the more intimate aspects of how the machine works. And besides, the magazine produced by the association was certainly not the ideal editorial space to propose an analysis of the internal dynamics of the movement. Rereading these notes ten years later, it seems to me that they effectively summarize the atmosphere of the Slow Food congresses and the transformations taking place in those years from the point of view of internal politics. In this chapter, I analyze the dynamics that led Slow Food to its current structure—dynamics that include the role of political bodies and the transformation of the governing responsibilities in the context of structural changes driven by leadership during the years of my research.

Congress genealogies

As the work of historians in very different geographical and temporal contexts encourages (among others, Durand 2021), the analysis of political congresses must take into account the ritual and symbolic dimension they embody, the discourses and worldviews they reveal, the individuals who participate in them, and the power relations that characterize them. The congresses punctuate the life of Slow Food, since the first founding congress, as happens in political parties. Remembered through the name of the city that hosted them, rather than through the date on which they took place, they allow members to trace the memory of the association's great changes. The 1994 Terrasini Congress, for example, was the one in which it was decided to invest in the international development of the association, which was then called Arcigola Slow Food, attributing to the Italian national structure the role of central operator of this development. To do this, it was decided at the same time to expand and consolidate the international structure, that is, the offices, so that they could guide the spread of the association in the rest of the world. The 2006 congress of San Remo was the one in which Carlo Petrini, until then president of both the international and Italian national associations, decided to leave the leadership of the Italian association to one of his designated successors while remaining as president of the international association. This change was not painless and marked the beginning of other transformations of the movement, as we will see in this chapter. The congress of Riva del Garda, in 2014, which I will examine in the last chapter, can be considered the concluding moment of this period of great transformations, which produced the association's new form of governance, which persists at the time of the publication of this book.

Slow Food Italia congresses alternate with Slow Food International congresses almost every two years.[1] The latter constitute a semipublic platform, which in recent years has been organized in conjunction with the Salone del Gusto and Terra Madre or in symbolic places for the movement (Puebla, Mexico, in 2007, or Chengduin, China, in 2017), where they serve to bring together the most distant countries and members. They provide a *trait d'union* between extremely heterogeneous elements of the international association. They show the different ways of doing Slow Food in different parts of the world and in doing so produce a kaleidoscopic effect. Political messages about new guidelines and descriptions of the themes to be developed locally and nationally over the next four years alternate with stories from the diverse membership. Each in their own language, they recount their experiences with Slow Food to the rest of the members and leaders present.

The members' narratives reveal a heterogeneous and diverse Slow Food, from militant movement to gourmet association, from promoting local productions to advocating or supporting projects in the Global South, like an NGO. The congresses of the Italian national structure play a slightly different role. Here as well, the political messages alternate with the varied experiences of *fiduciari* and of members involved in diverse regions of the territory, but the impression is that of a large, extended family reunion reclaiming a common sense of belonging. Even if diversity certainly exists in Italy, like regions or *condotte* particularly involved in political battles compared to others that are mainly organizing dinners and tastings, this heterogeneity is less visible, and their common points are more evident. Members are happy to see each other again and to interact with the *nazionale* (the national, those who work in the offices in Bra). This atmosphere is achieved, for example, by starting the congress with a festive welcome dinner for each regional delegation where delegates interact in a convivial setting (Counihan 2021). Friends from Abruzzi to Sardinia, from Emilia Romagna to Sicily, are proud to be there and show the achievements in their own *condotte* and regions. Although some regional and national politicians also take turns on the stage, the national congress is first and foremost a congress of the members and for the members. Much more so than the international congress, this is an intimate space and an event that acts as a connecting link, that strengthens bonds, that gives members the idea that the efforts and energies expended locally contribute to a common effort and common goals. At the same time, differences and tensions are quietly expressed: between regions, between *condotte*, between visions of the future of the movement, between the new and the old guard, between "Bra" and the "territory." These are tensions inherent in the association and that the congress exposes and sometimes exacerbates but allows the members to digest until the next congress.

From an enlightened monarchy to a (presidential) republic?

When I arrived in Bra, I had the impression that the Slow Food machine was being transformed. In reality, the political evolution of Slow Food had already begun a few years before. Compared to the early years, the internal structure had become more elaborate with various branches and hierarchies, invisible from the outside. The expansion and growth in complexity of the movement and its headquarters have also provoked gradual changes in the political structure of the association. Organizations are continually in "the process of formation [and] under constant modification and reproduction, although they can be temporarily stabilized" (Garsten and Nyqvist 2013: 10). But were these real structural changes? What was new about the system and why did the need for change emerge?

The system of the first two decades is often remembered by the "historical" leaders as a monarchy. An enlightened one according to many, but in any case, one built around the personality and the charismatic and partly authoritarian (though mixed with irony and self-deprecation) character of Carlo. The accounts of the political meetings and the internal workings of the association show an initial period in which ideas and projects followed one another. I collected a large number of anecdotes about official trips or meetings with foreign authorities in which untranslatable dialogues were planned, or about drunkenness that preceded the congresses, or late-night pranks. The meetings themselves extended into the night, with jokes and fun. The rules were few, and Carlin, the maestro of the orchestra, gave the association guidelines. Reflection centered around the following questions: How to develop the association? How to spread Slow Food in Italy and the rest of the world? What unifying tools to use? How to combine freedom of action and development strategies? The answers mixed political strategies, visions of the future, and initiatives that appeared extravagant, but for almost incomprehensible reasons they seemed to bring results in the end. Giuliano, one of the historical leaders, recalls the years of the first congresses:

> Our strength, our agility in those years was that the congresses were based on a series of intuitions that came from Carlin, and not only that, were divided according to the affinities that everyone had, and the congress was a time when it was said: you develop this, you develop that. They were moments of public elaboration. There was little written, few documents.

If the documents, in the memory of many, were limited in quantity compared to the congressional and pre-congressional production of the 2000s, the statutes outlined an association that grew from its headquarters and not from the base.[2] All social responsibilities were decided and attributed from the top, and the governing system provided for the concentration of power in the national headquarters.

"Initially," Antonio, a historical leader, told me, "the responsibilities were taken on for life. This allowed us to not worry about the elections or who was going to become president; we already knew it in advance." Another leader at the time joked to me about lifetime political offices when we returned from a meeting organized by Slow Food Toscana in the Tuscan islands, "Don't talk about it; it's absurd if you think about it today, but it made sense. It was the way to build a strong association. Otherwise, it would have broken into a thousand pieces." Lifetime political offices made it possible to maintain control of the association. In fact, not only were the positions in the national and international structure, as well as in the *condotte*, decided in advance "by Bra," but the votes in the various political bodies were known, and are still called, "Bulgarian votes" as an ironic admission of the consensual adhesion that characterized most of the political choices. Many still remember the amazement of those present and the dismayed nervousness of Carlo when during a meeting of the international council he put in a motion to vote, and two newly appointed American delegates who had not understood that they had to vote, nor how the political bodies of Slow Food worked, did not raise their hands. The president's proposal passed with twenty-three votes in favor and two abstentions. Carlin had asked aloud why (actually getting his English wrong because of the unexpected situation). The two American delegates understood even less what was going on. When I first heard this story, I asked, "This one goes with the *omissis*, right?" "No, no, you have to tell it," one of the leaders, smiling, replied. In fact, these unanimous votes continued to characterize the functioning of political bodies even during the years of my fieldwork.

When I began reconstructing the internal political dynamics while trying to understand the association's subsequent forms of governing, it seemed to me that starting in 2006 Slow Food had moved from a monarchy, with a charismatic leader, to an organization similar to a presidential republic. At the end of the fieldwork, I am tempted to say that what seemed like a monarchy was actually the government of a small group of four or five men, a sort of unseen oligarchy. This group sometimes wavered between the serious and the facetious, but it was dedicated to the development and diffusion of the association, even though it was already crisscrossed with internal tensions and power dynamics.

This system was characterized by strong solidarity at the higher echelons of the association, and local leaders participated even if they held less power than the leaders in Bra. But the system was also characterized by extensive freedom in the territory (regions and *condotte*) and generated aspirations for greater political and economic autonomy in some local areas of the association and among some leaders. These aspirations probably grew once Carlin decided to leave the Italian presidency to his successor and dauphin, Riccardo. In fact, that change was not simply about a different person in the presidency of the Italian structure; it was also a generational change. Although most of the historical leaders had supported this transition and continued to support it in various ways, the very possibility of a handover provided the opportunity for the tensions between the national and the local to be expressed more openly, creating opportunities for a redistribution of power that would give more recognition to the role of local leaders. Other figures could have taken on roles of responsibility at that time. The vice president was another charismatic figure of the early years, but he may have been too independent and less tied to the world of Braidese. "He wouldn't have worked out as president; he was always right and left, and he wasn't reliable," some historical leaders told me.

Some among the Braidese leadership were animated by a particular attachment to the object that they themselves had contributed to create. It is also likely that one of their goals was not to lose their own "for life" role that they had from the beginning or that they had acquired over time. More generally, the aim was to not lose control of the machine, to preserve "their" Slow Food. In fact, in the headquarters it was decided to opt for a succession that would remain anchored in the hands of people belonging to the Bra structure, who could act in a manner consistent with the internal political choices (such as the axes along which to develop the movement, or the modes of dissemination and communication). One of these leaders served unofficially as interim president, and at the same time a longer-term succession began to be considered. Compared to the fact that the positions had previously been considered "for life," this succession was aimed at not changing things too much.

Over time, other charismatic personalities have emerged within the headquarters and the inner group of leaders, but the system seems to have always reabsorbed any overly visible personalities, gradually refocusing attention exclusively on Carlo Petrini. Still today, no individual personality apart from its international President is projected or showcased. I have often reflected on the differences and similarities between the functioning of Slow Food and that of political parties, particularly those of the Italian left. The language and a set of terms are undoubtedly tributary to this political universe, but so are many aspects of the inner workings of the machine. Behind the appearance or disappearance of "historical" personalities in the different phases of Slow Food's history, a constant tension emerges between individual strategies and a collective dimension—a classical, continuous problem of anthropology—of which the association's offices and political instances constitute the space of expression.

Under Riccardo's presidency, the internal configuration of the association changed. Riccardo was not destined to become the new charismatic leader, a role that Carlo retained and still holds today. He was chosen to guide the Italian structure and to lead it towards changes that were probably already deemed necessary. His role was also to think about Slow Food's political strategy on a global level, regarding not only the Italian association but also the international structure and the way of governing this complex as a whole, in which Italy has always had a prominent weight. The new president of Slow Food Italy came from a fundraising position in the commercial branch of Slow Food promotion, seemingly further away from association politics. But among the members of the new generation, he was probably the one who had the most strategic and political vision. He was endowed with legitimacy but at the same time unlikely to overshadow

Slow Food

Carlo. In the first years of my research, some historical leaders who continued to have an important role in the association described the new president in a paternalistic tone: he was a young man with many qualities, who had yet to acquire the confidence expected of someone in his position as president of the most important national structure of the association. Others, especially those in the "territory," emphasized the greater transparency of government and sharing that Riccardo's presidency had produced compared to previous decades. To the contrary, other regional leaders criticized the fact that even in the transition from the old to the new generation, the governance of the association continued to be concentrated in the hands of Braidesi, and the role of leaders in the rest of the territory remained more symbolic than real.

From a formal point of view, the handover from Carlin to Riccardo had the effect of separating the international presidency from the Italian presidency. Less apparent to the outside world, this separation brought about a de facto separation between the offices and personnel of the international structure and those of the Italian national structure, which I will discuss later. To those who, like me, regularly frequented the quadrilateral of buildings between Via Mendicità Istruita, Via Vittorio Emanuele, Via Pollenzo, and Piazza XX Settembre, where the offices of Slow Food's headquarters are located, this estrangement was visible and palpable. With the symbolic separation of the leadership, the organization of work between the employees of the two structures was modified, and at the same time the existence of a small group of leaders, across the different components of the complex world of Bra (Slow Food Italia, Slow Food Editore, Slow Food Promozione, and Slow Food Internazionale), was consolidated. All the members of this group were men born in Bra, friends from childhood, part of the second generation of leaders. This group, undeclared and not identified as such in any organization chart, exchanged views and discussed regularly, before official meetings or decision-making, about internal policies and strategies concerning the governance of the association. Basically, a new oligarchy, as informal and invisible as the previous one, had gradually replaced the one from the association's early years.

The difference between the leadership group of the 1980s and 1990s and that of the late 2000s and mid-2010s is probably that the former, held together and motivated by the charisma of Carlo, was more heterogeneous (with very different personalities) than the new leadership group, although both came from the strong and cohesive Braidese core of childhood friends or comrades in political battles. Another difference between the first leadership group and the second, according to many, is that before they took themselves less seriously. "We didn't get lost in questions about offices and leadership positions as we do now," one of the historical leaders told me. Although there were many criticisms of the changes underway, evoking a sentiment that "before we had more fun," my notebooks are filled with notes, phrases, and situations that happened during my fieldwork and still make me smile or laugh when I reread them. I did not experience the atmosphere of the early years, but the feeling of a shared cultural intimacy mixed with self-deprecation certainly continues to characterize the relationships within Slow Food.[3]

This change in attitude was accompanied by occasional criticism of the concentration of decision-making power in the hands of this non-visible group, which some ironically referred to as the "politburo" (a term taken up by the members of the group themselves with equal irony). The existence of this group without an official role did not mean that Carlo was deprived of any real power regarding internal politics or the functioning of the structure. In fact, two levels of governance were created: a first level concerning internal policies, association policies, the structure of the offices and their interactions, and economic decisions, which were discussed within this restricted group before being put on the table of the various political bodies; and a second level concerning the major choices of the association,[4] in which Carlo's voice continued to be not only central but decisive, even if sometimes in disagreement with that of the other managers or leaders.

Carlo remained the undisputed and emblematic leader, both inside the movement and as its public standard-bearer. Today all the members grant Carlin the role of founding father, and public political relations with the outside are concentrated in his hands. Although his presence in the offices of the headquarters was perceived by some as too overbearing, he managed to appear detached from internal quarrels and even annoyed and bothered by the dynamics of power that animate the daily life at headquarters during my fieldwork. Nevertheless, he was always consulted whenever a major problem arose, either in the Bra offices or in relation to the policies of the association. Discreetly, he could be called on to resolve conflicts even if he was able to escape most of the daily internal decisions such as personnel issues or the reorganization of certain offices. His role resembled in some respects that of the President of the Italian Republic, guarantor of the constitution and *super partis* with respect to conflicts between factions or parties. Similar to what happens in Italian politics, Carlo seemed distant and often annoyed by the internal quarrels, but actually, he followed their dynamics and outcomes more than he pretended, suffering on certain occasions and intervening at some key moments.

Democratization?

Movements and mobilizations change over time, and the transformations I have observed within Slow Food are similar in some ways to those of other organizations in which a first phase, where an unstructured group aggregates around a charismatic figure, is followed by a second phase where professionalization produces internal hierarchies and new forms of governance. In the case of Slow Food, similar dynamics were certainly present, but more specifically, there was a constant tension between the different "souls" that made up the structure, and that aspect became more pronounced over time: center and periphery, association and movement, leaders and staff, paid members, and volunteer members. Several generations of leaders coexisted, while the exercise of power became increasingly invisible and contested, precisely at a time in Slow Food's history when a process of democratization was activated in the Italian association. What is the meaning and how was this "democratic" phase being implemented and why was it provoking discontent?

Democracy or the absence of democracy was evoked by many historical leaders. Carlo Petrini often said, "We are not democratic." This was also a subject during the regional

Slow Food

congresses. The lack of democracy can be at the same time a criticism and an avowed characteristic of the association. Pietro, a historical leader, who was behind the drafting of the first statutes with Carlin, told me that the textual formulas were used explicitly to prevent any form of democracy. There were not only lifetime offices: the *fiduciari* were like vassals who left heirs to follow them. "The first change came when the possibility of members distrusting the *fiduciari* (*sfiduciare i fiduciari*) was introduced, in 2000 or so." "We needed the statute to be that way at first, but it couldn't last forever, it had to change."

Before each Italian congress, every four years, the congress rules and then the statutes defining the organization of the association were reviewed and rethought during the meetings of the national board, and then during the governors' meetings. At the congress itself they were discussed and modified by a restricted group of leaders, some from Bra and some from the regions. The statutes do not seem to be a rigid instrument, nor do they faithfully represent the internal hierarchies; rather, they are the malleable result of the political direction given to the association, a reflection of some of its structural changes.

From the mid-2000s, under the banner of an internal "democratization," the Italian association's modes of functioning were restructured. This pyramidal process created different internal levels of political representation and governance, and the positions in the internal hierarchy of the association proliferated. In the beginning the association had a national base and local units everywhere in the territory (*condotte*). In the middle of this structure, a governors' committee, a sort of *trait d'union* between the *condotte* and the national structure, was composed of people who were selected from the top of the hierarchy and not directly elected by the members. In the first restructuring and "democratization" step, the association created regional presidents, assemblies, and regional congresses composed of representatives from the *condotte*.

During this process, the regions acquired increasing importance and additional representation. The focus on regions and the gradual establishment of direct representation of members responded to a demand that had coalesced over time: to give more autonomy and more power to the regional and local representatives (not necessarily the members themselves) and to bring "Bra" and the *territorio* ("territory") closer together and raise the influence of the latter. What was referred to internally as the congress process (*percorso congressuale*, in language inherited from the parties of the Italian left) served to prepare the association for the changes that the following congress would then sanction. The meetings of the board of governors (twice a year) and then the annual assembly of the *condotte* were important steps in sharing information about the changes. I use the term "sharing" because most of the decisions regarding the form that the association would take (after the sanction of the congress) had been previously discussed, refined, and then decided in a myriad of meetings. Some of these were formal, but many others were not provided for in the statutes. Meetings occurred between leaders from the main sectors of the association. These were sometimes precursory to the almost monthly meetings of the national board where the political choices were discussed. There were also informal meetings with historical leaders who were still presidents of regions or had regional responsibilities at the time. These were often individuals chosen

Power and Governance

as privileged interlocutors not so much for the official role they held as for the much more important role of a trusted political referent, a tutelary figure and guardian of the internal memory of the association.

My impression at the time was that the association, created almost out of nothing by an extended group of friends with sometimes divergent but complementary personalities, had arrived at a moment in its internal history that was almost as important as its national and international development a decade earlier. At that period the progressive professionalization of the Braidese structure and of those who occupied roles of responsibility within it marked a significant level of development. This period at the end of Riccardo's first mandate and the 2010 congress seemed to mark another great moment of caesura and transformation of the relationships between Bra and its members.

The process of democratization was translated and perceived by many as a process of bureaucratization. The language used to indicate the different parts of the associative structure was progressively modified: it moved away from the irony, and in some ways the originality, of the early years and assumed modes of expression closer to those used by political parties. Although the historical term of *fiduciario* remained unchanged, the *piccola tavola* (small table, the governing body of the *condotte*) were replaced by *comitato di condotta* (condotta committee). The *governatori* (governors), some of whom were from the Bra offices and others who were from the "territory," were replaced by *consiglieri* (councilors), elected members of the national council, the new name for the governors committee. In the first years of the association's life, when the role of governors was established, the body that assembled them was named the "*grande tavola*" (big table), then *consiglio dei governatori* (governors committee). In 2010, the name changed again, becoming the *consiglio nazionale* (national council), which also made the terminology of the Italian association and that of the international structure more homogeneous.[5] The change in terminology had a performative role aimed at supporting both the changes in image and the changes in the internal functioning of the association.

The first reason for these changes was to mark the difference between the association of the early years, in which the members were mainly gourmets, and the updated aspirations of Slow Food, which was increasingly a movement that fights in defense of local economies and small producers around the world. The "small table" describing the leadership of the *condotta* had too many connotations and was not very credible in this new context where Slow Food's leaders intended to affirm the political role of their association and to dialogue more and more with other institutional players. The second reason for the new terminology is linked to the process of "democratization" and "sharing" of responsibilities that the new Italian presidency along with several historical regional leaders sought to promote within Slow Food. This process was translated into a series of measures aimed at modifying the association's structure, such as increasing the number of people with roles of responsibility. These measures were intended to end the unique power of the *fiduciari* in the *condotte*, but also, at least in appearance, to reduce the power that the national office had previously exercised through appointment of the *fiduciari* and governors from the upper echelons of the association. Elections to choose the *fiduciario* and *condotta* committees were the first step in this direction, but the structural logics of the past continued to coexist with the new modes of operation, and the underlying control by Bra was not interrupted.

The congress and the new statutes also established term limits: an office cannot be held by the same person for more than two consecutive terms. This was the end of "lifetime" offices for those in charge at all levels. I remember that one of my first thoughts at the time was that the new president of Slow Food Italia, elected in 2006, was preparing to begin his second but also final term in 2010. The handover that had taken place when he was elected represented the move to establish the reproduction and reconfiguration of the association over the time, acknowledging that there would not be another charismatic leader like Carlo Petrini.

The consequences of pleasure

The Congressional document of Abano Terme (2010) was titled "*Le conseguenze del piacere*." The name winks at the film by the Italian director Paolo Sorrentino, *Le conseguenze dell'amore* (*The Consequences of Love*, 2004), and at the same time puts pleasure, one of the axes of the association since its creation, at the center of reflection. Where has pleasure taken us? The document, prepared in the months leading up to the congress, lists, alongside pleasure and conviviality, the other "values of Slow Food." Among these are complicity, fraternity, and the ethical dimension of Slow Food, which its leaders define as a commitment to make no compromises, even in the difficult and risky paths that the association is taking. The desire of Slow Food's leaders to have a greater say in decisions on agricultural, energy, and food policies is reflected not only in their involvement in national and international political battles but also in the projects carried out at a local or regional level. These projects require a growing commitment from members and their representatives. The *fiduciari*—those who have the "trust" of the national headquarters and the associative base and who manage the *condotte*—as well as the governors or national councilors and presidents, are urged not only to put the Slow Food philosophy into practice through new actions but also to penetrate and consolidate the association in the territory, to spread the ideas of the movement, to dialogue with local institutions and political powers, and to act to raise funds for the functioning of the association itself. Slow Food's increasingly political connotation means that it needs to find ways of financing the association so that it does not depend exclusively on public funding, which can be lost during political changes in the national government or particular economic situations. It also means a change in terms of the political commitment of members, who are increasingly encouraged to take a stand as activists "against" certain practices and policies.

How to move from a movement of people united by the pleasure of wine and food to a movement that, from head to toe, is committed to changing the system of consumption and food production on a planetary scale but starting from micro-local contexts? How to get the *fiduciari* and members of what for years had been the "small table," unbeatable in the organization of "classic dinners," to be active on several fronts—relationships with small producers, school gardens, training, relationships with institutions to promote and finance projects—and to push the rest of the members in these same directions? Above all, how can they remain inclusive—"Slow Food has never fired anyone," "Slow Food has never excluded anyone," I have been told several times in different circumstances—and at the same time remove roles and space from those who are not willing to adapt to change?

In the years of my research, there was no longer any talk of lifetime offices, even though in reality, many *fiduciari* retained almost unquestioned responsibility for their own *condotta*, from the moment of its creation. The Slow Food machine, characterized by slow moving gears, gradually invented new leadership roles and new procedures. These marked the end of the term of office for many of the historical leaders in Italy, and in certain cases, the end of their ambitions to continue in a prominent political role and possibly even assume the presidency of the association at some point. If a part of the old guard recognized, accepted, and in many cases promoted these measures that seem to guarantee the replacement of ruling groups and the end of a system in which power is concentrated in the hands of one person, others felt sidelined and consider the need for new viewpoints to be an unjustified pretext. Nevertheless, the change was experienced by many as too rapid and radical; they looked at changes and saw an association that was abandoning its heritage. Some of the historical leaders occupied leading positions for quite some time, either at the headquarters or at the regional level, but even if they continued to be symbolic as a reference, they gradually began to lose their leadership positions. Some have a more discreet but still important place; others were overshadowed by changing internal logics or left the organization.

Il pensatoio (the thinking room)

One of the new bodies created by the Abano Terme congress was the *consiglio di indirizzo* (guidance council), which was actually dissolved at the following congress in Riva del Garda in 2014. Some of the members who were asked to be on the *consiglio di indirizzo* called it "the thinking room." But others from the outside pointed to it with a hint of cynicism and called it "the museum of elephants." The guiding council was intended to be a place for reflection on the policies and future of the association. The members like Antonio and Lino were historical leaders who had played an important role and now were leaving the governance of their region to the new generation. They came from the same world of trade unions and left-wing political parties and had had important roles at the local level: both were presidents of regions and had been members of the *segreteria nazionale* (national board), one of the governing bodies of the Italian Association. Each of them had continued for years to maintain a role of "historical memory" and advice on the association's policies, sometimes with different points of view on the future of Slow Food and the relationship between headquarters and territory. Another prominent figure, Giuliano, the imaginative ideologue who had

Slow Food

been designated some years ago to take a central place at the head of the association, was contacted to become part of this new body but refused. He had been away from Slow Food for too many years and even though he maintained ties of affection and friendship with past companions of the adventure, he was no longer in agreement with the direction the association had taken.

The *consiglio di indirizzo* met three times, in three different towns, Abano Terme, Codigoro, and Orvieto, each time looking for paths of reflection that could re-imagine the future of the association. I remember, in each of the meetings, the time spent trying to define the role of this new body and how far the imagination of the association's future could go. And indeed, I could not avoid the impression that this group was almost a clearinghouse, a place for historical members to become accustomed to the fact that they had left behind the political roles they had occupied for so many years, a place where they could reconnect with others who had also drifted away from Slow Food but had occupied important roles in the past. The discussions that the presidency continued to have with some of them did not really require a new body, in part because those talks took place independently of the reflections of the "*pensatoio*." And indeed, the activities ended after the three meetings, and the *consiglio di indirizzo* was officially discontinued during the following congress. Perhaps it was not really destined to have the role that some within it thought it should have and perhaps some of the suggested directions came too soon (and did not come from Bra).

What was presented at all levels of the association as a process of adjustment to the political project that the association had given itself on a national and international level, in fact, introduced a system of control that contrasted with the freedom of action that for years had been left to the *condotte* and their local leaders. Almost monarchical for the first fifteen years of its existence, this pyramidal machine has gradually created different internal levels of political representation and governance. The regions indeed gained more and more importance, but the central control that "Bra" held over the *condotte* and the rest of the national "territory" became more pervasive. Behind the observed forms of control lies the difficulty of governing an association made up of extremely heterogeneous parts, local specificities, and varying forms of autonomy that seek to escape central control. Deep, trusting relationships were woven on a weft of proximity, love of gastronomy, and political engagement. But at the same time, fracture lines, friction, and ambiguities developed between the people with leadership roles and the simply salaried "workers." Outside those offices and relationships, this line also appeared in a larger sense between the seat itself and the "territories."

Notes

1. The congress is usually held every four years, but the dates of the congress can shift according to internal or external constraints.
2. Unlike other movements and associative structures, such us the AMAP in France, for example, see Lamine 2008; for other examples, see Koensler and Rossi 2012.

3. Although the level of playfulness had probably reduced over time, this climate was still in evidence during the trips and events or in the preparation of meetings in which I participated with Slow Food staff and leaders. In 2011, we spent a week in Hemavan, in the north of Sweden, with some of the staff and Italian and international leaders to participate in the international council meeting. The sun never set, nobody could sleep, and the staff would move from room to room, to discuss, drink, play, and joke around in a kind of humorous intimacy. In the middle of the night, Carlo made prank phone calls to discuss political topics with friends in Italy.

4. The emphasis put on producers, at the level of both the movement's philosophy and actions (investing in certain projects, such as the gardens in Africa or the Terra Madre meeting) or even the investment in the youth part of the movement or the importance given to the University.

5. The main political bodies of the international association were the international presidency and the international council.

Photo 4 Slow Food's headquarters: The entry of the Italian association offices, Bra (Italy), 2012. ©Franco Zecchin.

CHAPTER 4
INSIDE THE ITALIAN ASSOCIATION

In February 2011 in Pollenzo, two days of training were held for new *fiduciari* from all over Italy. The event took place in a large room where all participants were seated in a circle, each introducing himself or herself by quickly saying where they came from and why they got involved in the life of their *condotta*. After the introductions, Diego, a member of the Bra staff who was elected general secretary of Slow Food Italia the year before, goes into the theme of the first day:

> It falls to me to tell you how we are structured. We are an association made up of two souls, important and inseparable: a soul represented by the members, associative, and a more structural soul, *societaria* (corporate), at your service, which is the national headquarters. . . . We come from a history in which members were used to experiencing the association in a passive way. We decided to reverse this process and make the members an active part. The consequences of pleasure: we started from the values that come from our history, pleasure remains and will be the central point, together with the conviviality that makes us unique.

In the words of the general secretary, "the consequences of pleasure" meant giving more responsibility to members, making them active participants and not just passive members guided from above. Behind this binary vision assumed by both poles—the headquarters and the members in the *territorio* ("territory" refers to the regions and *condotte*), the Braidese staff and the volunteers—and behind the rhetoric of giving members an active part in the association, the actual functioning of the association is much more articulated and conflictual.

Some of these tensions appeared during the process of "democratization" that I analyzed in the previous chapter, democratization that involved a change in leadership, especially at the local level, but also created more bureaucratization in the Slow Food machine. In this chapter, I will follow some of the fracture lines and tensions that run through Slow Food's inner workings. The internal structure consists of a number of governing and political bodies that exist within the strong hierarchy in membership and leadership, a hierarchy which has always been influenced by the omnipresent friendship links that constitute the core of the association. Fracture lines appeared within these political bodies at different levels: between staff leaders and regional leaders, between small and large regions, between *fiduciari* and regional presidents, and finally within the *condotte*, the smallest units of Slow Food's complex political organization. These fractures involved autonomy and control, representativeness, money, and voluntary work. Tensions also involved the two souls of Slow Food, its identity as an association and as a movement, which at times are difficult to hold together. Using the Italian national association as a case study, I will analyze the way these elements emerged within the Slow Food political machine. The Italian association constitutes a model in several respects for the other national associations and to understand the way Slow Food functions on a global scale: the tensions and some of the contradictions that characterize the association in general appear here most visibly, and changes and possible solutions are often tested in Italy before being disseminated internationally to the rest of Slow Food's complex world. Evolutions in the philosophy and priorities of the movement emerged within the boundaries of Bra before being discussed in international instances. Finally, the Italian association continued to have a predominant role in the functioning of the entire movement.

Bra and the *"territorio"*

Since the beginning of Slow Food's history, the management system of the association has been designed to keep the concentration of power in what can be considered the first local unit, the national headquarters in Bra. The history of the association clearly shows how this happened. Slow Food was created by the "head," by people based mostly in Bra who established the headquarters before creating the *condotte*. For these reasons, it is somewhat artificial to distinguish the headquarters from the political bodies and the governance of the movement: the two are closely interconnected. Before the 2014 congress in Riva del Garda, the most important responsibilities—the national president, the international president, the general secretary, and so forth— were conferred to members who were also employees of the association and working at the Bra headquarters. These were the staff leaders, as I call them. They occupied the highest political positions, deciding the association's future development, its political lines, and its functioning. The staff leaders cannot just be described as employees who also play political roles. Nor are they simply members who have been assigned political responsibilities and receive a salary for their time. The core of the first generation of leadership includes the founding fathers of Slow Food. Although they created an association and a way to pay themselves for their work inside it, they were not just paid administrators. They were the intellectual foundation of the association, the political force behind the ideology and strategy of Slow Food. Over the course of time, this core reproduced itself, adding another group of administrative and political leaders. Some women began to arrive, but this second generation of leaders was once again composed largely of men, many of whom had first joined the association to fulfill a requirement of civil service (either military or civil service was compulsory in Italy until 2004).

Slow Food staff and leaders are called "braidesi" or "il nazionale" (the national) by volunteers in the rest of the peninsula (and referred to as "Bra" or "the international" by members in other countries of the world). "Those from Bra say that . . ." or "Bra let us know that . . ." are frequent expressions that have long been heard in the various Italian *condotte* (as well as in others countries). The national headquarters is described as a service center, a part of the machine serving the association on the ground, as noted in the quotation from Diego at the opening of this chapter, but above all, it assumes a political leadership role for the movement as a whole. The "national" or the "international" (which includes staff leaders and employees in all the headquarters' offices) is perceived and referred to by members and local leaders as a single entity, distinct from the "territories," often far from the needs of the *condotte*, and imbued with controlling and sometimes authoritarian attitudes. In reality, power and control, although largely concentrated in the hands of the Bra leadership group, have been exercised—perhaps even more pervasively—by other bodies in which regional leaders also participated.

Territorio, like "headquarters" and "Bra," is used by both of these "poles" as if it was an entity, but actually, it includes hierarchies and very different levels of involvement and responsibility. However, *territorio* still marks the distinction between national leadership and people who do not have the same level of political responsibilities. Local leaders have political responsibilities: in the *condotta* for which they are responsible (*fiduciari*), in areas of the association at the regional level (governors), or in the region as a whole (regional presidents). In some cases, they experiment with projects, partnerships, and different modes of action. Some are considered historical leaders, belonging to the group of "friends" from the early years, who have been close to the Bra staff and leaders and maintained that strong proximity even when they have assumed new roles. The association's growth has often been based on personal ties, friendship, and political networks and historical leaders have acted as links between Bra and the *territorio*.

The second level is made up of volunteers who get involved in the life of the *condotta* and in the events organized at the local, regional, or national levels, thus contributing to the daily life of the association. Finally, there are the "ordinary" members who hold the association's membership card, participate in dinners or events, and share the philosophy of the movement, but who have no political responsibilities or involvement in volunteer activities. They are important because their membership (the fact of having an association card) allows the association to affirm its strength and presence on the ground: an association with 30,000 members (the number of members in Italy during my fieldwork) is more legitimate and credible than an association with only a few thousand members. Below is a schematization of the different categories of members and leaders (Table 4.1):

Slow Food

Table 4.1 Members and Leaders

	"Il Nazionale" or "Bra"	*"Il Territorio"*
Leadership	Staff leaders (or Bra salaried leaders)	Local leaders: • Regional presidents • Governors • *fiduciari*
People without political responsibility	Staff (or Bra salaried workers)	Volunteers: • Members of the *piccola tavola* • Volunteers helping during the events Ordinary members

The regional presidents are considered to have a pivotal role in coordinating relationships between the *condotte* and therefore between the *fiduciari*. Their position was established in the early 2000s, but only in regions with more than 500 members.[1] These presidents are both the national association's representatives to local institutions and the national association's regional interlocutors. At the lower end of the spectrum of local leadership are the *fiduciari*: they are often at the origin of the creation of *condotte*, they have the trust (*fiducia*) of the national headquarters and oversee the territory through their activities. They recruit new members through *tessere* (membership cards).

The *governatori*, renamed *consiglieri nazionali* in 2010, have a role in representing portions of the territory or local activities within the national council. A historical leader, Pietro, humorously noted: "We don't really know what governors governed, but they were the representatives in the field." Initially, (local) governors were chosen exclusively from among the "best" *fiduciari* (active in their area, in conformity with Slow Food philosophy, and closest to Bra's leadership). But over time, they have been chosen from a variety of other positions of responsibility: today some come with the particular experience of working on the Presidia project in their region (in charge of dialoguing with local Presidia producers, and coordinating with the offices in Bra), or the "Orti in condotta" (a project for the creation of school gardens); they can be trainers in the "Master of food" courses that Slow Food organizes throughout the country, or they can be *fiduciari* with particular skills in local government (often, historical *fiduciari*). They are part of the *consiglio dei governatori* (renamed *consiglio nazionale*).

The most important body in the political structure of the association is the *segreteria nazionale* (national board), which assembles the presidents of the large regions (those with more than 1,500 members)[2] and a quota of members chosen by leaders inside the headquarters at Bra. The national board defines the political lines, the strategies, and the evolution of the movement. Its members are elected at the national congress (but in fact, the congress confirms choices that have already made). They are also part of the *consiglio dei governatori.*

The responsibilities differ depending on the governing level in which the leaders are involved, but at every level, leaders with responsibility perceive themselves and are represented as belonging to the decision-makers, as opposed to the "simple" members or members who may volunteer for various activities. "A good leader is one who has connections and who has ideas," one historical leader told me. People become leaders because they have a network of relationships and certain skills, but these need to be shaped over time. Many historical leaders recall with some embarrassment (in a discreet collective memory that should be preserved but not talked about) the abuses that sometimes resulted from the concentration of power, and the cases in which excessive autonomy has favored behavior and private interests whose economic or political consequences are still visible today. National staff leaders often believe that the local leaders and *fiduciari*, in particular, must be guided to ensure that they don't become too autonomous or deviate from the goals of the movement and the directives from the national and international leadership. They must be accompanied and trained in the evolving policies and philosophy of Slow Food, today even more than in the past. The need to guide those invested with responsibility is a widespread sentiment and is also expressed by non-Bra historical leaders regarding the new generation of staff leaders.

Normalizing and shaping Slow Food space

In 2009, a general assembly of the *condotte* in Fiumicino was organized to prepare for the 2010 congress. Regions, as well as *condotte*, were asked to focus their projects in two directions: educational projects and the defense of rural communities in their territory. Although *condotte* were required to produce an annual dossier even before, the task only became mandatory in the months leading up to the congress. The *dossier di condotta* was a programmatic document that summarized the actions carried out in line with the (new) principles of the association and presented the objectives to be achieved, including the number of members. Although the minimum number of members required to constitute a *condotta* had been thirty, a new objective was set at fifty people. This was the result of the process of "democratization" (analyzed in the previous chapter) advocated by the Italian national leaders: widening the leadership base, sharing responsibilities, creating a mechanism for historical leaders to step back and allow new leaders to emerge, and, finally, ensuring that projects and events organized at the local level were aligned with the evolution of Slow Food's philosophy and in particular with the importance of producers.

As Shore and Wright pointed out from a perspective of anthropology of policies,

organizations exist in a constant state of *organizing*, and that process revolves around the concept of policy. From universities and schools to public agencies and large corporations, policy is increasingly being codified, publicized and referred to by workers and manager as the guideline that legitimate and even motivate their behaviors . . . [Policy is] the force which breathes life and purpose into the machinery of government. (1997: 5)

Slow Food

At each meeting of the *segreteria nazionale*, the members would begin with the *dossier di condotta* elaborated by each *condotta* and then discuss the evolution of the association in each area of the country. The regional presidents are the ones who know which *condotte* are functioning well or poorly (with respect to the quantity and quality of projects carried out and their consistency with the association's policies) and can judge the appropriateness of an intervention (to open or close a *condotta*, for example, or to settle conflicts, as we will see later). The discussion often took the form of a map showing strengths and weaknesses (Low and Lawrence-Zúñiga 2003). Pages and pages of my notebooks report the exchanges during these meetings in which the geopolitics of Slow Food in Italy was drawn. If we continue with the reasoning of Shore and Wright, who in turn draw on Foucault, we can see two sides of a coin. The "objectification of the policy" produces an "objectification of the subjects of policy": applying this to the *condotte* and the *fiduciari* who govern and animate them, we can say that they become "the object of information" rather than "a subject in communication" (Foucault cited by Shore and Wright 1997: 5).

In September 2010, some months after the national congress, the members of the *segreteria nazionale* verified that the *condotte* who had been struggling had reached the objective of a minimum of fifty members, allowing them to continue to exist. On several occasions during the previous meetings, some staff leaders had reminded the other participants that the issue was not simply numerical: focusing on numbers was a way of avoiding problems with association policy with respect to the territory. But at this meeting, numbers were now being integrated as an essential criteria. Region by region, *condotta* by *condotta*, the members of the *segreteria nazionale* reviewed the situation, envisaging what action, if any, needed to be taken:

> Volture is a *condotta* that needs to be monitored. On Oct. 15, there will be a meeting to establish the Potenza *condotta*. We can see if we can merge it. Let's wait for the evolution of Potenza. . . . Parma has done a great job. We should merge Palmarecchio and Rimini. In Ferrara, there is a meeting tomorrow night with the previous '*piccola tavola*,' and there is a woman who could be a *fiduciaria*.

In some cases the members of the *segreteria nazionale* envisioned mergers between *condotte*, and in others they sought to identify new leaders. With the end of the long terms of office that had characterized the association up to that point, it was often difficult to ensure the renewal of leadership because the *condotte* had often been structured around the personality of the historical *fiduciario* who had initially formed the local group.

The representative of Lazio reassured his colleagues, "Cassino, Tivoli, and Latina are aligning. Cassino needs a different *fiduciario*. Terracina is already recovering. For Civitavecchia, the regional president has identified someone that she likes a lot." The national president confirmed: "Where there is already an interlocutor in place, we have to trust him." The *condotte* were judged on compliance, and the regional presidents or their representatives acted as guarantors of their conformity to the association's new rules. Trust in the new leadership teams extended to the whole *condotta*.

64

Another member of the staff spoke about Sicily: In one of the *condotte* there are 28 members; they have five *orti in condotta*, but "they don't make *tessere* (membership cards)." The national president recalled that they were already below thirty members at the end of 2009: "Closing the *condotta* to open the area to a new configuration is the solution, they will never reach 50 members. In consideration to those who respect the statute, we will close it. And we will write to the parents of the school gardens to explain." The local projects needed to be maintained. Interventions and their relevance in the local context were considered carefully. A regional president suggested convening the *congresso di condotta*, but the national president disagreed, "If the 'national' convenes the congress, it is the same as closing the *condotta*; it is better to close it directly; otherwise, they will contest [our intervention]." The discussion continued and another member proposed to merge the *condotta* with another one, but according to the national president this solution was worse: "All the *condotte* in Italy prefer to start from scratch rather than be merged. Then there is the problem of respecting rules, which in this region takes second place. Until we close the *condotta*, it is not possible to have a new *comitato di condotta* [meaning new leadership]. As soon as we close it, you'll see, it comes out." Closing the *condotta* in this case seemed to be the solution that would allow the formation of a new local group and ensure that the same rules were applied everywhere. The president of the region was not a member of the *segreteria nazionale*. This meant that it was not possible for him to take advantage of the exchanges among presidents who are also members of the *segreteria* and have the opportunity to act as guarantor for their own region. Moreover, Sicily appeared to be a difficult region to govern with problems far removed from the Piedmont perspective of Bra leaders. It is easy to imagine ironically historical analogies going back to the construction of the Italian state, a process that began in Piedmont with Garibaldi's army coming up from Sicily (which was under the crowns of the Bourbons) sewing up the various parts of the peninsula under the crown of the Savoy.

Between control and autonomy: the ungovernable Sicily

Sicily had already been object of discussion in the previous meetings of the *segreteria nazionale*, especially during a meeting in April 2010. At that time, regional presidents had to complete a dossier (*dossier regionale*), similar to the one prepared by the *fiduciari* for the *condotte*, outlining activities since the last congress and plans for the coming years, in line with the association's new directions decided one year before. Local leaders in Sicily were in conflict with each other and from the perspective of Bra, these conflicts were hard to understand. "The regional dossier was written by Pino [the regional president] in one night with the idea, 'let's do this dossier and then go on as before.' The Leopard cubed:[3] we change so that nothing changes. . . . I don't think it's the case to rush: however, they have gone from 1000 to 1400 members." "It's twelve years that there is a 'Sicily' problem," recalls another member of the board, "as [writer] Camilleri teaches us, Sicily is a particular 'continent.' However, either we archive Sicily, and what comes,

comes, or we start a program of political strategy for the association that someone from the national board will follow." "The only solution is to place side by side a fixed presence from the national," added another regional president. A member of the Bra headquarters then suggested sending a person from the Presidia office for three months, so that this flanking could take place from concrete projects and not be perceived as a simple Braidese control, which is difficult to accept. "There are two thousand potentials in the region, but as soon as you move away the potentials go away," adds the former. The president of another large region intervened in turn, "That someone from the national board goes to the regional committee, I agree, but let's not institutionalize it . . . Sicily is the most important region of our country [because it has the most Slow Food Presidia of any region], and we must make an effort in terms of political elaboration."

The discussion continued, some insisting on sending a "neutral" person from Bra, who would go to the region for other reasons; others objected that this person does not have the political cards to resolve the situation. The regional presidents did not seem to want to institutionalize forms of control that could then be applied to other regions and defend the idea of local autonomy, although they were aware of Sicily's problems. In the end, the members of the *segreteria nazionale* decided to create a sort of programmatic regional assembly that could allow a path of change within the Sicilian ruling group. This is an example of how the executive structures, which include Bra members and regional leaders, act in an effort to find a balance, never evident, between local autonomy and control from above.

When a problem emerges inside a *condotta*, it is the regional president who intervenes; if it is at the regional level, a "*commissariamento*" (commissioning) by the "national" may become necessary: in these cases, the general secretary or other staff members take charge of the situation until a new, reliable leadership team emerges. The "Sicilian problem" was resolved with the commissioning of the region a year after these exchanges and with the removal of the president, who had been in office since 2006, and who was suspected of administrative irregularities. During the period of commissioning, the "national" became the direct referent of the institutions and local partners (e.g., for initiatives to valorize island productions or events). At the same time, some in Sicily complained behind the scenes that "Bra" did not really care about what happens in their region and that it left many situations unresolved: a local leader told me that no one from Bra cared enough to intervene during the two years that a governor stopped exercising his functions. Beyond the specific occurrences questioning truthfulness or the mutual accusations and suspicions, which are more visible in cases like this, the important thing is that they characterize the life of the association in a more or less invisible way.

The limit between autonomy, claimed or practiced, and the effort to ensure that the association as a whole follows the same lines of conduct and adapts to changes in political direction, produces constant tensions and conflicts, and amplifies power dynamics. As Garsten and Nyqvist remind us, "To be a member of an organization, therefore, is to live with some measure of built-in-friction." "Rules are 'the talk' of organisations" and people "deal with these procedures in various ways: with acceptance, resistance, translation or ignorance." In fact, any "formal organization creates [not only] power . . .

[but] also authority." Membership in an organization implies "accepting being controlled to some degree without questioning authority" and at the same time there is a "zone of indifference where resistance takes hold" (2013: 11). This zone of indifference, in the case presented, is rather a space of claiming difference, in which the two poles seem not to understand each other and claim cultural specificities and differences. And above all, even though policies can be produced (such as the need to have a *dossier di condotta*)—pointing to "articulated fundamental organizing principles" (Shore and Wright 1997: 7) while simultaneously addressing an administrative and political issue—they are difficult to apply within an association that has been built on a very heterogeneous fabric and has indirectly encouraged extreme heterogeneity in the practices and realization of the philosophy of Slow Food.

The numerical problem of membership size was not only linked to the ability of local leaders to "make membership cards" (*fare tessere*). At the meeting of the *segreteria nazionale*, in July 2010, the national president recalled: "Our association is based on membership." A staff leader worried about the stagnation of membership in some areas:

> We all meet people who say they are Slow Food because their grandmother made ravioli by hand. But what if they add a membership card to the ravioli? People don't say "I'm WWF" if they don't have a membership card, but they do for Slow Food. Grandmother's ravioli is nice, but it would also be helpful to take a membership card.

The representative of Lazio region tried to analyze the problem: "The different perception between association and movement can determine the problem of membership. I am in favor of recovering the identity of the association by combining it with the ideas of the movement." He was referring to the balance between the dimension of movement—which Slow Food leaders seemed to assume more and more through initiatives like *Terra Madre*, supporting local producers and spreading the philosophy in the most diverse social and political environments—and the associative structure, which remained the backbone of the association. Slow Food needed to do more than simply maintain the number of members; that number needed to increase.

Staff leaders versus regional leaders

During the years of field research, I regularly followed the (almost monthly) meetings of the *segreteria nazionale* in Bra and the meetings of the *consiglio dei governatori* or *consiglio nazionale* (twice a year), which always took place in a different city in Italy. Outwardly, the *segreteria nazionale* gave the appearance of equality among members and common goals in the governance of the association. But behind this facade, there were actually tacit differences and lines of tension between those who were staff leaders (salaried) working in the national headquarters (national and international seat) and the regional leaders (volunteers) coming from the *territorio*. The element of distinction between these groups was not only their status as salaried or volunteer but also issues of autonomy, representativeness, and democracy. These emerge in the staff leaders' proximity to each other and with this central place of decision, that is the headquarters. Everyone was aware that decisions were made not merely, and not so much, within the official political bodies as in the invisible and informal spaces of the Bra intimacy, to be later ratified by those official bodies. Moreover, the control and the power exercised by the national headquarters (often addressed as "the power of Bra") were perceived by the *territorio* as more or less pervasive in various ways and were objects of claims and continuous adjustments. One example of this sentiment arose every four years, when the term of the *consiglio dei governatori* ended, and the members of the new *consiglio* were selected; at this point the balance between regional representatives and staff became an object of negotiation—or again, when the composition of the boards of directors of Slow Food Italy's component companies (Slow Food Promozione and Slow Food Editore) were renewed.

During the July 2010 meeting of the *segreteria nazionale*, Riccardo, the Italian national president, presented the proposal to assign the presidency of the two companies (s.r.l., Italian limited liability company), Slow Food Promozione and Slow Food Editore, to two historical leaders who were members of the previous board. They were joined by the heads of offices and staff of the Bra structure. Silvano, the Slow Food Italia vice president, explained the choice to propose staff people for these political bodies: "we are involving people who work operationally, their presence is not just to say 'let's put in people who already work [within the s.r.l.]' but it is an investment, to give these people a role in directing, a political role. The choice is to give a strategic role to people who are inside the machine." Another staff leader mocked his colleague, "*excusatio non petita*,"[4] under his breath. A regional president asked if they have considered including members of the national board on these boards. The answer was negative: "if they had been from outside [Bra] none of you would have succeeded. The people in these bodies are almost exclusively from Bra because the attendance fee [to participate to the meetings] is zero. We need to guarantee [the success of] the companies that we have created . . . The decision is not just about better management." And with that, the national president closed the exchanges on the issue. Behind the practical explanation (the absence of remuneration for this additional role, which justified appealing to staff members who already have a salary), two other reasons appear: the desire to keep control of the two companies in the hands of the Bra leaders (as ironically noted the staff leader with the Latin expression) and the level of professionalism that the management of the Slow Food machine requires (a level that some of the Bra staff members already have). This choice was indeed a way to give political responsibility (allowing career advancement) to Bra staff members, as the vice president suggested, thus linking the exercise of power and professionalization.

Balances of power between regions

Tensions concerning the balance of power and the representativeness inside Slow Food also appear among the regional presidents and in other parts of the association. Since the national board consists of presidents of regions with more than 1,500 members, smaller regions are not directly represented on the national board. In the years of my research, Sardinia, Umbria, Sicily, Calabria, Liguria, Abruzzo, and Molise were in this situation along with three other regions which had no president. Some of the presidents of these regions regularly protested during the meetings of the *consiglio dei governatori*, pointing out the problem of the absence of representation of the small regions, which they perceived as discrimination. The system in place, from their point of view, attributed a sort of merit to the regions with more members without taking into account other dimensions that affected the lower number of members and the difficulty in making more *tessere* (membership cards) in some territories.

The "Chiarini motion," informally named for the president of the Umbria region who proposed it, addressed the regional representation problem. We were in Trento in February 2010 for a meeting of the *consiglio dei governatori*. The president of Umbria, Sofia Chiarini, supported by the president of Sardinia and the president of Sicily reopened the debate by asking to discuss a possible solution to solve the problem of representativeness.

> Regions are different: you have to look at the ratio of the number of members to the number of inhabitants. Umbria [under the current criteria] will never enter the national board. The 2006 congress introduced a process of autonomy [creating the role of regional president], and now it is important to redefine representation. . . . Among the nine regions that remain outside the *segreteria nazionale*, we think that two more people can be added. The regions that are left out can decide the criteria. We should decide more generally how territorial representativeness is established.

The national president said he was open to the debate even though he was against the proposal and narrowed the scope of the discussion for two reasons. First, the statute could certainly be modified, but only in four years, and second, a board needed to be "streamlined" in order to make decisions, making it difficult to increase the number of members (already fourteen at the time). The presidents of the eight most important regions tried to bring the discussion back, claiming that the current system provided a good balance and avoided giving too much weight to the "braidesi," which is to say, the staff and staff leaders.

> The eight regions have a local support structure, that allows their representatives to attend [the board meetings] without interrupting their regional activities in the field . . . The criterion is not to represent the regions, otherwise we could have said four from the North, two from the Center and two from the South. . . . As for the nine regions that are outside [not on the *segreteria nazionale*] it makes no sense for them to decide who the extra two are. The need that is expressed is felt and is true, but this is not the solution.

One of Sicily's governors countered: "It is not that we do not feel represented; it is a problem of principles that must be expressed at the level of the statute and must be separated from

Slow Food

numerical issues. Our association must be one that chooses federalist criteria and not criteria linked to a business model." The ambiguous distinction between enterprise and association reappears in the internal workings of the Slow Food machine and in these debates.

A historical leader, president of a large region in central Italy, recalled that the criteria for the composition of the previous *segreterie nazionali* were quite different:

> The most capable leaders of the association entered the *segreteria*. . . . [Either we return to this criterion] or we accept an objective criterion that is functional for the governance of the association and is not a judgment of the merit of leaders. We [each regional president who is in the national board] represent a large part of the members of the country, and this is a criterion that gives credibility to the political body.

The discussion continued after the lunch break. Although the current criteria for the composition of the *segreteria nazionale* seemed to be much more democratic than those of the first years of the association, behind the questions of representativeness appeared the discontent of the small regions. They considered themselves excluded from political decisions that continued to arrive from above in a political vision of the historical leaders and the presidency defending a model that "guarantees" the association. This debate was reminiscent of the issue of lifetime offices, which, until a few years earlier, guaranteed the association's stability. Silvano, national vice president, said worriedly, "In the decision to give representation to the small ones, I see a dangerous mechanism. A group of regions get together to decide; in this way we create a parallel pseudo-elective mechanism . . . then there will be internal struggles."

The *segreteria nazionale* allowed the big personalities of the historical leaders to act in the interest of the common good (i.e., the association itself), thus acting as a cohesive force with respect to centrifugal aspirations. But the latter are always present at various levels of the association under the banner of autonomous decision-making or participation in the political decisions of the upper echelons. Lino, president of a big Northern region and historical leader, disagreeing with the arguments of the small regions as well as with the choice of the national president to have accepted the discussion, suggested, "Democratic moments are not those in which one can discuss, but those in which one can decide. Today we cannot decide. The discussion will not produce a concrete effect, I would not have initiated the discussion." In fact, the debate continued. The representatives of the small regions at the origin of the document tried to reduce its scope, "The document was intended to stimulate debate and it has succeeded. . . . This was intended to be a short-term proposal." The national president, probably confident of controlling the outcome of the vote, put the motion presented by Sofia (the Umbria president) to a vote, but contrary to what he had predicted, the motion obtained a majority. This was a result of the vote of some governors from the national headquarters who did not align themselves with the otherwise unified vote of the leaders from national and the most important regions. This "dissident" vote was perceived as a near betrayal by the president, which probably wounded his pride and certainly betrayed his expectations. He closed the meeting in an ironic and bitter tone, "I hope that at the congress no one will open the discussion on this, otherwise you will also find a new president." Later, the motion was often cited by some of the people who participated in that meeting as a moment in which a real fracture in the structure of decision-making and political representation surfaced, and the tensions between small regions on one hand and large regions along with the Bra leadership on the other became more evident. Although the motion had no immediate consequences, it opened a breach around the question of representation that was deeper than I realized at the time. Later, this breach also invests the functioning of the headquarters, as we will see in the last chapter of this book.

Political turmoil within regions: Lazio and Tuscany elections

In March 2010, the regions organized their individual congresses for the election of new regional presidents. This was done before the national congress, which was held in June of the same year and would sanction the new composition of the associative bodies. All the previous regional presidents had been nominated by Bra as they were when they were instituted for the first time in 2002. These were the first elections of regional presidents. But the choice of the new president still needed the consensus of Bra.

In those months I accompanied Riccardo, the national president, and two staff members, Dario and Mario, to Tuscany and then to Lazio to attend the congresses of the two regions. These two cases, although not representative of the diversity of situations in the different regions, provide a base for considering the political and associative characteristics of the Italian regions and help illuminate the existence of tensions that run through the entire structure of the association.

Tuscany, the avant-garde region

Tuscany is a region that the local leaders themselves have always considered avant-garde, "exemplary" compared to other Italian regions. According to the Bra leaders, it is a region in which the movement is extremely "strong" (about 4,000 members out of 30,000 at the national level) and in which many projects, such as the "Mercati della Terra" (famer markets), the *Presidia*, the *Orti in condotta* (urban gardens maintained by schools), the Masters of food, the "Bistrò del mondo" (bistro of the World),[5] and the Terra Madre Day, have been tested or realized earlier than elsewhere and in which the relationships with the local institutions are solid. Tuscany is probably one of the first regions that integrated the principles of Terra Madre: the importance of political action, the necessity of supporting small producers, and the idea that "pleasure is not real pleasure if it is not accessible to all." Those were the words of Luciana, the Slow Food Toscana outgoing president at the opening of the congress, placing the accent on the accessibility of quality food to all.

A staff member told me that when the outgoing president of Tuscany was selected, the choice made by the regional board, in coordination with Bra, took everyone by surprise because she was not well known: "It was a blitz, but then she did a huge amount of things for the association, and thanks to her, Tuscany is the region that most reflects what we are today." Historically on the Italian political left, the leaders in Tuscany have had experience or played executive roles within the PCI (Italian Communist Party), and, according to some, apply logics and practices close to those of political militancy. Mario, for example, the *fiduciario* of one of the most numerically important *condotte*, near to Florence, is a figure of reference at the regional level. "Mario is the 'grey eminence' of Tuscany,"[6] some people from headquarters told me. Member of the regional board and husband of the outgoing president, Mario started his political career and participated in the PCI until the logic of the party, which he didn't appreciate, forced him to step aside. For many years he was involved in Slow Food at the regional level, working "door to door" to recruit members.

In March 2010, Luciana and the regional board designated her successor: Sabrina was the regional vice president and would now assume the role of regional president. She was presented to the members of the regional congress by Mario, who noted the institutional positions she had held outside the association in her city, San Miniato, "the most slow-food town in Italy," where she had been councilor and vice-mayor. Her presentation at the regional congress provoked discontent from a part of the assembly. Some *fiduciari* complained about the outgoing president's lack of communication on the choice of the successor and the fact of that they didn't "know" the future president. Others complained about the proliferation of positions on the regional board and the disconnection from the life of the *condotte*. It is true that the region had experimented with a new intermediate level between the presidency of the region and the *condotte*: *nodi provinciali*, provincial nodes, with people in charge of coordinating relations between the *condotte* within the territory of the provinces.[7] Once again, the tension was evident between the leadership (in this case, regional leaders) and the base, represented by the *fiduciari* and the *condotte*. "We consider the autonomy of the condotte fundamental, we don't like prevarication and decisions from above," said a *fiduciario*. Part of the discontent was probably linked precisely to the militant dimension embodied and pursued by the region's leadership, which some perceived as too rigid and others as a path taken too quickly and ultimately translated into the pursuit of goals that everyone did not (and still don't) share. Behind the scenes, some criticized the "single-mindedness" of the outgoing presidency. But others declared their blind faith in the proposed choices for succession or pointed to the consistency of projects carried out by the presidency and the link she was able to establish with projects developed at the micro-local level. Tensions were concentrated around two models of doing politics. One model was described as very close to the pattern of functioning of the PCI during Berlinguer's[8] era, in which austerity and rigor coexisted with loyalty to the party and its guidelines. This probably left less room for other sensibilities, but at the same time was extremely active and in line with the most advanced ideas of Slow Food. The other model was more open to different interpretations of the associative life but at the same time more attached to an obsolete and less militant structure. But part of the discontent was surely linked to the important place that the *condotte* had inside the association since the beginning (before the creation of regional leadership).

After the remarks made by the *fiduciari*, the national president intervened. In an effort to shift the focus from local conflicts to the larger political objectives of the association, Riccardo asked everyone to remember, "The consequences of pleasure are local scale policies, the defense of food sovereignty, soil, landscape, education for the future, the defense of memory, and the fight against waste." Finally, he emphasized that although he personally did not know the candidate, he had complete confidence in the choice of the regional board, and further reminded the other congress attendees that his presence, and that of a responsible and the future general secretary from the association office in Bra, "shows the role we attribute to Tuscany." Certainly, the presence of three people from Bra, and particularly the national president, did not happen at all regional congresses, and the fact that they were at this congress was linked to the importance of the region in the policies of Slow Food and also to the internal tensions within the region, known by the regional and national leaders. The presence of leaders and staff from the *nazionale* in this case aimed to pacify those tensions. Although the successor of the outgoing president was identified by the current board, the choice was shared with the national presidency before submitting it to the vote of the Tuscany regional congress. During the sessions of the congress, the general secretary moved around, pausing next to the members who seemed unconvinced, trying to convince them to vote in favor of the propositions preferred by the regional and national board. "He does the dirty work," one congress member told me. The vote confirmed the election of the new president, Sabrina. Like the outgoing president, she was a woman, but this time, the new president would be the first female member of the *segreteria nazionale*. The outgoing president had selected a man, another member of the regional board, to be the regional representative on the *segreteria nazionale* rather than taking on the role herself. This evolution was not anodyne in an association where most of the leaders are men.

Lazio, the rebellious region

In the nearby region of Lazio, the situation was much more complicated: the region was divided into two factions after the resignation of the outgoing president. There were two women candidates for the succession, one supported by the small *condotte* of Sabina area, in the province of Rieti, and the other by the *condotte* near Rome, the capital. Lazio was one of only two regions in this first year of real elections that had two candidates on the ballot. In an attempt to understand the functioning of the association, the interest of this congress is twofold: the two candidates revealed the fractures that existed in the way the association was conceived within the *territorio*, and the congress highlighted the particular role of Lazio within Slow Food. The national capital of Italy is in this region and therefore it is home to the ministries and the associated advocates and political interlocutors. Slow Food leaders have long considered Lazio region to be both complicated and strategically important precisely because of the presence of Rome and the national political powers with which the association needs to maintain relations. At that time, the Rome *condotta* had "only"

Slow Food

500 members (actually very few for a city of four million inhabitants, if compared to the *condotta* of the outgoing president of Tuscany, which at the same time had almost twice as many members in its municipality of 50,000 inhabitants). Rome is considered by the "national" as a historically "rebellious" *condotta* which has experimented with different modes of governance. It was the only *condotta* in which the *fiduciario* had been salaried in the past, with "disastrous effects." This was the situation that some historical leaders were referring to when they invoked the uncomfortable mix between private and associative interests that this choice entailed. The night before the 2010 Slow Food Lazio congress was held, coming out of the restaurant where we had gone to dinner, the national president told me in a critical tone: "This is a place of politics, there are and always have been too many interests. There is too much money and too much politics going around." During the next day's session of the congress, a member of the Roman *condotta*'s committee used similar words to say, "The Roman condotta is a good example of how the action of Slow Food can also lead toward personal interests. In Rome there is politics and bureaucracy."

During the congress, the attitude of the national president was noncommittal with respect to the division of the *fiduciari* and the two candidates on the list. Although his support went to one of the two, this candidacy—which would later turn out to be the winner—seems difficult to grasp. It was not a candidacy really prepared in advance nor in the continuity of the previous government, and in this case the "national" seemed to have little control. Rome and Lazio are even more distant than Tuscany from the logic of Bra. The candidates for the new leadership in the two groups had professions linked to the world of food, which hinted at possible conflicts of interest.

In Lazio, many of the *fiduciari* present and their interventions during the congress seemed far removed from the militancy of nearby Tuscany. A staff leader, originally from Rome, told me in a whisper that things were changing, but that until recently the association in Rome seemed more like a Rotary club than Slow Food. Then, smiling, he said, "To be put with the *omissis*," and proceeded to tell a story about "Bra" asking him to take charge of an office, either one in Bra or Rome, to which he responded, "No, not Rome!"—because the *condotta* was so complicated to manage—and accepted without hesitation the assignment in the headquarters in Bra.

During the congress, autonomy is one of the notions that was often mentioned in the discussions of two Lazio "factions." Many expressed discontent with the national and regional boards, both of which represented power from above. "We must not focus on top-down actions and let the ideas and energy that come from the base be lost," recalled a *fiduciario*. Much as in the congress in Tuscany, the dialogue among the two parties revealed the different conceptions of associative commitment and the conflicting relationships between the *condotte*. It seemed that the need to defend their own prerogatives and their own territory was even stronger here than in other regions. In this spirit, the *fiduciario* of the Roman *condotta* officially affirmed that he would put the city squares at the disposal of the association, but with a clear caveat, "We will not accept invasions [from other *condotte*, nor from 'national'] that have not been previously discussed."

In contrast to his discourse at the Tuscan congress, the national president reminded the Lazio members that the region was among those well behind in terms of the Slow Food system. There was little cohesion, and the *condotte* had often operated outside their own territory without consulting each other. How could Lazio be kept attached to the rest of the association? "Lazio is the most visible region," he told the local leaders, "Politicians see what is happening here, this is a responsibility, and you have to assume it. I have to give you something more, but you have to do the same." The Slow Food headquarters has never moved from Bra, and unlike other national and international associations, there were no offices in Milan or Rome. It was precisely the strategic position of the region and the *condotta* of Rome that the president was trying to leverage by proposing to delegate the contacts with local institutions to local representatives for whom it might be logistically easier to manage. At the same time, it was precisely in this proximity that ambiguous relationships could be created, along with the risk of collaborations with institutions not approved by the national Slow Food headquarters. The vote took place in a chaotic situation in which the members of the congress quarreled over the method of voting (secret or open vote). In the end, the national president managed to get an open vote, the result of which was probably easier to control, and the candidate who had the support of the "national," even if discreet, obtained the majority. But the reflections on the situation they left behind continued during the return trip of the Braidesi leaders, who wondered what consequences the election might have. After all, even the new Lazio executives that had their support would introduce an operating style that was far from that of Bra, and they would probably aspire to even greater autonomy.

What do these two congresses allow us to understand about these internal tensions? The process of democratization and regionalization takes place in very different ways in the various Italian territories. The national presidency did not directly choose the new local leaders but took a position of approving or disapproving. The "style" of the presidents characterizes the image of their region: rebellious Latium, ungovernable Sicily, Veneto faithful to the line of Bra, or Tuscany that tries to revolutionize some parts of the association, which "is ahead" in many respects but acts as if it follows communist party logic and too autonomously. Tensions run through all levels of the association, and strong regions are sometimes a counterbalance to the *nazionale*, sometimes in alliance with certain members of the Bra leadership.

Money, volunteerism, and commitment

Another tension inside the Italian association concerns the relation between money, volunteerism, and professionalization. "The structure in Bra has become too heavy now," an historical *fiduciario*, told me one day, "There are too many people working within it, many of whom are employed in reproducing the machine itself, making it function more and more ineffectively." According to him, "It should take half the number of people." The funds necessary to keep the Slow Food "machine" running has been a recurring theme in my exchanges with other local leaders as well. In fact, the "national" absorbs a

Slow Food

large amount of resources because of the huge expenses for office rents and, above all, the salaries of the 130–170 employees (depending on the period).

Financial "pressure" also appears in other forms and sometimes it clashes with volunteerism. Progressively, local leaders, and particularly regional presidents, were encouraged to increase fundraising and seek resources not only to finance events in their region but for the association as a whole. Some complained and argued that fundraising should be practiced by paid professionals. Although the regional leaders were reminded during every regional congress and often in the meetings of the *segreteria nazionale* that the association is made of volunteers and that one should not superpose the associative commitment with money—to avoid conflicts of interest—the commitment required from these local leaders seemed more and more important and time-consuming. Leadership in the association was provided by professionals from various fields, often not directly related to the activities of eno-gastronomy. These doctors, agronomists, retired business managers, accountants, and restaurateurs often struggled to manage all the activities their leadership role required. Often, they said they were exhausted after a few years. When their work was close to the issues addressed by Slow Food, there was always the risk of taking professional advantage of their associative role and the visibility of Slow Food. Professionals who had networks of relationships in their *territorio* that they use for the development of the association obtained intangible advantages in terms of recognition and, to quote Raymond Firth's classical book of economic anthropology (1939), the maximization of personal prestige.

Sometimes local managers were at a point in their life where they were trying to change professions or find a new job. The associative commitment was possible because they had more time, and volunteerism was an opportunity for a bridge between the two professional phases. The new president of Tuscany, elected in 2010, for example, was in a complicated period of her political career, opposed by the lobbies in the town where she was vice-mayor, when she was "intercepted" and recruited by the previous Tuscany president. Another example was the Cagliari *fiduciaria* who took over the leadership of the *condotta* in 2011 when she was in a phase of transition in her working life, the ideal time to invest herself full-time in the association. Besides the symbolic or sometimes material advantages, volunteering has a "cost" in terms of time, energy, and the absence of money otherwise earned. Although the first generation of historical leaders was able to serve for years inside the association, I had the impression during my research and afterward that the term of leadership was becoming shorter, no matter what the statutes said about the length of the term. The forms of volunteering have changed, and the amount of work required has also changed, leading to a more rapid depletion of energy and associative momentum.

A Bra staff member, at a regional meeting, used the term of "gift," the gift of volunteerism. The association is a nonprofit structure, and this element was used often by the staff leaders to explain why local leaders could not and should not receive a salary. But gift of volunteerism and commitment seemed to be limited for many local leaders. A *fiduciaro* explained, "Nonprofit yes, but there must also be recognition of what we do." This situation is similar to that analyzed by Rakopoulos in the early 2010s within Greek food distribution cooperatives where paid work and volunteerism were the subject of discussion and tension: "Labor arises as a major *food value*; indeed, it stands as a *mesure of value* for contemporary food systems and a field of contestation within food activist groups" (2019: 157). Inside Slow Food, some association activities, such as that of master trainers, often carried out by *fiduciari* or *governatori*, were already remunerated, but the political ones were not. And the idea that certain volunteer activities should become professional was increasingly widespread, even if a job with a salary was not the subject of direct claims, partly because most of the local managers were professionals who already had jobs. This is basically what happened with the founders of Slow Food who created a profession out of volunteer work.

Tensions within the *condotte*

In September 2010, a delegation of the new leadership of the Roman *condotta*, elected before the regional congress, some months before, came to Bra for a few days of training. This was not a collective meeting, but a training dedicated exclusively to the three members of the delegation. The first member of staff to introduce the new leaders to the mechanisms of the association was the general secretary, Diego, who began his speech by retracing the steps of Slow Food's history and its most recent evolutions. The founders of Slow Food appeared one after the other in Diego's story: his father Francesco, then Silvano, Giovanni and Mario, Carlin, and Giorgio. The names of the historical leaders allowed to draw the plot of the family ties and friendships on which Slow Food was built, which do not belong only to the past but are part of the daily life of the association, as it is lived in Bra today. Then, he traced the history of the *laboratori del gusto* and other major events, the guides, the Presidia, until 2006 when "the association had to make a leap from being 'Carlin-managed'" to another kind of association. This was the beginning of the process of democratization:

> With very few exceptions like Piero and a few others, everything here was conceived by Carlin, even Terra Madre was born from an idea of Carlin. The leap that needed to be made was to give ourselves a different structure with real political bodies that can influence the actions that Slow Food is going to take. It's a journey that is not yet over. We started with the *segreteria nazionale* and the *consiglio dei governatori*, then, with the last congress, the *condotte* . . . This story is linked to a strong national association, but now we would like the *territorio* to be the real engine of Slow Food. Not the *fiduciario* who does everything wrong or who does only one thing. Responsibility in the *territorio* now lies with the *comitato di condotta* . . . In some cases this has meant changing people, because a person who has been working in one way for twenty years is unlikely to change. Then you have to ask them to take a step back. Some have taken it on themselves to identify a successor.

The members of the Roman delegation, in turn, intervened to ask questions or share with the general secretary the problems they perceive at the level of their *condotta*,

Slow Food

"the impression we have is that Slow Food has evolved so much but the perception that nonmembers have is that it's a clique of gluttons." "It's a place where a lot of money goes around," added a colleague. "A lot of people think of the association as a way to get benefits." Their comments echoed those I often hear when I said I do research on Slow Food: they seem incongruous to me when looking at the machine in its inner workings but still significant as signs of contradictions with which Slow Food staff and members cohabit.

The delegation was then received by the education office, followed by the Presidia office, Slow Food Promozione offices, which organizes the Salone del Gusto—in full swing just one month before the event—the Italian association office and finally the *Centro studi*. I accompanied them on this tour of the different branches of the association, taking notes and observing how the staff members, with whom I was already familiar, after more than a year doing fieldwork, presented themselves and their activity to the new Roman leaders. The gap between the Braidese organization and the vision of the members of the Roman group, who come from a *condotta* distant geographically and also in terms of associative history, was enormous. I had the impression that, in spite of the good will on both sides to explain in the most pedagogical way possible the association way of functioning and to receive the maximum amount of information, the translation was complicated, as they did not represent the same association. The staff members described ways of functioning that navigated between the associative and the professional, in an environment where one breathes the long history and the presence of the heart of the association with its web of close relationships. The Roman group, animated by energy and good will, discovered a context that was unfamiliar to them and that could not be reproduced elsewhere, where the work is entirely voluntary and the local logics so different.

Six months later, in February 2011, the enthusiasm and the energy seemed to have disappeared and the internal tensions of the Roman *condotta* took over again. The national president traveled to Rome for a meeting aimed at resolving the ongoing conflicts. I accompany him to the meeting, which was held in the home of a member of the *condotta* committee. The president of the Lazio region and her representative in the *segreteria nazionale* were also there. The national president opened the meeting by reminding, once again, as at the regional congress a year earlier, that the Roman *condotta* is extremely important in the Italian chessboard, "what happens here falls on the other *condotte*. In the two previous *condotta* leaderships there was an absence of confrontation [with Bra and with the regional president] and people demanded more autonomy, we do not know the reasonwhy." The leaders of the *condotta*, one after the other, began to list the progress made in terms of the number of members and activities carried out. During the meeting, the treasurer, who was part of the delegation I met in Bra some months before, announced her resignation, which follows that of another member of the board (communicated by email). The other members of the *condotta* committee simply "registered" her resignation and with apparent indifference proceeded with the agenda they had established for the meeting. The owner of the house, a member of the committee and close to the *fiduciario*, twice said, "then I'll be the treasurer," and then again, "I had ambitions, but I left the place to the young people. I am precise, I can be treasurer." But the president of the region pointed out that the resignations were the sign of a problem and, noting that indeed it is difficult to manage Rome, he asked the members of the committee, "are you still having fun?" The national president added, "I told you that if you don't have fun, it's not good." What had happened since the September meeting six months before? Inside *condotte*, there were often different ways of maintaining and participating in the association and pockets of small local powers that are difficult to dismantle. In places like Rome, more than in others, the associative machine had also been used or perceived as a 'brand' at the local level and it was necessary to regain control: "In Rome there are more solicitations than elsewhere, and you risk standing in for the 'national' or even the international. First do things that allow you to enjoy participating as a *condotta*, from the *classiche cene* (classic dinners) to the rest, otherwise you become a business," said the national president towards the end of the "crisis meeting" in words that seemed to be the opposite of those expressed at the national and regional levels. Although the message largely given to members and local leaders was "let's stop with the dinners and let's get political," it was a message that carried risks in a big and important town like Rome where money and politics permeate relations with institutions, where scandals and cases of corruption and malversation are frequent. Control was difficult to maintain from Bra, and the machine and those driving it needed to adapt their strategies to the extreme heterogeneity that exists within Slow Food.

The power and weakness of volunteering

The Roman example shows also that the enlargement of the leadership involved in the life of the *condotta* or the change in leadership sometimes comes up against forms of resistance from members of the previous management. The renewal of local leadership that Slow Food required from the *territorio* and the sharing of responsibilities by a larger number of people were intended to reduce the weight and scope of local potentates and lone individuals who participated in the association in their own way and thus make the association more "democratic." But it was also linked to the increasing complexity of the associative machine: more than the number of members, the projects, the political presence of Slow Food and consequently the needs in terms of associative commitment and resources have increased.

In this process, political cases increased, and as some people within the headquarters and some of the historical leaders pointed out, the regions had become an intermediate level between the *fiduciario* and the headquarters, a level that wanted more power. The "fiefdom" model embodied by some *condotte*, often extended to the regions where leaders (regional presidents and governors) applied models of action and forms of defense of their space and autonomy, similar to those of the *condotte*. Within the latter, the creation of the *comitati di condotta*, composed of a minimum of five people with the task of helping the *fiduciario*, multiplied the number of people invested with associative roles, increasing the number of local leaders from about 300 to more than 2,000. Although this

Slow Food

allowed a greater number of people to feel more involved in the life of the association, and to redistribute roles, it also increased the spaces of power and, consequently, the need for control and "normalization" by the national leadership. A smiling older staff leader said that Slow Food is an association of managers and leaders.

The tensions observed within the Rome *condotta* also appeared in other parts of the association and are probably linked to the characteristics of volunteerism within Slow Food. What is particular about this specific type of activism? The emotional and affective dimension seems to be an essential component for the most part of the *fiduciari* and people involved in the *condotta* activities. Both leaders and volunteers in the territory claim that fun and the need to continue "to have fun doing things" (*divertirsi facendo*), as well as carrying out the actions and principles of the association, are considered constitutive of militancy within Slow Food. Alongside these, a term often evoked is "friendship": it appears to be the engine of involvement and a characteristic of the way local groups function, at least ideally. The way the association was born—a group of friends who enjoyed themselves through political commitment and a series of cultural and recreational initiatives—impregnated the way members joined and became involved: people who loved being together, who defended pleasure, conviviality, and the pleasure of conviviality; friends and "friends of friends" (Boissevain 1974) who enjoyed the *classiche cene* ("classic" dinners), the "gioco del piacere" (pleasure game), the tastings. During a dinner in Benevento, in November 2009, after a meeting, one of the governors of Lombardy told me that he was always uncertain whether to continue to stay in Slow Food or not, but then he had so much fun that basically that's why he stayed. The jokes, the irony, the sarcastic jokes, the teasing, characterized all the moments spent together, even after the more serious meetings when the discussions were tense at times. For a long time, this way of operating allowed the association to spread and take root in the territory, through a sort of "contagious conviviality." Although the leadership now claims that Slow Food has always participated in politics, this has certainly not been the case in all manifestations of the association, nor in the same ways, and certainly not all members have adopted the same militant posture at the same time.

The change in the leadership base, pushed by the national leadership, produced other effects: the historical leaders were motors at the local level and at the same time had a relationship of familiarity and direct "friendship" with the national leaders, which allowed them to act as a transmission link between the two parts of the association. Many of them also contributed to reflections on Slow Food and its changes. If the arrival of new leaders, of young forces, allowed a new impetus to be given to contexts in which problems accumulated over time, the ties between the national leadership and the local ones became less direct than in the past. Volunteering continued to be experienced in a pervasive, daily, and involving way, but its duration had shortened, and the turnover among leaders become more frequent in some places of the association. The associative network was weakened by the tension between the declared sense of friendship and the move towards almost professional volunteerism, and in some parts of the association, faults appeared.

Notes

1. Friuli-Venezia Giulia, Trentino-Alto Adige, and Marche did not have regional presidents. Molise was linked to Abruzzo (with only one presidency) and Sardinia no longer had a regional president after 2014.

2. Regions with presidents on the national board were Piedmont-Val d'Aosta (with only one presidency), Lombardy, Veneto, Emilia Romagna, Tuscany, Lazio, Campania-Basilicata (with only one presidency), and Puglia. The regions not represented on the board were Sardinia, Sicily, Calabria, Liguria, Umbria, Friuli-Venezia Giulia, Trentino-Alto Adige, Marche, Abruzzo, and Molise.

3. The ironic analogy refers to the novel *Il gattopardo* (*The Leopard*) by Giuseppe Tomasi di Lampedusa (1958) and to the famous sentence pronounced by the nephew Tancredi to the prince of Salina during the clashes that prepare the landing in Sicily of the Thousand led by Garibaldi: "If we want everything to remain as it is, we must change everything." "Leopard cubed" means that the Sicilian leaders, even more than the protagonists of the novel, pretend to adapt so that nothing changes.

4. The Latin expression in whole is : *excusation non petita, accusatio manifesta*. It means "an unsolicited excuse is an obvious accusation." The first part of the sentence alone is sufficient to implicitly suggest the second part.

5. The Bistrò del Mondo is a project started in 2008. It is a cultural club of the Slow Food Foundation for Biodiversity located inside the Acciaiolo Castle in Scandicci (Florence), consisting of rooms where events, book presentations, and Slow Food training and educational activities (Master of Food and *Laboratori del Gusto*) are organized. Local products and Slow Food Presidia are sold in this space.

6. *Eminenza* (Eminence) is the title of honor due to cardinals. *Eminenza grigia* (Gray eminence) means secret and powerful adviser to some high personage.

7. These infra-local responsibilities are in some cases a way to gain experience in associational responsibilities. Describing two of the candidates for the regional board, Mario told me, "They are young and are an investment for the future. They were responsible for provincial nodes, now we have to make them grow."

8. Referring to Enrico Berlinguer, Italian politician, general secretary of the Italian Communist Party from 1972 to his death in 1984.

Photo 5 A political meeting of a French convivium, Gap (France), 2012. ©Franco Zecchin.

CHAPTER 5
AUTONOMY AND DEPENDENCE
THE INTERNATIONALIZATION OF SLOW FOOD

> This is the Slow Food family assembled here; we have much in common, and like all families, we also have disagreements and conflicts. But the links that bind us together are what count.

These are the words that Louis, one of the French members of Slow Food's international council—and a former board (*conseil d'administration*)[1] member of the French association—used to address representatives from the thirty French *convivia* (local chapters) that were gathered in a small meeting room in Paris's fourteenth *arrondissement* on December 4, 2010. It was cold in the room, and snow would soon blanket the streets outside. The members present at this meeting had come from various regions in France, responding to a call to participate in a debate on the future of Slow Food France which had been in crisis for several months. Luca, an Italian leader and general secretary of Slow Food International—in which Slow Food France participated as a national association—had come from Slow Food headquarters in Bra for this meeting. When his turn came to speak, he began with a historical reminder:

> Slow food was born in Paris, in a meeting room like this. It was the month of December, twenty years ago. None of the participants of that meeting could have imagined what Slow Food would become. At the last Terra Madre [meeting] there were delegates from 161 countries: the network has truly become global. The impact that Slow Food can have on the future of food is truly important. The agri-food system in place for the last fifty or sixty years has failed; we must change it if we want to preserve the future. . . . Slow Food is now a full-fledged actor in the debate over food policies, from the United States to Africa. . . . In ten days, we will be meeting with the European agricultural commissioner to discuss what we believe should be the new agricultural policy.

He then changed the style of his discourse, preparing the terrain for the subsequent debate on the viability of the French association itself. He spoke about Slow Food in general, but his words implicitly referred to the particular situation of Slow Food France and its weaknesses: low number of members, limited public awareness, and inadequate economic resources.

Slow Food

> But we remain convinced that if we have the ideas, the other problems can be resolved. And we must approach these weaknesses with the acknowledgement that resolving them is hardest at the level of national structures.

What Luca meant was that the difficulties France was experiencing could not be solved by the French leadership team. Today, in the public sphere and at different scales—local, regional, national, European, international—the association's staff and leaders present Slow Food as a single, international, or transnational movement that now includes more than 100,000 members throughout the world. With only 1,400 members at the time of my field research (between 2007 and 2011), the French association was one of the smallest of eight national structures existing at the heart of Slow Food. Each of them autonomously managed its own programs and membership and translated its own specific versions of certain aspects of the movement's philosophy and initiatives, all while maintaining a complex relationship with the international structure.

In this chapter I analyze the process of Slow Food's diffusion from its headquarters in Italy to the rest of the world (particularly in the Global North). I will use the case study of Slow Food France as one of the autonomous, national associations participating in the international structure and one that has held economic, political, and symbolic links in its relationship with the Italian headquarters. This approach enables a better understanding of the different forms that the movement has taken outside of Italy, and also what I call the "international relations" of Slow Food, as well as the friction and conflicts that emerged within them. The internationalization of Slow Food makes the internal hierarchies and the tension between its two dimensions as an association and a movement more visible. It also makes the association's strong Italian roots appear and brings out the heterogeneity of Slow Food's modes of appropriation and the problematics of their cohabitation.

Comparative view

Both a movement and an association, Slow Food operates through a diverse collection of actors, volunteers, employed workers, political authorities, and leaders. As we have seen, these actors represent diverse points of view and different types of support and involvement. The international relationships in Slow Food reflect this internal heterogeneity. The form that it takes in each country is linked to the interactions that the founding individuals established in each context and to the history of the movement in its entirety, its policy of internationalization, as well as its internal politics. The social configuration of the membership—from simple food-lovers to militant food activists—varies, not merely from one country to another but from one local unit to another, as we have seen in the Italian context. It also has changed over time, with political reorientations and the evolving philosophy of the movement. This evolution has provoked changes in the relationships between the international structure and its components located in other countries around the world.

The early years in the life of the association were marked by the founders of Slow Food traveling all over Italy looking for local productions and places where they could taste "home-style" and regional cuisine, uniting gastronomic criticism and the promotion of "traditional" products with their goal of expanding the territory of the association. Starting in the city of Bra and the Langhe wine region, they wove links with intellectuals, artists, journalists, and food critics, gradually venturing further afield and enlarging their network well beyond the Piedmont and Italy. In the vocabulary developed by the association and the narratives of the early activists and architects of Slow Food, we find a mixture of political ideas, irony, and self-irony, as seen in the text of the *Manifesto dello Slow Food*. But from the beginning, this apparent lightness of dialogue seems to camouflage a veritable political design with a strategy of expansion which followed two paths. One led to national development and a goal of establishing the *condotte* throughout Italy, the other to the diffusion of the association on an international scale. Changes in the association's name within the space of a few years marked the intention of making it more universally recognizable: the name, Arcigola, strongly associated with Italian political context, became Arcigola Slow Food, and then Slow Food Arcigola, and finally it was shortened to Slow Food (see Chapter 2).

The creation of an international association was first accomplished on paper, at the signing of the Slow Food Manifesto in December 1989. The event took place at the Opéra-Comique in Paris, surrounded by entertainment celebrities, journalists, writers, artists, food critics, and intellectuals seduced by the movement and its political positions.[2] The ceremony was also attended by "delegates" from other countries in Europe, the Americas, and Asia. These "delegates" represented fifteen countries: Argentina, Austria, Brazil, Denmark, France, Germany, Japan, Italy, the Netherlands, Spain, the United States, Sweden, Switzerland, Hungary, and Venezuela. Since the association did not have an international structure at the time, representation by an official delegate did not yet exist. However, in the documents and in the memories of the people who took part in the event, we can already see the language and terms that would later be used to define the various links in Slow Food's national and international structure. The founders of Slow Food saw this gesture as a way to reinforce and valorize their links with France, which they considered important to the development of the movement. The event was also performative, announcing the creation of the international association even before it actually existed. Like a free-trade treaty, the signature of this manifesto opened the way for the diffusion of Slow Food outside of Italy. The creation of local groups in different countries would begin later, first in Europe and then in the United States.

The geopolitics of the movement

During the process of developing the international movement, Slow Food's founders and leaders followed the model of diffusion which had been applied in Italy. In each country they chose individuals, well regarded in their region or in their city, who would be able to spread the principles of the association and foster membership. They became the intermediaries of Slow Food on the ground. Less diffused and capillary than in Italy, but always following the model of social-political networks, this expansion proceeded in a less-balanced manner. The goal was to avoid taking themselves too seriously and expose two of the association's founding principles, pleasure and conviviality. The official investiture that Carlo Petrini gave to these local intermediaries was inspired by distinctly libertarian principles. But adherence to the ideology of this "slow" revolution in the world of food supposed, and supposes, actual membership cards, dues, and statutes. Seemingly contradictory, these two characteristics (a movement that spreads by leaving much freedom to its followers and an association that needs to establish rules) contributed to the construction of Slow Food's position as a political actor that became recognized and included in the international debates on food issues, but they are also at the source of other contradictions that can be seen at work in the case of France.

The diffusion process in Italy and then abroad was accompanied by a progressive transformation in both the internal organization of the movement and the movement's philosophy. From the end of the 1990s, the ensemble of Slow Food structures became more consolidated, the political policies became more structured, the statutes more precise, and Slow Food headquarters transformed. The leaders of the international office began to encourage the creation of national associations in Europe, the United States, Japan and Australia, where Slow Food's diffusion was most successful. Slow Food Germany was the first national structure created at the beginning of the 1990s. Slow Food Australia was established at the end of the 1990s. Then came Slow Food USA in 2000, Slow Food France in 2003, Slow Food Switzerland and Slow Food Japan in 2004, and Slow Food UK in 2006. The launching of the University of Gastronomic Sciences in 2004 with its many international students fed into the global expansion of Slow Food.

Theoretically, a formal national association could be created when the international presidency considered the number of members and local chapters to be sufficient. But in practice, the process has depended on both the combination of the local leaders' motivation and ability to build a national structure, and the strategic plans of Slow Food's international leaders to reinforce the association in one country or another. Actually, well before the creation of the international association, the emergence of national structures corresponded to a combination of the local leaders' desire to enlarge the movement's place in their own country and their sense that the time had come to create a national structure that mimicked the one present in Italy from the beginning. Some believed the creation of a national association would give them a stronger voice in decisions while improving Slow Food's visibility in their country. The leaders of Slow Food International shared this desire to improve visibility and reinforce the association: national structures were envisioned as being capable of interacting more directly and effectively with local institutions, and also of providing a source of funding, a part of which would serve to finance the central structure (the headquarters and the projects it also carries out on an international scale). In addition, the existence of several national associations would reinforce the legitimacy and reputation of Slow Food, contributing to the image of a veritable international association. Gabriel, a longtime leader of Slow Food Switzerland, described how Slow Food developed in his country:

I became the leader of Zurich, then of German-speaking Switzerland, and finally I was able to unify the three existing independent organizations. First, Ticino, then German-speaking Switzerland, and I helped create, or I was there, during the foundation of Slow Food in French-speaking Switzerland, Slow Food Pays Roman. It functioned autonomously, and then in 2004 we had a conference founding Slow Food Switzerland with the three existing structures. The gossip held that I was able to put together the three organizations because in reality I am not originally Swiss, I'm Swiss by adoption.

During the establishment of the movement, all foreign countries have not been equally favorable to consolidation. In the 2000s, the United States association rapidly increased membership numbers, in part through a media campaign which proposed membership for the "political" price of one dollar. The campaign was launched by the president of Slow Food US who was particularly mindful of the more "militant" dimensions of Slow Food's message. The increase in membership was so rapid that the leaders of the Italian association, behind the scenes, were momentarily worried about the primacy of their own structure at the heart of Slow Food.

During the same period of time, the United Kingdom association was losing membership, even though a series of media initiatives gave the image of an organization in full expansion. In reality, the two components of the English association—on one side, the national operating structure with salaried workers, some of them with very high salaries, in contrast to the salaries of the staff at headquarters, and financing for communication campaigns, and on the other side, local structures operated by volunteer workers and centered on ground initiatives—were beginning to distance themselves, the one from the other. In other countries, such as Spain, political divisions slowed or prevented the creation of a national structure. At the beginning of the 2010s in Germany, the national association's introduction of a new group of leaders and the creation of an office with personnel was followed by a progressive augmentation in membership and increased visibility. The new president, Ursula, an intellectual woman with an academic international background in literature studies, introduced new ways to be political.

This contextual diversity in Slow Food's expansion has engendered a political geography of the association. In Italy this geography is characterized by the coexistence of "strong" regions with respect to the presence of Slow Food and the political capacity of its local representatives, and "weak" regions where the social-geographical fabric is thinner, with active local groups but little form of regional structure. At the international level, varying geography can be seen in the contrast between "strong" countries where the association is firmly rooted, and countries where Slow Food has never developed as much as the international leaders would have liked, even though there may be an active base. Whether the local groups function "well" or "poorly," and their ability to maintain an appropriate presence on the terrain, depends on the specific configurations of each context and evolves as a function of changes in the political line espoused by Slow Food headquarters. In addition, this ensemble of processes is not exempt from conflict and tension; much of the contrary is true, as can be seen in the case of the French association.

Slow Food

Center and peripheries

France has always occupied an important place in the vision of the leaders of Slow Food and of Carlo Petrini in particular. It is the country of Jean Anthelme Brillat-Savarin, author of the *Physiologie du goût*, which was published in 1825 and whose tenets are part of the foundation of Slow Food philosophy. France was long thought of as the country of gastronomy par excellence. Certainly, French cuisine had an important influence on Italian bourgeois cuisine of the nineteenth and beginning of the twentieth century, and notably on regional cuisine in the Piedmont—the region of the founders and leaders of Slow Food. These reasons explain the choice of Paris as a symbolic place to launch the Slow Food vessel into international space. But from the start, the French association encountered difficulties in establishing itself and developing.

The French national structure was not created until 2003 even though convivia had already existed for some time. Slow Food's earlier presence in France was established through the efforts of local leaders in several southern regions: Béarn (now part of Nouvelle-Aquitaine), Languedoc-Roussillon (now part of Occitanie), and Provence-Alpes-Côte d'Azur. As teachers, researchers, farmers, and professionals, these leaders were well anchored in their respective regions and notably associated with food production by virtue of their work or personal interests. But even as the movement grew, there was no general consensus among the French membership in terms of the need to create a national structure. Many remained decidedly skeptical of a new echelon being interposed between the *convivia*—administered by volunteers and aimed at local projects—and the international structure. Even if all the French *convivia* were associated with the philosophy and global projects promoted by the international movement, individually these convivia were, and are, very different from each other, with distinct "styles" and interests. Paradoxically, the rather lineal development model of the Slow Food "machine" did not appear to sufficiently account for the enormous diversity of social and political contexts that the libertarian approach had pretended to integrate.

Throughout the existence of the French national structure, it was marked by a permanent strain in the relationship between its *conseil d'administration* and the convivia. One of the reasons for this strain seems to be linked to the history of the movement in France. Contrary to the sequence of events in Italy, where the association's headquarters was established before the local chapters and remained the primary engine of development both nationally and internationally, the French convivia came into being well before the creation of Slow Food France. At the time of my research the general feeling in the convivia was that they alone were in a position to develop and sustain the movement in France. The question of the distance between this membership base and the national structure often emerged among the board members themselves. On various occasions one of the administrators, speaking more in the voice of the convivia than his colleagues, pointed out that certain projects seemed completely unrelated to convivia initiatives conducted locally and seemed to have fallen from above, ignoring members' interests and actions, like certain campaigns promoted by Slow Food International or some projects of the French national board: "We mustn't forget the convivia." "There you are completely ignoring the perspective of the convivia." "It is the convivia that do the work and then we seize the benefits!" This same criticism surfaced when volunteer work was involved in the framework of projects or initiatives aimed, at least in part, as a source of funding for the national structure (such us the organization of national events and salons). At the local level, the members themselves had difficulty feeling as if they were represented by the national board, and this strain appeared in both formal situations such as general membership meetings and in informal ones such as workgroups (communication, coordination, etc.) that were formed during the last year of the national association's existence. Caught between varying demands and expectations Slow Food France appeared to be a disconnected entity, sometimes in opposition or in any case out of phase with the life and efforts of the association on the ground.

The case of the convivium in Gap, France, is one of the examples of an ability to promote the movement even without the particular support of a national structure. At their own rhythm, and often in anticipation of decisions taken at the national level, the leaders and membership of this local unit have always managed to invent new and original ways to promote the movement and translate the global changes of Slow Food to fit the local terrain. Almost every year, for example, the Hautes-Alpes convivium, in association with other local groups and producers coming from various regions of France and Italy, has organized the salon *Savoirs et Saveurs de Montagne* (Mountain Knowledge and Flavors). This initiative has adapted the movement's most significant and militant messages to a precise region through stands maintained by small producers, educational programs for children, cooking workshops, and the discovery of regional products. In this initiative, the convivium's members have combined both the political dimension and economic action on a scale closer to the consumers and producers than the large events organized by Slow Food International. In the words of the convivium's president, François, during the 2015 edition of the salon, "This is the Slow Food spirit, to bring people together, in community, around a cause."

This discrepancy between the central and local structures, while a common trait in the complexification of social movements, is also probably related to the particularly centralized French context in which most of the economic and political activity, as well as the headquarters of associations and institutions, are located in Paris, the capital. Born out of a desire to oppose the standardization and loss of variety in food production, and advocating Carlo Petrini's concept of an "austere anarchy," would the organizational forms of Slow Food in France rebel against the hierarchies imposed by the "mother house," as they often called the international headquarters? And in turn, would the local chapters project the same attitude towards the French national structure? Certainly, these aspects were present behind the constant criticisms that emerged within some convivia and were directed against the French national structure and members of the *conseil d'administration*, and in the latter, against Bra and the international.

Slow Food

Translations and resistance

Between 2007 and 2011, I regularly attended board meetings, annual general assemblies, and salons organized by Slow Food France. Meetings of the *conseil d'administration*, one after another, passed with the participants concentrating on how to make the association more visible in France. The subject of identity and the specificities of the French association were almost systematically introduced: "What is our identity?" "We must build our specificity." "We have to understand who we are, and then propose clear ideas to the members." Like a leitmotif, this questioning was a recurrent theme: "We need to find our flagship project." "We need to find stable funding." In fact, my notes show that the modes of funding were frequently linked to these discussions of the movement's image and the search for their own specific projects to develop in order to obtain funds and visibility. In the eyes of French administrators, the implementation of specific projects (e.g., setting up farmers' markets or school gardens, organizing courses) seemed to be less attractive because they already existed in France and were supported by other environmental associations, agricultural unions, or local institutions. The creation of a national structure had not prompted an increase in membership, and economic resources remained weak. For the French leadership the central problem was one of communication and translation: local leaders had to constantly explain to political actors and sponsors why they needed an English name and an Italian movement in order to talk about quality production and "eating well" in France.

Indeed, the "translation" of the movement is one of its principal problems. From the time of its birth in Italy, and then abroad, the founders encouraged members to appropriate the messages and philosophy of the movement and to implement them through specific autonomous actions. They encouraged liberty, but only within a pact of fidelity toward the association and its principles: "In your region, do as you would like, but do it in the name of Slow Food," said Carlo Petrini when ordaining the position of someone as founder and leader of a local group in Italy. The same instructions were given to future local leaders in other countries where Slow Food has attempted to spread the association. But the equilibrium between liberty (of action) and fidelity, between appropriation and respect for the philosophy of the movement, is difficult to find and maintain, especially when it involves national structures.

During a September 2009 meeting of Slow Food France's board of directors in Marseille, the participants discussed a new initiative launched by Slow Food: the *Terra Madre Day*. On December 10, the association would celebrate the twentieth anniversary of the signing of the Manifesto, and the international council had decided to institutionalize this date as a day each year when all the members throughout the world should celebrate at the same time. The other goals for this anniversary would be the support for the Terra Madre network of small producers which had an increasingly important place in Slow Food philosophy, actions, and strategies, and the reinforcement of the movement's visibility through local coordinated actions. For the members and leaders of Slow Food, Terra Madre also enabled the adoption of a posture that is increasingly attentive to the problematic of agriculture (see also Petrini 2010). Dinners, events showcasing products or producers, presentations in the schools—the type of event was not important, but everyone was to be invited to participate in an action that would promote the movement and its principles. The national structures, in countries where they existed, were obviously encumbered with the task of designing and coordinating the activities surrounding this event.

Somewhat reluctantly, the president of Slow Food France presented the initiative to the other board members at their meeting in Marseille: "It is already difficult to talk about Slow Food, then Terra Madre, and now, Terra Madre Day; that makes for a lot, and the risk is that nobody ends up understanding anything." Others echoed his sentiments: "We are already occupied with other projects, other activities; we don't have to add still another one." "The Terra Madre Day wouldn't be understood." "Terra Madre is already confusing, and now we add an English word to an Italian expression!" Even though the decision to establish Terra Madre Day was technically made by the international council, it appeared evident to the French administrators in this meeting that the initiative originated inside the headquarters located in Italy. A young Italian woman who would later assume the direction of the administrative services of Slow Food France suggested that in light of the fact that the decision had already been made, the most important consideration was that everyone participate in the event. But her opinion was passed over, and recalcitrant members defended the idea that ultimately the French were not really obligated to participate and that "the dictate coming from Italy, well, enough is enough."

This brief exchange is an example of tension in relationship between Slow Food International's central administration and its national components. Although messages and projects initiated by Carlo Petrini are often incorporated as theoretical references and essential incentives for action in Italy and abroad—"Carlo Petrini said," "as Carlo says"—their practical implementation follows protocols, mechanisms, and regulations that the international structure endeavors to disseminate and enforce, an aspect which the French often resisted. The need for national structures to find their own style and autonomous means of existing often conflicted with their relationship to a hierarchical international structure in which the place and importance of the Italian leaders tended to dominate.

Reinterpretation or misunderstanding?

Contrary to Italy, France did not have a particular location identified with the association. The *conseil d'administration* meetings generally took place alternately in each administrator's city of residence. During the eight years it existed, the French national structure's headquarters were moved several times to accommodate the mutual desire of successive members of the Administration Council to resist the French penchant for centralism. The headquarters was in Montpellier for several years, then transferred to Toulouse, and just before the definitive dissolution of the national structure, it was in

Tours. For several years, the cities of Montpellier and Tours were the sites of Slow Food exhibitions inspired by the Salone del Gusto de Turin (*Aux origins du gout: Salon des Terroirs du Monde*, organized in the 2000s, and then *Eurogusto*, which had only three editions between 2009 and 2013). Following these exhibitions, the regional public administration provided offices in the city of Toulouse, after which it was the turn of the municipality of Tours. In each case, a combination of specific political links explains the presence or absence of official association offices. At the same time, the logistical questions which reflect the capacity to create links between the association and the regional political arenas point to the difficulties in establishing stable political links at the national level.

In 2009, the French council members began several months of discussion on a new project developed in the French context. The "high quality food" project (Haute Qualité Alimentaire, HQA) was conceived to accompany local communities in promoting "the improvement of food and farming practices." This seemed to respond to the dual necessities of conducting an initiative originating with the French association and interacting with other institutions in order to "sell" the messages of Slow Food. "The French association used its HQA campaign to target food that values quality of taste, responsible production, respect for the environment. Local production, pleasure, and conviviality are the main objectives of the High Quality Food" (HQA working document, 2010).

"We will be able to integrate HQA in everything we do," explained Jacques, the president of Slow Food France at the General Assembly of March 2010. "HQA is a coherent project, and it's our project; it doesn't belong to anyone else." He then laid out the list of cities and regions that had become closer to Slow Food in search of "original ideas and training, they are looking for new perspectives." The first were the cities of Millau and Bègles, communities situated on the progressive left wing of the French political map. Millau is also a symbolic place known as the location of a number of political acts taken by the *Confederation paysanne*, such as an attack on a McDonald's restaurant installation led by José Bové (Heller 2013). This coincidence is particularly interesting: From the beginning, Slow Food's leaders—Carlo Petrini in particular—attempted to maintain their distance from actions carried out by the *Confederation paysanne*. They intentionally concentrated on positive initiatives rather than critical confrontations and pointedly aggressive actions. In one of his writings, Carlo Petrini addressed the protests of José Bové: "The French union leader . . . who is today one of the leaders of the antiglobalization movement has voiced ideas that have often cast a spell over us. But, when he adopts a strategy of direct action, he chooses a path leading to head-on confrontation with the multinationals, the path of the guerrilla fighter, that we prefer not to take" (Petrini 2003: 26).

In the eyes of the French leaders, "Good, clean, and fair, is too vague. . . . It needs to be something concrete." The HQA project was an attempt to translate Slow Food's messages into concrete actions likely to catch the attention of actors in France's food service and production industries and especially the actors in public or large-scale catering (schools, hospitals, etc.). The project was presented at internal meetings or at local collectivities, and professional groups, but it never got off the ground. The terms used to present it—"a model for responsible agriculture and food," "responsibility in supply and consumption," "quality taste, and responsible production, respectful of the environment"—were not more concrete than the triad of "good, clean, and fair" promoted by Slow Food International. In the end, the bureaucratic dimension of the project seemed both far away from the spirit of the movement's key words, and too close to examples of other associations and movements already present in France.

If we closely examine the way that the Slow Food vocabulary and expressions are translated and applied, we can see a slight distortion of their original sense in the effort to make the principles pertinent in the French context. These expressions had not been specifically conceived for France, but rather for export worldwide. In HQA's draft charter for example, "good, clean, and fair" is explained in dimensions that were not present in the concepts initially developed by Carlo Petrini (2005): The sense of "good," which originally was only related to the organoleptic qualities of a product, was extended to include a reference to its authenticity; the notion of "fair" which reflected the idea of social justice and fair remuneration for farmers was translated as "fair trade and equitable compensation and working conditions, from production to consumption." Just as we can observe semantic shifts and the migration of ideas from one movement to another in the wider field of food activism, we can also observe the circulation of ideas within these movements themselves (Siniscalchi 2015; Rakopoulos 2015; Palomera and Vetta 2016).

Although these migrations of terminology (moral economy, food sovereignty, food justice, slow) can enhance the ideas and sometimes modify their initial sense, the processes of translation are never linear. In some cases, they become the subject of dissent; in others, they may give rise to a lack of understanding. The case of HQA clearly reflects this. Even more than the specific document and the failure of the project, the French association added the position of the consumers to the notion of fair, particularly with the perspective that a price should be fair for both the producers and the consumers. Although some of the international leaders found this extension humorous and scoffed at their transalpine colleagues' relationship with money, this dimension was eventually integrated in the messages of Carlo Petrini and Slow Food International. This evolution was, however, closer to the concept of "food justice," which affirms "good, clean, and fair" food for all, and not just for the gourmets and economically privileged people.

Filiation, affiliation, and the "French" problem

Along with Slow Food's political, cultural, and translating issues, other elements in France have contributed to the difficulties that hamper the association's development. Beyond the successes and failures of national and local organizations, difficulties at the level of the movement's global organization also involve the movement's funding needs and the organizational methods that have progressively been established to govern a complex mechanism—or *dispositive de pouvoir*, in the terms of Foucault—and make it functional. At the December 2010 meeting in Paris, Luca, the general secretary of

Slow Food

Slow Food International from the Bra headquarters, continued his presentation with the following:

> Why do we need national structures? For three reasons, but should any one of the three fail, we might as well do without these structures: firstly, to support each convivium, secondly, to maintain a dialogue with ministries and public authorities, and finally, to support the international structure because we will never be able to change the agro-food system in France if we don't also change it in Africa. We are all in the same boat, all 161 countries, and the countries who are capable must aid the others.

In 2004, the Terra Madre event was also established, allowing the extension of the international association to be visible through the network of producers who participate in the event. Slow Food's presence in 161 countries, as shown by the maps that appear in the association's documents and communication tools, often takes place simply through a few *convivia* or members, or through producers linked to the association and projects of the Biodiversity Foundation to support the local economy (especially in the Global South) as we will see in the next chapters. "Supporting the international structure" means contributing financially: the national associations are required to pay a subscription, the amount of which is fixed by the international council and is independent of the number of members. In France, certain administrators and convivium leaders regarded this contribution as an unjustified tax. From the perspective of the international leaders, it is justified by the necessity to contribute to the functioning of a central structure (headquarters' offices) that serves the worldwide membership. In addition, they contended that the contribution of each country enables the organization to fund projects and develop the movement in countries on the southern continents. Ironically, a historical leader told me, "Luca [the General Secretary] charges for what Carlin used to give for free [Slow Food membership and freedom of action]."

Indeed, the large events organized by the movement's international structure are a means of spreading the messages of Slow Food, of educating consumers and speaking to political authorities, advocating for the future of local economies and the environment through the themes of food production and consumption. Clearly, the international structure as well as the local associations have to find the means to pay for personnel and the development of Slow Food projects. As an economic model, this implies a combination of funding sources: membership dues; national public funding for large events and local government assistance for specific projects such as community gardens, regional labels, and promotional initiatives like food tourism; European funding for even larger projects; and finally the dues paid by the national associations that together constitute Slow Food International. At the Italian headquarters there is a group of employees whose work is dedicated to fundraising activities. In the other national structures it is often volunteer elected members who take on the responsibility of looking for funding. At each French board meeting in Corrèze or Marseille, Auvergne or Paris, the board members devoted hours of discussion on strategies to make Slow Food France more visible and increase the membership and thus enlarge the possibilities of obtaining funding. In France as in Italy and at the international scale, the numbers (the number of members, the number of countries in which Slow Food has members or projects, the number of Presidia, and so on) are always an issue for Slow Food leaders: more members means not only an increase in revenue from dues but also an increase in legitimacy that improves their ability to win support of institutions and attract still more members in a sort of perfect virtuous circle. Although this process based on expanding the structure and professionalism was successful in Italy at a particular time and in a given economic context, it was not necessarily reproducible everywhere else.

In the crisis that struck the French association, budgets became a central element in the negotiations between the leaders in France and those at Slow Food International. To justify the contributions that France owed to the international structure, the general secretary of Slow Food International said to the members of the French national board during a meeting in June 2011:

> The countries where Slow Food is stronger must support those in which Slow Food is less strong. So it was decided that where there was a national structure, there had to be a contribution. . . . In order to be sustainable as a national association, membership fees are not enough. The problem in France is that we did not find other funds.

Ever since the international council decided to institute an annual subscription to be paid by each national association to Slow Food International (€50,000), not all of these structures have been able to respect the decision, and the Italian association has paid for countries that were not able to meet their contribution. But the transfer of funds from one structure to another is not without consequence: it defines political relationships, autonomy or dependence, or even the primacy of one structure over another, thus becoming part of a political language. The relationships engendered through loans and debts (involving Slow Food International and Slow Food Italia) have indirectly contributed to confirm Italy's political preeminence over the other associations. These budget issues reveal "genealogical" links between the Italian national association and those of other countries, and highlight the balance, or imbalance, of power between them. Ultimately, the relationships between the international association and the affiliated national associations of different countries are governed not only by the statutes but also by these budgetary ties.

Southern Europe was especially affected by the financial crisis of 2007, but the consequences were not as strongly and immediately felt by the association in Italy, with its strong Slow Food presence, as they were by the associations in countries like France, where Slow Food was less well known. The French national structure struggled to achieve the visibility necessary to increase membership and never succeeded in establishing a dialogue with the public authorities. Following the national association's December 2010 meeting in Paris, a series of meetings between the French Slow Food president and other administrators, members of the board, and international leaders was organized. It became clear that the French national association was no longer sustainable, and French leaders agreed to its closure. The accumulated debt to Slow Food International was canceled, and the French national association officially disbanded.

Financial problems and the difficulties that they engender are among the consequences of the movement's political complexification, and France is not an isolated case. During the same period (in the early 2010s) in Japan, Australia, and the United Kingdom, various crises occurred, following different scenarios that ended in the suppression of structures that were not viable. The initial impetus and support for the creation of national associations was frequently followed by these difficulties, and as a result, Slow Food International's leadership changed strategy. Without necessarily disbanding all the existing national associations, at the end of the 2000s Slow Food stopped encouraging their creation on the grounds that they were too difficult to fund and manage. The international leaders seemed to be looking toward other types of organization: For example, in 2015, the Slow Food national structure in the United Kingdom was transformed into a confederation, "Slow Food in the UK," composed of four national units (Scotland, Wales, Northern Ireland, and England) with a single administrative council.

In spite of the energy deployed by the leaders and administrators of both the national and international structures, the creation of Slow Food France in 2003 never produced the desired effect nationally. One reason for the difficulties leading to its demise is an elaboration of the fact that the French terrain was different from that of Italy in the 1980s and 1990s. For example, when Slow Food established itself in France there were already existing projects which closely resembled those that had been implemented on the Italian peninsula. These projects were initiated by other associations (environmentalists or gourmets) and had widely varying aims such as environmental education, the promotion of regional products, urban gardens, and support for alternative production systems (organic, biodynamic, etc.). At the political level there were also the *Confederation paysanne* (Heller 2013) and the Colibris movement founded by Pierre Rabhi, both of which are similar to Slow Food in some initiatives, and both of which have a recognized or legitimate presence in France.

This is probably one of the reasons that Carlo Petrini came to France several times between 2009 and 2012 to participate in public discussions with other politically active personalities and scientists (Edgar Morin, Serge Latouche, and Pierre Rabhi, among others). The intention was to kick-start the movement in France by motivating its base membership that was embroiled in internal quarrels linked to problems in the French structure, engaging the media, and participating in public discussions. But an additional objective was simply to talk with other recognized intellectuals and leaders of social and political movements in France—including political leaders like José Bové, with whom Carlo Petrini had maintained a distance over the previous decade—in order to find complementary aspects and potential links that could raise the visibility of Slow Food on the French sociopolitical scene.

In an article dated November 13, 2014, in *Le Monde*, Carlo Petrini responded to questions from a journalist:

The French speak of gastronomy on one side and the food economy on the other, without ever addressing the link between them. . . . As much as I love France, this is a veritable thorn in my heart. This is the country of Brillat-Savarin, my intellectual mentor, the one who actually defined gastronomy as a holistic science that touches not only nutrition but also biology, physics, history, economy, [and] politics. . . . The French adore the aphorisms of Brillat-Savarin, but they have completely forgotten the substance of his thinking (my translation).

For Carlo Petrini, the demise of the French national association represented a failure, and even worse was Slow Food's stalled development on the French terrain in general. More than once, when discussing the subject, he said to me, "The militant activists in France are gloomy, they don't know how to enjoy themselves." The issues accumulated: resistance to the hierarchy, translation problems, ill-adapted funding efforts, difficulty combining progressive, social and ecological activism with gastronomy and pleasure. Are these the only reasons for the "French problem"? Is there a certain reticence on the part of the French to modify their habits, as Slow Food encourages? Should we evoke the power of the agro-industrial sector? Is it the difficulty of combining left-wing activism, ecology, and eno-gastronomy, as Slow Food has been doing since the beginning? All of these explanations are probably valid, but it is more in their articulation that I find the actual cause of the difficulties in establishing Slow Food in France.

Producers and activists

Since the beginning of the 2000s, the philosophy and actions of Slow Food have shown an increasing commitment to the integration of environmental and ecological themes, and to concerns for the living and working conditions of producers. In the triad of the movement's slogan and keywords, "good, clean and fair," the notion of fair refers both to the access to "good and clean" food as a universal right and to the producers right to fair working conditions and fair prices for their products (Petrini 2005). The most utopian dimension of Slow Food's philosophy can be seen in their attempt to change the food system by building a network of all small producers, attributing them all with a harmonious relationship to Terra Madre. In the vocabulary of Slow Food, "food communities" refer to food actors—producers, processors, and consumers—linked through commitment to a quality product, and the idea of "slow" has grown so far as to encompass the battles against unbridled capitalism, land grabbing, seed patents, nuclear energy, and the privatization of public utilities.

In line with these changes, Slow Food's international council decided in 2014 to condemn the agricultural and livestock practices that are contrary to an animal's quality of life, and force-feeding in particular, which is an integral part of *foie gras* production. Many French members viewed this decision as direct interference that signals an inability to understand the cultural context in France, "traditional" products, and the concerns of small livestock-farmers. After heated exchanges, the leaders of the international structure and the Slow Food Foundation for Biodiversity decided to suspend the decision and allow the French members time to find their own ways to apply the principle. But the debate continued, notably at the same year's October manifestation of the Salone del Gusto-Terra Madre in Turin.[3] During the meeting of the French delegation to the event, the producers spoke out forcefully. Robert, a livestock farmer, said:

> Slow Food is attacking the small producers instead of defending them. The major problem is [not small foie gras producers but] the industrial force-feeding, which in the future will mean the production of foie gras coming from China. With this attack [on small French producers], Slow Food is going after those who spread the Slow Food message and embody the French culinary tradition.

François, a goat farmer went further, saying, "Slow Food should be advocating less meat consumption instead of attacking this production which is ultimately only a small portion." The debate continued and ended with the hope, expressed by both sides, of better coordination and collaborative work on a sensitive subject. Upon leaving the meeting, Mariella, a discouraged staff leader from Bra said to me, "They are never ready to change, to discuss their practices and consider the problems from a global point of view." Beyond their historic and contextual character, these examples illustrate the tensions that punctuate the life of the movement and illuminate some of the internal contradictions.

If we interpret these conflicts strictly in terms of cultural differences and misunderstandings, we risk remaining on the surface and failing to understand the functional dynamics of the movement. Outside of the specificities of the French situation, there are effectively two ways of existing at the center of the movement that confront each other in this episode. One side is comprised of producers, acting on the terrain, and the other of movement professionals, acting to make Slow Food more and more recognized as a political force. We find the same divisions in some of the events that Slow Food organizes, such as Terra Madre and the Salone del Gusto. Sometimes the association has difficulty taking account of the day-to-day problems of farmers and recognizing the local dynamics. And sometimes, the projects and the attention focused on small producers in countries from the Global South can divert the attention of association leaders from closer realities in the countries where Slow Food is present.

This case also denotes the existence of two different scales of action: on one side, the local realities with economic and social characteristics related to a situation where the actors sometimes feel ignored and unrecognized for their specificities, and on the other, the European policies and regulations of food production, which Slow Food seeks to influence. To operate successfully, the leaders of Slow Food have to exhibit a unique position, understandable by both the public authorities and the other actors of this vast field of food and environmental policies, while at the same time distancing themselves from the perception of nostalgia, or a sentimental attachment to local traditions, or a denial of modernity as directed at the movement by certain journalists and researchers (see among others, DuPuis and Goodman 2005). Even though the autonomy given to national and local groups (*convivia*) has allowed, and still allows, Slow Food members to elaborate original methods for spreading the movement's messages in each country, or region, or simply within their own convivium, this autonomy inevitably collides with their obligations to a single centralized association. The internal structure of this association—also on a global level, regarding the relationship between national structures—is hierarchized and characterized by the dependence on political and economic relationships linked to the history and geopolitics of the association.

Even so, the difficulties encountered by the national structure in certain countries do not necessarily affect the membership base at the local level. Since the dissolution of the French national structure, the association's presence in the country has been referred to as "Slow Food *in* France," and it remains active through initiatives conducted by the local chapters. The more capable among them continue to spread the movement's messages, sometimes in partnership with other organizations or associations, through tastings, product promotion, education, and exchanges with chefs and restaurant owners about the principles of "good, clean, and fair." In practice, the demise of Slow Food France is not necessarily seen as a failure, but rather as a part of the local process of translating the movement in a way that takes other forms than those envisioned by the founders. These forms are the local articulation of the various Slow Food initiatives, which are both political and economic, and which take place in the interstices of the neoliberal system. It is this local articulation that characterizes the international movement today as we will see through the projects involving producers (see Chapters 7 and 8).

Notes

1. The *conseil d'administration* is the governing body of the French national association. It consisted of the president and five members from different *convivia*, elected by Slow Food France general assembly and serving four-year terms. According to French regulations, an association must have a president, secretary, and treasurer, who are part of the *conseil d'administration*.

2. This is the same event to which the leader of Slow Food International was referring to in his discourse quoted at the beginning of this chapter.

3. Previously, they were treated as two distinct events even though organized simultaneously, but in 2014, Salone del Gusto and the meetings of Terra Madre took the form of a single event (see Chapter 9).

Photo 6 Banner "Casa Slow Food" (Slow Food house), in Via Mendicità Istruita, the location of Slow Food's headquarters, Bra (Italy), 2017. The banner was installed when the association launched the purchase of part of the headquarters buildings, which until then had been occupied on a rental basis. ©Franco Zecchin.

CHAPTER 6
THE "BLACK BOX"
HOW DOES THE SLOW FOOD MACHINE REALLY WORK?

In 2012, I was doing fieldwork in Sardinia when my five-year-old son, who was at home, telephoned me for information about Santa Claus. Christmas was approaching and he had a lot of questions about how Santa Claus found out what presents the children really wanted, about the techniques he used to get into houses without anyone noticing, and so on. In a bookstore I discovered a book in English, *How Santa Really Works* (Snow 2005), which seemed the perfect gift for him after my weeks away. The reading of the book had two consequences: my son stopped believing in Santa Claus, and page after page, I found hilarious analogies with the functioning of the Slow Food headquarters.

In this chapter, starting with these analogies, I will explore the inner workings of the Slow Food machine, particularly the most intimate of them located in Bra headquarters, or the "black box" of the association and the movement. I will look at some of Slow Food's characteristics that are less visible to the outside world in order to understand the logic and tensions that permeate it and how those who work there experience it. Some of the modes of functioning and contradictions that appear within the Bra world may appear simply as the specificities of a "service center," as staff members sometimes present the Bra offices to the rest of the members in Italy and in other countries. Bra is far from being simply a service center. It is the place where the movement's philosophy, its communication tools, and a large part of its projects and actions are elaborated (even though they are related to what happens and emerges from local implantations). And it is the place where the functioning and governance of the association is designed to reach far beyond the Piedmont or Italy. My hypothesis is that the elements that characterize the world of Slow Food, as well as its specific history, influence the way Bra's headquarters functions at the local level and reproduces itself over time.

Santa Claus is a man with a big belly, a white beard, and a look that is both friendly and stern at the same time. He lives in a small, sober house. But "Where does Santa work?" asks the second chapter of the book. "Beneath his living quarters is everything he needs to make Christmas happen. There are factories, warehouses, transport facilities, a communication center and many other vital and necessary departments" (Snow 2005: 6). "Who helps Santa?" the book continues.

> Santa has many helpers. Most of these are elves. Elves lives all over the world, but when they grow up, a lot of them get jobs with Santa and move to the North Pole.

> Each year more elves are recruited. The new elves must undergo extensive training before they start to work. This is done at the CCR (Christmas college for elves). . . . These courses teach them how to do a specific job in one of the departments. (Snow 2005: 8)

The book then goes on to illustrate the different departments, such as the one dedicated to "research and development," where games are invented, some based on ideas that come from the children, others designed in the offices of the headquarters. "How does Santa know if you have been good?" asks another chapter of the book, "This is done for Santa by the CIA—the Christmas Intelligence Agency. All over the world, an elite squad of elves gathers data on children. It then relays the information to the CIA's office back to the North Pole. . . . As you can see on the next page, they are very busy" (Snow 2004: 12).

I wish I had written a picture book similar to Snow's book about Slow Food. Not having the qualities of an illustrator, nor those of a humorous writer of children's books, I simply evoke some analogies to how Slow Food works. I hope Carlin doesn't mind the comparison with Santa Claus: the character in the book is quite likable. Carlin is a charismatic character who plays a central role in the workings of the machine, and who lives soberly, in the center of Bra, not so far from the Slow Food offices. Indeed, even though Carlin seems to have become the only visible personality, the personification of the movement, and omnipresent in the press and media platforms, there were other historical figures, visible and present, at least in the years of my research (which is of course different than the world of Santa Claus). "He has to be very flexible to get in some people's homes, so during the year he does lots of bending and stretching exercises. . . . He is in good shape for a man of his age," says Snow about Santa Claus (2004: 29). Carlin's work rhythms and his ability to dialogue with actors in extremely diverse contexts (from international politics to small producer communities) also require flexibility and elasticity. He is surrounded by dozens of people who make his enterprise possible. Among those working in Bra, some come from territories where Slow Food has a presence, either Italy or other countries. Some have trained by working with Slow Food activities or have been volunteers. Others come from the University of Gastronomic Sciences. Bra, as a location, is in the North of Italy and in the Global North, even if not in the North Pole. As the headquarters, it is composed of an articulated set of offices and services in which employees work and learn to manage specific tasks. They are not very visible to the outside world, and for all of them, the work within the headquarters is a training exercise in itself. The games, such as Slow Food's projects or prizes (the Prize for Biodiversity or the Game of Pleasure, see Chapters 7 and 8), are designed partly at the headquarters and partly through the inspiration of people in different parts of the Slow Food world. A network of volunteers in the territory (local leaders and simple volunteers), like the elves of Santa Claus, transmit information on the good behavior of everyone, making it possible to dispense rewards and gifts (such as the right to be included in some projects, the Presidia project, the Ark of Taste). In previous chapters I have already analyzed leadership in the regions and the way in which regional presidents, with staff leaders, operated as a chain of transmission to Bra on the one hand and to the territory on the other. But thinking about analogies to gifts, I also remember when some historical leaders would tell me about the membership campaigns of the early years when, in Italy, members were entitled to packages with products to taste, now replaced by Slow Food magazine or some of the guides, depending on the period. And finally, the tremendous amount of work required to prepare for Christmas, the rhythms of which get faster and faster as the date approaches, reminds me of the busy months and weeks leading up to major events, which often ended with dinners among staff members (or among volunteers who helped during the event). Not to mention that afterward everyone would take a few days off.

Bra

Bra's headquarters is not only the place where most of the communication tools or their contents are conceived—after all, Slow Food is first and foremost a machine that produces ideas and projects on and from food and food politics—but it is also the place where the identity of the staff and those who are part of the association is forged. Within Slow Food, work and voluntarism are combined, both for local leaders and for staff members. The tensions between work and voluntarism mirror the specific configuration of the headquarters where work was often all-consuming, with each sector building its own way of working. In a now-classic volume on the Anthropology of Work, Sandra Wallman reminded us that when analyzing work, it is necessary to consider "what activities are called 'work'" (1979: 2) and how work is thought about. Work is not just about the production of material goods or economic transactions, it is also about "the ownership and circulation of information, the playing of roles, the symbolic affirmation of personal significance and group identity—and the relation of each of these to the other" (1979: 7).

I studied Slow Food's headquarters as a classic anthropological object, paying attention to roles and internal dynamics, friendship, kinship, and marriages. When I had breakfast in the morning, in the kitchen of Giovanni's home, where I lived during fieldwork in Via Mendicità Istruita, I was accompanied by a buzz of familiar voices coming from the pedestrian street where the house was located. In the building next door were the offices of Slow Food Editore, halfway between the offices of Slow Food Italy, a few meters down, and those of Slow Food International, around the corner at the top of the street. Bar Converso, a little further away, or the bar on Piazza XX Settembre were meeting places for breaks and before going to work. The people from Slow Food offices crossed each other and discussed right under my windows.

The headquarters was made up of a dense social fabric, a weave of interactions between people on the staff, some in the role of employees, others, at least for a few years, in the role of leaders. There was the work in the offices, the meetings, the lunches together, sometimes in small groups in the Boccondivino restaurant, located in the

Slow Food

courtyard of the Italian association building or in the other cafés and restaurants in the area. When I went to eat with some of them, for lunch or dinner, it was natural to meet their colleagues as well. These activities began early in the morning and often continued until after dinner; they were a mix not only of comradeship, friendships, and working relationships but also of frictions and conflicts. And this world was also characterized by a few romantic relationships, some stable, others "secret" but known to most.

Perceived and often represented by the local members as a compact whole, Slow Food's headquarters—often called "Bra" or "national" by Italian members and "international" by members and leaders from other countries—is actually extremely differentiated internally. Dozens of people work in the offices and in the different services or components. Most of these people are hardly or not at all visible when compared to the international president, Carlin, or to some of the historical leaders such as Silvano or Piero. Silvano, who was at one time vice president, was a dedicated leader in the Slow Food world, ever faithful to the association and most of all to Carlo; Piero, the president of the Foundation for Biodiversity, has been one of the most committed leaders on the environmental front, which over the years has become one of the main axes of the association's work.

This first generation of Slow Food staff and leaders was made up of people from the same social context, even if not always from the same cultural background, who shared political commitment and cultural adventures and who had forged, precisely through these experiences, their organizational skills and the first elements of Slow Food's philosophy: always having fun. The second generation was composed largely of people who learned by working in the offices, acquiring specific skills related to the sectors and projects that were gradually developed; some of them learned by working alongside the historic leaders. "I grew up with Carlo." "Diego and Fausto are Silvano's men. That's clear." "I was a kid when I came in here." Those are typical of the comments I noted during the research. Slow Food became a professional school and life for many who exemplified precise "styles" of work and specific approaches to the association. These links allow us to reconstruct a kind of agnatic genealogy that follows male lines: "He is the son of . . . ," "He comes from . . ." In some cases the reference to filial relationships was real (the children of some historical staff members or leaders work or have worked in the Slow Food offices), in others it was a filiation in professional or associative terms that appeared in the way they did things, sometimes even in their physical posture (in the way they walked for example) or in some expressions that they used. Generational belonging was not determined by age but by the time of integration within the machine. In the first generation, for example, some were very young, like Gianni, who directed the publishing house for years, or Mario, who was the president's secretary before moving on to communications office and the photo archives.

"It is from the University that the new ruling class will come," Carlo often repeated, after the creation of the University of Gastronomic Sciences. Indeed, in recent years many young people have joined the Slow Food offices in Bra. This third generation is made up of people who have done university studies, who speak several languages: some have been trained at the University of Gastronomic Sciences; others have come from local branches of the association. Many of these younger people work in the international structure or in the Biodiversity Foundation, following the projects developed in different parts of the world. It is this entire group of people from three generations, heterogeneous in their motivations and their professional backgrounds, who constitute the association headquarters, who make it work, day after day.

Organization chart

During my first week in Bra in June 2009, I had the chance to attend a general assembly of the staff that had been organized by the Slow Food leadership group in the large hall of a local bank. I had wondered if this was a regular meeting or something more exceptional. Although meetings of this type were held on occasion, this one had its own peculiar character. During the general assembly, a Slow Food organization chart was distributed and presented. It consisted of ten pages, two of which summarized the main decision-making bodies of the International association, the Italian national association, and each of the Slow Food components (foundations, university, companies). One page schematized the "institutional structure" of Slow Food with the nine national associations and its different components. Another page outlined the "operational structure," which included the main offices and internal structures with their areas of responsibility. And finally, six pages detailed the composition of the internal structures with the names of the people working in the various offices or areas and the names of the heads of each sector or office.

It was the first time that such a tool, which was more common in the corporate world, had been distributed to the staff. The fact that until that moment there had been no organization charts, or at least that they had not been distributed to all employees in the various sectors, and that suddenly the structure produced one, were two elements of extreme interest to me in my effort to understand how that mysterious world of the Slow Food headquarters functioned. In addition, an organization chart seemed to me to be a very useful tool from a practical point of view, to know who the people were, where they were, and what their role was. I soon realized that a few days after the meeting, the organization chart had already been forgotten. For me, this was a third element of interest regarding this object. When I brought up the subject with the people I interviewed, to my surprise, they seemed to have found no use for it. Many told me that it was useless because it did not correspond to the reality of the offices and because it did not describe how they really worked. Over time, more and more people confided in me that this document said nothing about the real way decisions were made and power was managed within the structure. And soon I too began to use it just as a reminder not to forget to interview someone or as a working basis for my meetings with the director of personnel, Beatrice. She helped me at various times during the research, as I had tried to follow the internal changes, the new hires, and those who had stopped working in the offices. What was the reality in the offices? And if the information in the document was useless, why did they spend time to draw it up and distribute it to everyone?

Slow Food

The organizational chart arrived at a particular moment in the life of the association in which there was a need "to put some order" (*mettere ordine*) into the structure, to rationalize the organization of personnel and budgets. Fausto was at the head of the administration department and the person in charge of this. He told me that Carlo had entrusted him with the task of rationalizing the internal structure but had told him, "please, we are not a company (*azienda*), do not turn us into a company." The task was not going to be easy with an organization made up of 160 employees in the city of Bra alone, two affiliated companies (Slow Food Promozione and Slow Food Editore), a university, two nonprofit foundations (Foundation for Biodiversity and Terra Madre foundation), and an international association (Slow Food International) composed of Slow Food Italia and eight other national associations. In fact, the headquarters seemed to work as a company in certain situations and spaces (organizing salons or preparing budgets, and administrative or consulting offices) and as an association in others (membership or Presidia offices, and producing guides). The coexistence of elements from both associative and business environments is a reflection of the way Slow Food has developed over the years. From a small association with a headquarters that initially functioned almost like a hobby or game for the participants, it grew rapidly in size and complexity, spreading to many countries around the world, multiplying projects and fields of action, and evolving into a large organization requiring extensive administrative offices and staff. What happens when a militant association, composed by friends, becomes a professional structure? What is lacking in the organization's charter? And what kinds of tensions does this system produce?

Fissions and mergers

For weeks and months, I followed the daily life of the headquarters and participated in dozens and dozens of meetings in councils, preparatory meetings, nonofficial encounters, meetings inside and outside the offices and during international events. I also accompanied the staff on official trips "to solve problems" in the rest of the "kingdom." During this time, I saw a considerable amount of movement among offices and people within the association: inside the offices, from one office to another, from one building to another, from one function to another. Why were people moving? And according to what logics?

At the beginning of my fieldwork in Italy, I found a staff photograph on the final pages of *Il Dizionario di Slow Food*, written by Ruffa and Monchiero and published in 2002. It listed the names of each person and the specific headquarter's office in which each one worked. No hierarchy appeared in the list, but it represented a sort of organizational chart, very different from the one given to the staff in 2009. Now, as I look back at that photograph, it seems to me that the relative position of each individual was not an accident. For example, the four historical leaders, Carlo, Gianni, Pietro, and Silvano were sitting next to each other in the center of the photograph.

Most of the people portrayed in the photo continued to work at Slow Food, but not in the same offices. Slowly I began to reconstruct their internal trajectories and the history of internal changes within the structure. As we have seen, the gradual expansion and growth of the movement's complexity has provoked gradual changes in the political structure of the association, and this evolution can also be seen in its headquarters. The end of the 1990s and the beginning of the 2000s was a period of professionalization of the movement: the Braidese structure employed more and more people, leaving behind a sense of interchangeability where almost everyone was able to do almost anything. A progressive specialization gradually became the norm, and roles seemed to become more strictly defined. But these changes did not stop when the structure reached its present size. Fissions and mergers—think of segmental systems, such as the Nuer studied by Evans-Pritchard (1940)—have continued: some offices are unified or their purpose is modified to include other projects or services. Sometimes their name is simply modified; other times, new offices and sectors are created. This process takes place according to a mechanism of expansion or reduction and then reorganization that follows the chronological and thematic evolution of the projects of which an office is in charge. Usually, the stated aim is to "rationalize" the work and the relationships among the various parts of this Braidese world, to "make the structure clearer" for members and for those who work in the offices. But often this process is linked to the undeclared aim of favoring or breaking the alliances and collaborations that are part of the internal power dynamics. From time to time, certain people leave, and others arrive, but there is a core group (which in the meantime has incorporated younger people) that remains relatively stable. In the organization chart distributed in 2009, many people can be found in several boxes at the same time or even at different hierarchical levels depending on the sector in which their name appears. Inside the physical working spaces of the offices, people from different sectors are grouped together in a logistical system linked to projects or the complementarity of certain tasks rather than an organization chart. The latter seeks to formalize and schematize situations that in reality are extremely fluid where people work together according to the practical or political logics of the moment.

I keep in contact with some of the people within the association and the headquarters and they regularly send me news, informing me of how they are and how things are going. This information combined with my own inquiries to see how the roles have changed over the years has confirmed that movement continues to characterize the functioning of the headquarters. If we consider the Slow Food world from a bureaucratic perspective— like it is often critically reviewed, from the outside looking in—the goals of this fluid bureaucracy described above do not correspond to those of Weber's sense of bureaucracy, which seeks equal treatment, rationalization of decision, and neutrality of administrative actions. But neither do the goals of most social organizations that apply bureaucratic principles, as Weber himself knew (Herzfeld 1992). People move according to the needs, to the skills that an increasing number of tasks allows to develop, but also according to internal conflicts and power dynamics. A classic text by Crozier and Friedberg on the sociological analysis of organizations reminds us that "any structure of collective action is constituted as a system of power. It is phenomenon, effect and fact of power" (1977: 25, my translation). And again, the two authors emphasized that power is a relationship that is first based on having skills, then being able to control uncertainties, and being able to "play the

Slow Food

indispensable role of intermediary and interpreter between different, even contradictory, logics of action" (1977: 86). In fact, only a few people in the years in which I frequented the headquarters seemed to possess this ability, necessary in a context in which the different sectors were built over time and almost as autonomous spaces. "The organization creates power simply by the way it organizes communication and information flow between its units and between its members" (1977: 87). Finally, the rules and the possibility and ability to create them are a source of power (1977: 90). We have already seen how the redefinition of rules and statutes has characterized the more recent period in the life of Slow Food. I tried several times to graphically represent the way the management team, not visible, functioned through small concentric circles of information sharing, but none of these schemes is really effective at showing how power is distributed within the machine. After all, one characteristic of power is its apparent invisibility. Nevertheless we know that it is embodied in specific relationships and interactions (Wolf 1990). Over time, some offices became like "castles on a hill," others were divided up almost like the partitions of "fiefdoms" and spheres of influence. Many offices or sectors were built around the personalities of those who later became their staff leaders.

Citadels

The political separation between the national presidency and the international one, which occurred when Carlo ceded his national position in 2006, coincided with a clear separation between the offices and staff of the two structures. But actually this separation was the result of other internal dynamics and tensions. The day-to-day governance of the international offices was entrusted to a staff leader while the Italian association became the charge of its new national president. This division, in turn, was at the origin of another change that occurred shortly before I began my research: the offices of the Italian Presidia, which were previously located within the rooms of the Foundation for Biodiversity in the same spaces as the international Presidia, had been moved into the offices of the Italian association at Via Mendicità Istruita. The international Presidia remained in the offices of the Foundation, adjacent to those of the international structure. Some of the staff criticized this decision because, in their opinion, the Presidia should have remained a unique project instead of being divided into two projects. Others justified this decision in terms of coherence: The Italian Presidia are part of the associative network which signals products that can be considered for the project or follows the projects in the field. It involves producers in the events of the *condotte* and acts as an intermediary between producers and the "national." In fact, beyond the motivations in terms of coherence, this reorganization had displaced people who used to work together—who apparently lost daily contact with the projects for which they had been responsible—and had created new proximities between sectors that in the past had rarely communicated. But the change in the internal geography of the association probably did not produce the desired effects, and a few years later, after my intensive fieldwork, the Italian Presidia reintegrated into the Foundation's offices. These shifts were sometimes described with references to the structural "fiefdoms" created in those years. Although the people at the head of each "jurisdiction" (such as the Italian association, the International association, and Slow Food promotion) had had offices in close proximity, the work of those offices had become increasingly separated in terms of operations, and employees from the various camps were thus less aware of what was happening with their neighbors, and even with the people working in the offices in the building next door or on the next street. Still, some more maliciously suspected that the origin of the separation of the Presidia office had more to do with a desire to break the unity of a sector of the association that seemed too independent.

The Foundation for Biodiversity was a prime example of a fortress created over the years. Located in nineteenth-century buildings between Piazza XX Settembre and Vicolo Chiaffarini, its offices were linked to those of the international association by stairs and balconies along the courtyards. Even though it was linked to the international structure, not only in terms of location but also through projects (actions in the Global South) and in its connections with the Italian structure (the Italian Presidia), the foundation was perceived as a fortress apart by members of the staff working in other offices. Its functioning was built around the charismatic figure of its president, Piero, the most intellectual and at the same time the most autonomous of the first generation of leaders. He was often traveling, always intolerant of the hierarchies and constraints of the structure, and maintained a critical voice on environmental and food production issues (pushing for more radical changes) from within the headquarters. At the same time, Piero's office communicated with Milena's office (in charge of the international Presidia) which of course had a geographical focus, outside Italy. On the balcony, just opposite, was the office of the Secretary General of Slow Food International with whom Milena also worked. On the second floor, also accessible from the stairs in the courtyard, was the office of the International President, higher up than the others, in front of the office of his co-author, and next to the press office—not surprisingly, these three offices were contiguous.

The *Centro Studi* (Research and Documentation Center) was another fortress located in a separate building, one floor up from the education office: this was where the conferences and scientific meetings were conceived and programmed for events such as Slow Fish, Cheese, or Terra Madre. The office had been conceived around the figure of its director, one of the second generation of people joining Slow Food. Chiara was another intellectual personality, author of several books contributing to the shaping of Slow Food philosophy, and a teacher at the University of Gastronomic Sciences. She had had other responsibilities in the years before my arrival in Bra. In 2006, when I participated for the first time at Terra Madre, she had been in charge of the event and relations with the academic world. And four years before, in the pages of the *Dizionario di Slow Food*, she appeared in charge of the *Premio Slow Food per la biodiversità* (Slow Food Prize for Biodiversity). The *Centro Studi* worked and did research on some of the issues on which Slow Food was building its expertise in those years: GMOs, fishing, and seeds were issues being addressed through projects in the Global South by the Foundation for Biodiversity. But this office appeared as another almost separate

Slow Food

working space. Unspoken tensions among the new leadership group were probably at the origin of the creation of this office and the changes in responsibilities of its director.

In the first months of my research, changes were also taking place in the offices of Slow Food Editore, the association's publishing house: a person who had worked in the international structure in the past had been reintegrated into this part of the headquarters after a few months of absence. With her arrival and that of a new manager in charge of "*Editore*"—as this part of the machine is referred to—the offices that were located on the second floor were transferred to the ground floor and vice versa. I had thought that this internal move was driven by the desire to connect the different parts of the structure together. But Gianfranco, the current head of the "*Liquidi*" office (where the people in charge of the wine guide worked), explained to me: "Until the beginning of 2000, this was a garage. The publisher was already here, but before he only occupied the upper part of the building. In ten years I've done seven moves, first here, then there, then up, then sideways, then down. Maybe five moves in this building alone." Despite all the internal moves, the "*Liquidi*" office remained a separate space from the "Guide" office (where the people in charge of the *Guida Osterie* worked).[1] It seemed to be a space apart from the others because of its specific functioning and to facilitate the direct relationship, almost daily in certain periods of the year, with wines and winemakers. At certain times of the year cases of wine regularly arrived for the tastings that would be held to choose the wines destined to be mentioned in the Guide. "This was an atypical office. We were six people: three of us were here in Bra and the others were external. Although external they were all employees, they also worked on the wine masters; they organized the lessons and found the wines," Gianfranco told me. The autonomy of the "*Liquidi*" office and its employees, often talked about by those from the other offices, seemed to be connected not only to the specific rhythms imposed by the production of the guide and to the fact that three of the six employees did not permanently reside in Bra, but also to the historically important role of wine within Slow Food and to the way this office lagged in adapting to the changes in the association's philosophy.

Friendship and moving

Even in this simplified picture, the internal articulations were more complicated than a spatial diagram or organization chart could show. Over time, some staff members lost status and power while others gained them; new alliances were forged and sometimes those in positions of responsibility were moved aside or voluntarily relinquished responsibilities for various reasons. Sometimes the evolution in a family was the reason for changes: some married and had children and women in particular chose family over role of responsibility they had in the past. Family life seems to be incompatible with the relentless responsibilities of management at headquarters that are especially time-consuming for the staff leaders. Some argued that Carlin, whose life is entirely devoted to Slow Food, constitutes an implicit model for involvement in the "mission" of the association.

The roles of responsibility in Bra seem to both require and create strong links and solidarity with the association. Being stronger in comparison to others, the links of friendship within the Bra structure sometimes play a role in the attribution of responsibilities. In the years of my research, a non-Braidese rarely became part of the most internal (and less visible) nucleus of the leadership, where work relationships were often mingled with relationships among family or friends. Even if someone without these prior relationships was recruited for their special skills, they rarely integrated into the Bra culture. The positions of the first- and second-generation leaders were consistently linked above all to the elements of solidarity and proximity resulting from their years together in the association. Strong ties also appear with some of the employees who can be defined as "historical employees." These are people who did not hold leading political positions but who were part of the first generation of people who joined Slow Food, part of the same Braidese environment. The position they occupied was often tailored to their skills and passions. But they were not exempt from changes in the office structure and sometimes from the frustration that some changes brought.

Although the quadrilateral layout of the historical buildings in which Slow Food's offices are located occupies a well-identified space in the urban center of Bra—Via Mendicità Istruita, Via Vittorio Emanuele, Vicolo Chiaffrini, and Piazza XX Settembre— the social space extends well beyond the four streets in which these buildings are located. This extended space encompasses more than just the contemporary work and social life of the employees and managers of the structures that make up Slow Food. Along with the cafés and restaurants where members socialize, this area also represents a space of childhood friendships among a number of them who grew up together in Bra.

The new director of Slow Food Editore was introduced during a board of governors meeting. A previous resident of Rome who had recently moved to Piedmont to work in the offices of Slow Food, he introduced himself by saying, "I live in Bra now," and a chorus of voices from the staff in the audience corrected him by saying "not in Bra, in Turin!" Somewhere between seriously and jokingly, he was regularly reminded in this way that he did not belong to the "original" world of Bra—not to mention that he had chosen to live 60 kilometers away—which probably contributed to his slow integration into the headquarters' social and working environment.

Company or association?

"Slow Food moves money; it moves a lot of money." "Slow Food has become a company." "They got rich." Those were all comments I heard from some of my colleagues in Italy when I started working on this research project. They are also expressions that I sometimes heard in the field. Such a large structure absorbs money and, as in other cases of associations that professionalize (see Gross 2014 among others), a part of the energy of those who work there must be dedicated to projects that bring in money to pay for the work and reproduction of the machine itself. Even if parts of Slow Food have become a company (particularly Slow Food Promozione), people with high-level associative or organizational responsibilities have salaries far below those in private companies (including the international president, whose daily lifestyle remains sober, despite his important political role and extreme media visibility), salaries that I define as being "militant." Here lies one of the contradictions of Slow Food: on the one hand, a public image that suggests a company dedicated to business, and on the other, a militant structure, even from an economic point of view when one considers the lower salaries and the importance of volunteerism. But in the years of my research, another contradiction appeared.

In the 2000s, fixed-term and precarious contracts dominated the Italian labor market (for young workers in particular). At that time, the neoliberal policies, which had developed in the 1980s and 1990s, began to systematically attack the social protection system which had been codified in the 1970s.[2] These "project contracts" or fixed-term contracts were also used in hiring Slow Food staff. Some people inside the association pointed to the fact that they represented precariousness and a contradiction to the "fairness" that the association and its local actions promote for producers. At least in part, these contradictions are probably a direct result of the way the association was created, without the structure or the culture of a company. The first generation created and then consolidated, along with the second generation, a system that allowed salaries to be paid to everyone in Bra. Although low, the salaries provided a "decent living," as some historical staff leaders told me, and members of the administrative offices pointed out that contracts were almost always renewed. "Slow Food has never sent anyone away, never fired anyone," I was told repeatedly. In reality, the contradiction, which was experienced by some members of the staff, lay not so much in the presence of precarious forms of work as in the co-presence of corporate and associational logics and models. Slow Food is not a corporation and its leaders and founders do not want it to become one, but at the same time the number of employees, the need to comply with current regulations for structures of its size, and the economic model that staff leaders have developed compels them to follow corporate-type procedures. Clearly, it was difficult to find a balance between the worldwide assimilation of neoliberal logics in this era of "flexible capitalism" (Kjaerulff 2015; Mollona et al. 2021) and those of an association started by a band of friends. Associational and volunteer-based logics continued to function and guide internal policies, even with respect to more recently employed people who had not experienced the initial stages of commitment mixed with fun. Some of them came to work inside Slow Food because they were fascinated by this world; but others see it as just another job, and contrary to many of their colleagues, it is difficult for them to understand the dynamic of the Slow Food machine, mixing work and volunteerism.

Lino, a historical leader, president of one of the regions where Slow Food had an important presence, and for many years an important figure in leadership, described the inner workings of the headquarters this way:

> What I see inside the association, with the generational change, is that they do not have the experience of a movement, of an association, not so much because they

have not been part of associations but because they had never had a leadership role before. Carlin comes from ARCI, they [the historical leaders] all come from the world of political parties, of trade unions. Silvano has trade union experience, all of us [have had experience], either one in ARCI, like Giuseppe, or like Antonio in politics. Mine were in the trade union world; all of us [have had these kinds of experiences]. For us, the organizational aspect of the association has always been important. This has always been the positive anomaly of Slow Food: it has not just been a publishing company, it has not just been a gastronomy club, it has been all these things at the same time because it had this strong associative aspect that no other structure has.

Although Slow Food has spread internationally and increasingly appears as a global movement, these origins, rooted in the Italian left cultural and political context, deeply permeate its structure and internal logic. For example, no one is really trying to build a career inside Slow Food; and the leadership positions appear to be governed by logics other than those of career advancement. Still, Lino told me:

Now there are new people; they are competent people, but they lack this background. All of them are young, but they are not new to the association [they have worked inside the offices of the association for several years]. This is the big problem of Slow Food, of having young leaders who find a job inside the association. The association is their workplace; it is their factory; so they must have [career] opportunities. The financial gratification will never be there; for a few, the role you have is the gratification, and there are more and more [people] who are acquiring skills, which have a market value. This is a dangerous but also natural relationship with the market [competent people leave to go elsewhere]. The contractual framework is affected by the association's ideological approach.

Lino reminded me that many of the staff had the same kind of contracts whether they were employees with skills and responsibilities or those doing simpler office work or secretarial work. They were working inside an association that did not have a system of career advancement like private companies. And often, they did not have experience in associational leadership outside of Slow Food, as the first generation had. For these employees, according to Lino, work should provide rewards that the system does not, or that it only provides for certain workers. "The people who organize events [Salone del Gusto, Terra Madre], they represent a lot of value. But they are put in the same box [they have the same kind of contract] as Michele [working on membership office]. If he does not send the *veline* [the membership receipt] today, he sends it tomorrow, but if those organizers forget a step, the podium comes down," explained Lino. The fact that the contractual framework was the same for people with different skills and responsibilities, combined with the work in close proximity and the advancement of some who acquired political responsibilities in addition to organizational ones, created tensions: "They were

Slow Food

all recruited at the same time, doing the same things. Now some are presidents, some have become secretaries, but they were all doing the same things [at the beginning]. What authority does a leader have? They grew up together and don't have different contracts," analyzed Lino. The political role assigned to some staff members became a way to allow them to move up the ranks, in the absence of other systems of advancement: at the same time, the assignment of political roles produced hierarchies among people who were hired at the same time to do, initially, the same thing.

Although Slow Food has never sent anyone away, many have left and many continue to leave today, even among people who have been working in the structure for many years. Some leave precisely for the reasons highlighted by Gianni, or because of internal tensions, or because their role is suddenly no longer recognized. But they rarely leave for a higher salary. Others leave because they are disappointed with some of the internal logic or disagree with the direction taken by the philosophy of the movement. Others simply have a desire for change or can no longer tolerate a totally consuming job that leaves little room for private life, particularly for those in leadership positions. At the same time, those who walk away rarely cut ties forever. Most of those who have left Slow Food maintain a strong bond that often mixes affection with a critical gaze and sometimes a touch of bitterness (a common characteristic of all those who have had experience of work and leadership or responsibility within Slow Food). Many return a few years later in other functions, often with external collaborations that leave more freedom and a chance to avoid being "trapped" in the internal mechanisms of the machine. Some have opened activities related to the world of food, often restaurants, and remain in a sphere of proximity. Marco, one of the two owners of Boglione, a bistro near the Slow Food headquarters frequented by many of those who work in the offices, worked for years in the communications department of Slow Food and the publishing house. Andrea, past director of events, now has a restaurant in a town near to Bra. Edoardo, past director of the international office, today collaborates with the wine guide. The examples are numerous.

These bonds maintained well beyond the duration of a work contract remind me of other contexts on which I have done research in the past, such as that of the sharecroppers in the Campania region. Beyond the criticism they might express towards the owners of the land, they maintained a strong affective relationship and social proximity that lasted well beyond the duration of the contract, a relationship that many defined as a "family" bond (Siniscalchi 1995). Although the context of Slow Food is very different from that of the Campania sharecroppers, here too the working relationship takes on connotations that are different from those of a simple labor link. Many of those who are employed in the headquarters have a strong affective relationship, at least in the first years, with Slow Food, with its mission, with the image and philosophy of the movement, or with the associative dimension that continues to pervade the offices. This associative dimension does not necessarily have a positive connotation. Most leaders dedicate their time almost entirely to the association: the boundary between work and volunteer work is difficult to draw, not only in terms of time dedicated to the association but also in social terms, in which working proximity and friendship (sometimes sentimental relationship) often blur together. In some cases, the link between work interests and kinship relationships is so close that some, sarcastically, speak of endogamy. For many of them, weekends are devoted to meetings, events, or traveling for association and the limits between private life and professional life don't exist. "Slow Food is the first thing, it's my life," some staff members explained. "My wife, yes I see her, sometimes!" said Silvano, a first-generation staff leader. Another former staff leader talked about this close relationship between private life, associative commitment, and work, and said to me: "I have never liked having only Slow Food as a job, a hobby, and a political commitment. However, take someone like Silvano, if you've asked him to make a membership card and his wife falls off a wall, he says to her, 'Wait, I have to make a membership card.'"

Isaia, another former staff member, who later became responsible for a country where there was a national Slow Food structure, told me, "Carlin used to say, 'our weapons are sympathy and friendship, and they don't cost anything.' And when an employee once complained that [she or he] was working twelve hours a day during the Salone del Gusto, he jokingly asked [her or him] 'What do you do during the other 12 hours? You have to work 24 hours!'"

Not only does work pervade private spaces, but the rhythms of work are contrary to the slow dimension that Slow Food defends, and this is another contradiction in the functioning of Slow Food: "Summer is the time of the year when we suffer the most, the rhythm slows down, there's a kind of blank," Francesco from the association office explained to me, "We work well under pressure." In fact, the urgency, the speed of action that Slow Food needs to continue to exist as an association and movement, in political arenas and through concrete food projects, requires constant availability and almost absolute dedication: "Slow Food's activity has always been fast-paced, almost frenetic, despite our name," recognized Francesco. Another staff manager, compared their time to that of the University of Gastronomic Sciences professors, whose research results are often not concrete enough or arrive too late to be useful in the development or implementation of Slow Food projects: "We are self-taught, but we get things done, we move forward. And we have a capacity for rapid reaction," she proudly announced.

"Do they believe it or not?"

"Colleghi e compagni" (Colleagues and Comrades) is the name of the headquarters' internal mailing list: work colleagues and political comrades (*"compagni"* is the classic communist illocutive formula). The question of who had a membership card and who did not was a regular issue discussed in informal meetings or discussions between staff leaders. According to some, having a membership card was an essential element of commitment that distinguished working at Slow Food from any other job. Although in fact there was no obligation, some employees discreetly claimed the right not to be members of Slow Food, like they discreetly voiced their disagreement with certain internal dynamics of the structure. While some presented the fact of having a membership card as a sign of sharing the philosophy of the movement, seen as necessary to carry out their

Slow Food

work (some even have a lifetime membership), others perceived this requirement as interference in their private choices. And if the card became indispensable—as someone noted—shouldn't it have been given for free to the employees?

Was believing in the "mission" really indispensable for employees? The term "mission" refers to both the mission in the religious sense and the "company" mission. The work in Slow Food was presented in some staff meetings by the managers as a "mission," meaning both the corporate mission and the ideal mission of the movement, in other words, acting in order to pursue the goals of Slow Food. According to Valentina, who was the head of the education office, most of the people who worked at Slow Food were first emotionally involved with the causes the association champions and then became passionately involved in working and spending time together. One evening, in Trapani (Sicily), after a day of international board meetings, I went for a drink with some of the staff leaders. One of them, Claudio, showed me a piece of paper where he had written something and asked me, "you who are the Spy, can you answer my question? According to you, who believes it, and who doesn't?" *Chi ci crede e chi non ci crede*, meaning "Who still believes in the ideals of the movement, in what we do as Slow Food?" On the paper, which I still keep in one of my notebooks, there was a little diagram with three possibilities: (1) She/He doesn't believe it; (2) She/He tries to believe it; and (3) She/He believes it. We began to joke about these three possibilities and refine the typology: among those who "don't believe it," we distinguished between those who "pretend to believe it" and those who "don't believe it and make no effort to dissimulate the fact." In the middle, between them and those who try to believe it, there are people "who used to believe it and are now disappointed." Finally, among those who "believe it," there are those who are happy and those who, while believing, have the feeling of losing out. I didn't put any names in his diagram, but Claudio was naming his colleagues and trying to imagine where they could be placed. The tensions that I discussed in Chapter 4 about the commitment of local leaders being required to become increasingly professionalized and have more and more time for association, which was difficult to juggle with their real-world professional activity, can now be seen more clearly. The game that Claudio submitted to me reveals the tension that permeated the entire association, the offices as well as the "territory": the commitment to pursue the "mission" required of both the leaders in the regions and the staff in the offices is always greater, always more time-consuming, yet often the gratifications are few and the effect is progressive demotivation.

A former manager of one of the sectors of the structure told me, "The problem is that they are always over their heads." In this complex machine, on the one hand the projects have multiplied over time always requiring new skills, and the work in the various projects has been like training school for many; on the other hand, the growing notoriety and the commitment to new battles have confronted the limits of the staff's knowledge and strained their ability to train themselves and the members. This feeling of not being able to meet all the commitments, running behind time, and running to acquire the needed skills is another example of the contradictions of a movement that defends the notions of slow and pleasure.

Women

In the narratives of the historical members of the association, women are always absent, as many of the historical leaders have acknowledged. Looking closer, women's names do appear, but it is always later, and they don't seem to have had a place in leadership. With the complexification of the headquarters and the association, women began to arrive; some came from the publishing world and others from the world of the local press. "In order to enter Slow Food you have to know how to write," some of the women on staff told me. "The first thing that I was asked was whether or not I was able to write," said Marta, who worked in the administration office. Everyone must know how to write if they want to work in Slow Food, and many women (from this second generation) told me that they were recruited "to write" even if later they went on to other tasks.

During my fieldwork, inside Bra offices, 55 percent of the employees were women, but no woman was part of the inner governing body or very high in the spheres of decision-making, even if some of them were responsible for certain offices.[3] Except for a few rare cases, the women who did have responsibility in certain sectors did not have a family. And the reasons for leaving often corresponded to a change in private life (for men also but more often for women). Sometimes the birth of children pushed women away from jobs of responsibility or prevented them from taking them.

The rhythms of Slow Food required flexibility in schedules and a commitment that went well beyond working days. Roles with responsibility required almost complete dedication, which is hardly compatible with a family life, as I was told by both male and female employees. It wasn't happenstance that I left my family at home when I started my research in Bra: at the very beginning of my research I realized that I could not follow the same work rhythms if I was not alone in the fieldwork. Being alone made it possible for me to be included in the myriad of meetings, gatherings, and travel that required an extreme flexible schedule.

The administrative office, where most of the employees are women, probably more than in any other office, is a one of the few Slow Food spaces in which women seem to be able to have private lives and children. But as Beatrice, the staff director, told me,

> When we had to find another head of the administration sector, Fausto asked us what kind of person we were thinking about. Marta and I, immediately answered, without consulting each other, that we absolutely needed a man. These [roles, such as the head of the administration sector] are not roles for women. He has to be an available person who can stay late on weekends.

Even if, on the eve of a national or international council meeting, administration employees can spend the evening or a part of the night preparing budgets and documents for the next day, this is a service in which, with the exception of the director, the employees very rarely need to travel. At the same time, this service was rarely mentioned by people with whom I spoke when they were describing the internal changes or simply

Slow Food

the internal structure of the offices. It was as if it had a status apart, or as if it were practically "invisible."

"A man can devote himself more to this work, he is more comfortable in meetings with other men, but this isn't a rule. One day a woman could be president, why not," said Beatrice. However, once as we were coming out of one of the many meetings I had attended equipped with notebook and pen, Mario, who worked in the Italian association office, stopped me with a laugh: "You know Slow Food better than all of us: dozens and dozens of meetings and interviews. What are you really going to do with all this?" I answered him jokingly, "Maybe, one day I could become president," to which he replied, only partly joking, "That's impossible! You forget that you are a woman."

The case of the *direzione operativa* indicated by members as the "*direttivo*" (board of directors) is a clear example of the gender dynamics inside the headquarters and more generally inside the leadership of Slow Food. During the June 2009 meeting, in which the organization chart was distributed to the staff, this board was presented as an extension of a previous unofficial board composed of four or five men, each in charge of one of the large sectors around which the headquarters were organized. The board had been made official through the organization chart with a goal of transparency and democratization. The new and enlarged form was now composed of twelve people, and four women in charge of important sectors in the association (the administration office, the Fondazione per la Biodiversità, the Centro Studi, and Slow Food Editore) had been included. They had been "recruited" inside the *direttivo* by one of the men of the first unofficial directive board. But the two goals—make the leadership team visible and include women in a more democratic spirit—failed. This new body functioned only a few months, very quickly losing any political function. It had been presented as the place where political strategies were to be developed and decisions made affecting headquarters, but it became a place to discuss logistical issues without much importance, such as the use of company cars. It may be that the larger number of members caused it to lose its role of a decision-making space by diluting the number of issues that needed to be considered. But I would not exclude the possibility that one of the reasons was the inclusion of women. The board soon stopped meeting, and instead, a small group of the men continued to work unofficially. "We did not know how to function as a governing group," said one woman who had been a member of this directive board, suggesting that the group's failure was the responsibility of the women. Were women refusing roles of political responsibility, having assimilated gender inequalities and power relations, or did they express commitment differently?

During other office meetings or transversal meetings in which the participants were primarily women, it seemed to me that the political issues and governance "strategies"— that are very much part of the other more formal or informal meetings of men—were curiously absent, except in a few cases. "Women have a more practical, concrete side, they work on projects," said Valentina, who was in charge of the education office. "We are busy with the large number of tasks required to make this work," added Milena, speaking about her position at the Foundation. Following a pattern found elsewhere, the men and women inside the headquarters seemed to construct different spaces for themselves, and

The "Black Box"

the women's spaces were devoted to more concrete action: Claudia or Monica in the organization of big events, Ornella in the publishing house, Chiara in Centro Studi, and so on. This made some people like Edoardo, a former staff leader, suggest that the real power was in the hands of women:

> In reality, women are the decision takers in Slow Food [because] they are in places where things are accomplished. A woman manages the [Slow Food] review; another leads the most important sector of education; a woman is the head of the *Osterie* [publishing] office. . . . Women are very important; they do; they act, and they really decide. But it is true that they aren't at the head of big structures which characterize the organization of the offices in Bra.

Both points of view capture a part of reality. In fact, even in the 2009 organizational chart, women occupied strategic sectors of the association, but when the chart indicated that a woman was in charge of an office, a man's name was always listed above her name (the president, general secretary, and so on). The difference between the kinds of engagement expressed by men and women within headquarters corresponds to what Carole Counihan (2014, 2019) has observed within some *condotte* and in other spaces of food activism in Italy. The women analyzed by Carole Counihan expressed a capacity to act that was related to a national context in which women's work continues to be penalized or at least does not receive the same recognition as that of men, in terms of salary as well as career (see also Counihan 1999, 2004; Molé 2012).

Indeed, the gender issues inside the offices were not so different from those in the "territory." At the regional and local levels, the leadership remained strongly masculine in the years of my fieldwork. As Antonio, a regional president, told me, "At a given moment in our history, women began entering the territory, becoming *fiduciairi*, teachers of masters of food, but still there were few women in the leading organizations." Looking inside the composition of the national political bodies, the presence of women was extremely small. Between 2006 and 2010, only one woman presided over one of the larger regions, Tuscany. As a regional president, she could have been a member of the *segreteria nazionale* (the national board), but she decided to leave her place in this political body to another governor of the region, preferring to concentrate her time and energy on regional activities. Other women were regional presidents but in "small" regions. The only woman on the national board during that period was a member of the staff, the director of the education office. After the congress of 2010, the situation evolved slightly through the framework of the "democratization" process: this time two women were elected as regional president of "large" regions (Tuscany, again, and Lazio, see Chapter 4); with this role, they were both eligible, but only one decided to join the national board. The other relinquished her seat to her vice president, a man. The imbalance seen in these examples was the same inside the international presidency and international council.[4]

The strongly gendered history of the Italian association continues to have a bearing on the configuration of Slow Food and its political bodies, even if two women were appointed as vice presidents, Alice Waters[5] and Vandana Shiva,[6] at the 2007 International

119

Slow Food

Congress in Puebla (Mexico). But international representativeness is another question, more symbolic, linked to the philosophy of the movement, and once again, less in touch with real political decisions. Those two vice presidents were not actually involved in such decision-making. In fact, in more recent years, as Slow Food leaders began to pay increasing attention to the world of production and to local economies around the world, women have appeared as political subjects but in a particular perspective. In his speech at the opening of the Salone del Gusto and Terra Madre in 2010, Carlo Petrini said:

> Indigenous people, peasants, women, and the elderly should not only be listened to; they should also be at the front line of the challenges . . . but in reality, these people are the least listened to by politics and by the media. We have left these people behind as if they were the last part of the planet. But to the contrary, they are the ones who will show us the right road, the right way; the most marginalized people are the ones who preserve the earth.

Thus, alongside farmers and indigenous people, women became the symbol of the relationship to the land, to knowledge, to food. On the stage of the Palaisozaki,[7] where the closing night of Terra Madre was taking place that same year, Vandana Shiva represented all of these dimensions: the rights of small farmers, indigenous people, and women, and as a woman, she was an icon of the new philosophy of the movement. And since she was an intellectual, she allowed the women who are vital to the daily functions of the association inside the territory to think differently about the role of women within Slow Food.

Notes

1. Osterias are small, family-run restaurants that use and value local recipes and products (see Chapter 10).

2. Italy is a "democratic republic, founded on labor," or so states the first article of the constitution drafted after the twenty-year fascist period. Treasuring the antifascist struggles and profiting from leftist intellectuals and politicians, labor legislation drafted in the 1970s protected workers from dismissal. One of the instruments was Article 18 of the Labor Code, which was later revoked during the development of neoliberal policies because it was considered a brake on business development. See among others in the English-speaking literature the work of Molé (2012).

3. Women were the heads of only five of the fourteen offices indicated in the organizational chart. The number of women working in the other offices and functions of the association dropped dramatically: the members of the boards of Slow Food promotion, the University of Gastronomic Sciences, and the *Amici dell'Università* (Friends of the University) association were all men. On the board of Slow Food Editore there was one woman, along with five men.

4. Before 2010, the eight Italian members of the international board, included one woman from the staff in Bra, another who represented the Foundation for Biodiversity, and a third woman from the University. Of the other thirty-one international board members who represented the various countries in the world where Slow Food had an established presence, only five

were women. The proportions changed slightly with the Italian national congress in 2010 and then the international congress in 2012.

5. An American restaurateur and chef, author of several books, and owner of the restaurant Chez Panisse, in Berkley, California.

6. In the chapter dedicated to Vandana Shiva (Piron 2015), T. Hougton describes her like this: "A scientist, philosopher, activist, and feminist activist, the Indian alter-globalist is seen as a leader in the ecofeminist movement that advocates a return to purer values within our society by putting women and nature at the heart of the struggle against the neoliberal agribusiness" [my translation].

   https://scienceetbiencommun.pressbooks.pub/citoyennesdelaterre/chapter/vandana-shiva
   -1952-inde/

7. The building is an indoor sport arena, with a capacity of about 16,000 people, that was built in Turin for the 2006 Winter Olympic Games. It is named after Japanese architect Arata Isozaki.

Photo 7 Aromatic herbs' smell workshop, Cagliari (Italy), 2011. ©Franco Zecchin.

CHAPTER 7
GASTRONOMIC BIODIVERSITY
HOW ARE THE ENVIRONMENT AND FOOD CONNECTED?

During the 2014 Terra Madre, I was passing by the central space of the Oval, where large meetings take place, and I came across a huge wooden structure in the shape of Noah's Ark. At the Ark's bow, apples of ancient varieties from different parts of the world were arranged to form a snail which was then surrounded by legumes, plants, and fruits with labels indicating their origin. Behind a counter situated on the Ark, Foundation of Biodiversity staff were welcoming people carrying samples of their products, the fruit or cheese, or jar of seeds that they sought to justify as belonging on the Slow Food Ark. But the Ark is much more than the large wooden platform that was built for this occasion. To understand what the Ark is, we need to take a step backward.

In this chapter I approach Slow Food philosophy through a few of the association's projects that reveal what kind of environment is at the core of Slow Food's actions. These projects support and enable the development of new ideas and vice versa. From an analytical point of view, they constitute spaces of tension and expression of the two dimensions, economic and political, that in my view characterize Slow Food from its origins. But I hypothesize that the projects related to the theme of biodiversity (and gastronomic biodiversity, which Slow Food leaders elaborate) do even more: they enable the transformation of Slow Food into a transnational movement, spreading even in countries where there are no local groups, let alone national structures, while retaining a strong associational structure deeply anchored in the Italian political and cultural context.

Saving tastes from the "great flood"

Concern for producers and the environment is now seen as characteristic of Slow Food's mission, but their apparition at the core of Slow Food was a gradual process. It wasn't until the end of the 1990s that they could clearly be seen, almost in tandem, as two fundamental matters of interest to the association's leaders and members. The process integrating these issues began with the shifting of attention from products—the food, family cooking, and wine—to production methods and environmental aspects.

Created in 1996, the Ark of Taste was conceived as an inventory of "forgotten" products that merit attention and are in danger of disappearing. The *Manifesto dell'Arca del gusto* (Manifesto of the Ark of Taste) was written in 1997 and is one in the long list of *manifesti* that Slow Food has elaborated over time. It defines the Ark as an instrument "to save the flavors of the planet," and outlines several objectives: to protect small artisanal productions of high-quality foods from the deluge of industrial standardization; to prevent "fast food" from devouring and annihilating endangered animal breeds, cheeses, cured meats, wild and cultivated edible herbs, cereals, and fruit; to promote taste education; to make a stand against the obsessive concern over hygienic issues, which kills the specific character of many kinds of production; and to protect the right to pleasure.

In the Ark's manifesto the opposition between slow and fast assumes a particular flavor: "fast" production represented by industrial agriculture is seen in opposition to "slow" food production that is respectful of the land and natural growing seasons as practiced by small, artisanal producers and acts in favor of preserving the diversity of species and products. "Fast" reflects the standardizing effects of globalization, whereas "slow" directs attention to the production specificities of various contexts and their climatic and environmental characteristics, which are considered crucial to the quality of products. The Ark is thought of as a lifeboat that saves producers and products from the homologation instituted by the food industry. Its goal is to preserve all the products (vegetal, animal, or processed), country by country, that are at risk of being lost.

The Ark of Taste project helps us identify the contours of this new field of action for Slow Food built through the notion of gastronomic biodiversity. This notion is integrated into the association's actions with salvific language that blends biblical images and military terms, which can also be found in other more radical ecological movements such as Greenpeace. However, within Slow Food these terms have always been used with a sense of irony, even if a more direct and militant posture seems to have taken the upper hand from time to time. During my first conversation with the president of the Slow Food Foundation for Biodiversity, he explained Slow Food's perspective on the notion of biodiversity.

> When we became involved in the field, the image of the gourmet as a visionary was limited to what arrived on his plate. But as we started looking at what occurred "before" the food arrived on the plate, what occurred in the fields and in the production centers, we began to think about biodiversity. Our largest initial challenge was that of affirming biodiversity as not only forests, pandas, eagles, or tigers but also sausages produced by man, species and cultivated varieties, domesticated over 10,000 years of agriculture. . . . All this is biodiversity. It has the same environmental and landscape values as spontaneous biodiversity. In fact, it is thanks to our work that the agri-food world was integrated in the concept of biodiversity; this is to our credit.

Biodiversity is conceived above all as gastronomic diversity, and the Slow Food vision of the environment includes not just fields, pastures, and vineyards but also the knowledge and techniques of food production. Although today these statements intersect with those of other associations and movements and certain scientific positions (Alkon and

Guthman 2017; Dubuisson-Queiller 2009; Gross 2014; Schlosberg and Coles 2016), at the end of the 1990s, they were original in the Italian context, as Gabriella, the head of the Italian Presidia office, explained to me:

[In 1998] at the Salone del gusto, we introduced the Ark of Taste products, and something unexpected happened. Most of the media and journalists covering the exhibition became more interested in these "lost" products than in anything else. There were these taste laboratories: the *Lardo di Colonnata*, the *Pecorino di Farindola*, etc. There was already existing research [on these products]; we published a catalog of products facing extinction. But that was only a catalog; we still didn't know where that would take us.

This process shows the performative character and the unexpected success, almost fortuitous, of certain initiatives taken by Slow Food. The association leaders have gradually assumed the role of experts. Along with the Ark, Slow Food leaders used this new space dedicated to biodiversity to launch the *Premio Slow Food per la difesa della biodiversità,* known as *Premio della bodiversità* (Prize for Biodiversity). The award was first presented in 2000 and was aimed at recognizing and rewarding producers or other professionals with activities that Slow Food considered as contributing to maintain agro-alimentary diversity in the fields of agriculture, livestock rearing, and gastronomy. Between 2000 and 2003, approximately thirteen awards were presented each year to the associations or producers determined to be exemplary for their production activities or research contributing to "food biodiversity." The award given to virtuous producers, the *Premio della biodiversità*, allowed Slow Food staff and leaders to build specific communication aimed at highlighting the exemplary cases selected each time. But it only lasted a few years before it was replaced by the Presidia project.

This perspective continued to evolve over time, weaving together the economic, political, and legal dimensions, and in 2003 the nonprofit *Fondazione Slow Food per la biodiversità* (Slow Food Foundation for Biodiversity) was created. The foundation enabled Slow Food to obtain funding, often European, and invest in the defense of biodiversity, primarily in countries of the Global South. Moreover, it made it possible to concentrate the movement's environmental initiatives in a single structure and at the same time rendered them more visible.

Defending the environment through food

Slow Food philosophy preceded and then accompanied these changes. One of the changes is summarized by the "Good, Clean, and Fair" formula, which was introduced by one of Carlo Petrini's books in 2005 and has become the synthesis of the philosophy of the movement. "Good" refers to the taste and organoleptic quality of food products. It is not quality in an abstract sense, defined once and for all, but quality as perceived by consumers who are "educated" to recognize it. In a seemingly contradictory way, good is relative; it is linked to the context, the consumer's experiences, and knowledge. Thus, for those with the proper experience and knowledge, "good" refers to "natural" products that have not been standardized by the food industry. Carlo Petrini's book, titled *Buono, pulito e giusto* (Good, Clean, and Fair), outlines Slow Food's perspective on these ideas.[1]

> "Clean" is a far less relative concept than "good.". . . Clean, too, corresponds to a criterion of naturalness, but in a different sense, or at least in a different conceptual development from that which we have described in the case of good. Naturalness here is related not to the intrinsic characteristics of the product, but rather to the methods of production and of transport: a product is clean if it respect the earth and the environment, if it does not pollute, if it does not waste or overuse natural resources during its journey from the field to the table. . . . A product will be clean to the extent that it is sustainable from the ecological point of view. (Petrini 2007: 114–15)

Indirectly, this aspect of the philosophy values local and artisanal production, which it considers as the only means to preserve the diversity of products, their taste, and even the environment.

> Our definition of "fair" is closely linked with the crucial concepts of social and economic sustainability. . . . The fair, socially speaking, means fairness for the people who work the soil, respect for those who still love it and treat it with respect, as a source of life. . . . "Sustainable" means promoting quality of life through dignified jobs that guarantee sustenance and fair remuneration. (Petrini 2007: 135–6)

Production, distribution, and consumption can be defined fair when they respect the rights and dignity of producers and support fair wages and working conditions. In some respects, this discourse and its key words (sustainability, dignity, fair remuneration, and fair price) are close to the rhetoric of Fair Trade (see, among others, Grimes 2005; Luetchford 2008; Lyon and Moberg 2010), integrating power relations and consumer power into the discussion in order to give a more equitable place to producers, not only from the Global South but also from Europe. This perspective is also similar to other "social justice" discourses (Gottlieb and Joshi 2010): in the Slow Food world, "social justice" means, first of all, justice for producers in terms of economic, working, and living conditions. From another point of view, justice considered through the notion of "fairness" is a universal notion, close to human rights: "'Fair' is sustainable; it creates wealth, and establishes a more equitable order among the people of the world" (Petrini 2007: 143). The notion of "fairness" as justice also makes it possible to affirm that the right to food is a universal right.

We can see the "Good, Clean, and Fair" triad in a chronological order reflecting the place that these three words occupy inside the movement's evolution. In the mid-1980s, the movement's first concern developed from a consumer viewpoint. The "Good" was all about good food and good wine. The following decade saw a shift in focus toward products, which was clearly affirmed with the creation of the *Premio della biodiversità* and the first Presidia projects. "Clean" marks this continuing transition and the introduction of ecological concerns in the actions and discourse as Slow Food's interests expanded to include livestock breeds, plant species, production methods, and their environments. Finally, with projects involving small producers and local economies and events like Terra Madre highlighting their value, Slow Food philosophy and actions embraced the issue of justice in producers' living and working conditions. "Fair" represents this commitment to and integration of producers, not only in the movement's philosophy and interests but also in the ranks of the association itself. This period of history also witnesses an increasing change in the perception of Slow Food from one of an "association" to one of a "movement," a semantic shift which accompanies and drives its transformations.

The three terms "Good, Clean, and Fair" create and demarcate new political spaces of action that are simultaneously concerned with consumers, producers, and the environment. But which environment are they talking about? The environment targeted by Slow Food actions includes agricultural activities as well as the "food" dimension. This is one of Slow Food's specificities as compared to other ecological movements. The environment is conceived as collective good including the animal and plant species necessary for food: in the Slow Food perspective, supporting good, clean, and fair products and production means contributing to the preservation of the environment. At the same time, this support depends on the individual and private choices made when producing and consuming food. These choices imply a responsibility, and this notion increasingly appears in the dialogue of staff members and text of official speeches. Of course, as Narotzky (2012) reminds us, this rhetoric emphasizing individual responsibility, characteristic of a range of experiences conceived as "alternatives to capitalism," is also characteristic of neoliberal economics. In the case of Slow Food, as with many different movements and forms of mobilization in the field of food activism, individual action is all the more effective when it is collective, and accountability is an injunction made not only to individuals but also to the political classes. At the same time, the actions undertaken by Slow Food are not immune to overlaps with market logics, as we shall see.

The Ark selection process

Soon after its creation in 1999, the Ark was endowed with a scientific commission to address the requirements of putting together a catalog. The commission was coordinated by the association's leaders in charge of identifying "exemplary" cases that merit

Slow Food

recognition or being placed on the list of products to be saved, and included experts from the fields of agronomy, botany, and zoology that were selected from the circle of close "friends" of Slow Food. Over time, Ark national commissions were established in several other countries where the movement was active. A national commission could exist also in countries without (or who, like France, no longer had) a national association, where they were still able to contribute to the effectiveness of the movement's presence on a national level and in a more institutional sense.

During the years of my research, the meetings of the Ark committee in France brought together a large number of scholars and experts who committed themselves to long days presenting and discussing the assembled characteristics of each product proposed for inclusion. In April 2010, the meeting took place in the castle of Suze la Rousse, in the Drôme department, where the headquarters of the *Université du vin*, a structure dedicated to training in the field of wine not directly linked to Slow Food, is located. Among the nine members of the French Ark of Taste, there were academics and researchers, food historians, and agronomists; the others had roles in the national structure of Slow Food France, including the president, Jacques.

This was the second meeting of this new committee. It began with a discussion of a variety of wheat, which had been signaled by the Parc Naturel Regional du Luberon. The members discussed the number of producers involved but were especially concerned about what products were made from this wheat. The discussion became lively around the possibility, or not, of bringing a variety of wheat into the Ark without connecting it to a specific product. Some members compared this to a breed of cattle, questioning the need to always have a link between a specific product and the variety or breed. "It's the race, it's the line chosen by the international, it's the race that goes into the Ark" recalled Laurent, one of the members of the Slow Food France *conseil d'administration*, referring to the political position he thought was taken by "the international" (the Bra headquarters). Another member of the committee, a researcher, corrected him: "It must be good. The breed is a concept, but it is about the meat of the breed." "A vegetable will be eaten as it is, but no wheat will ever enter the Ark because it is not eaten like that," Laurent argued. The president of Slow Food France, who was the person who had the most contact with the international headquarters, said "In Italy, cold cuts cannot enter the Ark if there is no interesting breed." Another researcher, who was the president of the committee, intervened to underline that there was a strategic and political issue for Slow Food in this case: "the project is serious, it is carried by a park and it seems strategic to me to enter into a kind of alliance with these structures, the regional parks, the national parks. In my opinion we can say yes." He was trying to reach a consensus through arguments linked to the potential strategic local alliances that the inclusion of wheat could have. The president of Slow Food France then suggested adding food considerations as a condition and to follow this same line of conduct whenever there is a race or a case like wheat that is discussed. This would mean adding to the product's admission formula "from a food perspective." The member of the *conseil d'administration* of Slow Food France then proposed to add this same formula to the specifications, but other members of the committee reminded him that the specifications are an instrument of the Sentinelle project [the name in France for Presidia] and not of the products of the Ark. The discussion continued and they finally agreed to accept in the Ark the "flour from wheat milled in Apt" [the city of production] as an Ark product because the wheat producers made flour (and the final product was the "bread of the Luberon.").

This excerpt from my field notes on the French Ark committee allows us to see another example of the problems encountered with translations of the devices that Slow Food diffuses in its various communications. It also highlights the attempts to comply with international policies while finding an interpretation that accounts for the local situation and actors (in this case a regional park.) In terms of the relationship between cultivated plants and food, however, this meeting is even more enlightening because it provides an example of the Ark's product selection process and accompanying discussions in which committee members reflect on the links between biodiversity and food. At the same meeting of the French Ark, members discussed several cases of products that had been included in the Ark and had begun to advertise or indicate their Slow Food Arc membership. Did producers have the right to indicate their Ark status on their label or not? "We don't have a commitment to them, and they can't put that on their label." "We ask too many questions," added another member. "Yes, but how do we control and guarantee that they don't make their products with GMOs?" resumed the former. "But among these products this case does not exist," replied the Slow Food France president, "We are halfway between Italy with 200 Sentinelle and the US with zero. It just needs to be explained that the Ark does not have specifications, but the Sentinelle do." Speaking in the same vein, another member of the *conseil d'administration* of Slow Food France added, "The Ark represents identified products, the Sentinelle represent accompanied products." Finally, the members discussed the need to organize more tastings, the need to meet with at least one producer for certain products they were reviewing, and the possibility of asking members of the convivium, who are in the area of the product discussed, to do complementary research. Each of the fifteen products analyzed during the day-long meeting provoked discussion and some degree of disagreement.

We can look at these discussions as a case study of "politics in the making" (Shore and Wright 1997; Shore, Wright and Però 2011), in which the different actors involved interpret the project imported from the "Italians in the 'Mother House,'" as Slow Food France's president described the staff members in Bra to the administrators of the French structure.

Over the same period, these cataloging activities, which represent the core of the Ark project, appeared to lose importance in Italy. The wide range of projects initiated by Slow Food has evolved. Some were abandoned after a few years, others were newly developed, and still others transformed. Actually, in spite of succumbing to the rise of the Presidia, the Ark has continued to function and in more recent years has even recovered a measure of its political importance, as shown by the installation in a place of honor during the 2014 Terra Madre event described at the beginning of this chapter. This recovery probably happened because of its flexibility and economy when compared to other projects that are much more expensive in terms of staff and bureaucracy. By

Slow Food

contrast, although the Presidia project has been modified over time, it has never been abandoned, and Slow Food continues to invest in its actions.

Presidia of food biodiversity

At the beginning, the Presidia project was conceived as a "natural" evolution of the Ark of Taste and the "Prize for Biodiversity." Shortly after its inauguration, this new project and its purpose were described in *Il Dizionario di Slow Food*: "After the research and cataloging of productions at risk of extinction, we could have left the 450 products selected in a drawer, forgotten, but instead we decided to do something: to intervene directly to save them. This is the sense of the Slow Food Presidia" (Ruffa and Monchiero 2002: 130). It is a labeling project intended to defend and valorize quality products—also referred to as Presidia—considered "in danger" from both a social and environmental point of view as well as that of economics. Here, too, we find a salvific and military language: the word *presidio* in Italian refers to a military garrison with a contingent of troops that is stationed in a place for control or defense, and by extension it can also mean protection and in the sense of public health, safeguards. The same dictionary defines a Presidium (a single Presidia product) as being a number of things at the same time: "a rare and excellent product; a project of protection; a group of farmers, livestock producers, and fishermen; a record of specifications and rules of production" (2002: 130).

When Slow Food staff members select a presidium product, they are attentive to local varieties, but they are also concerned with the area of production and the ecosystem. The director of the Italian Presidia office told me: "Environmental goals are part of each presidium. Each [Slow Food] product specification asks producers to eliminate or reduce chemical treatment, ensure animal well-being, safeguard local races and native varieties whenever possible, and privilege the use of renewable energies." Indeed, during the first few years, the project's stance placed the accent firmly on the environmental dimension. The environment may be composed of vineyards, pastures, and cultivated fields, but the human production activity remains the focus.

Alongside the environmental objectives, Slow Food staff members are also intent on emphasizing the Presidia project's "cultural" goals, "strengthening producers' cultural identity, and promoting production areas" (Battaglino et al. 2012: 22). Although Presidia label does not legally protect the products or their individual names, the collective dimension, the valorization of knowledge, and the transmission of that knowledge are elements common to both the Presidia and the PDO European label.[2]

"The Ark was about products, the Presidia are about producers," affirmed Piero, the president of the *Fondazione per la Biodiversità*. In the last few years this aspect has become more obvious, and the association's guidelines, "How to create a Presidium, establish relationships with the producers, and organize project activities" (2014), state that a Presidium can serve to protect not only "a rural countryside or ecosystem in danger of disappearing" and a product but also "a technique or traditional practice in danger of disappearing (fishing, raising livestock, processing, crop varieties)." More recently, one of the last editions of the Presidia brochure clearly integrates the evolutions of the Slow Food philosophy.

> Slow Food Presidia . . . save the good products, meaning high quality products, rooted in the culture of the region; clean products, which are obtained with sustainable techniques and with respect for the land and the region; fair products, achieved under conditions respecting individuals, their rights, and their culture, and guaranteeing fair remuneration. (*Presidia* brochure, 2017)

Products carrying the Presidia label are often endangered because they are no longer profitable. Many of these products have lost any market relevance because of marginal production; their producers need guarantees of economic viability in order to continue their activity, which was the case for the *Lenticchia di Santo Stefano di Sessanio* in the province of L'Aquila (which grows in the Abruzzo Apennines at an altitude of 1,000 m). "The Presidia project remains vital for many producers. Indeed, Presidia have been a means of setting in motion an extremely important mechanism," declared Gabriella, the head of the Italian Presidia office. Sometimes there are simply not enough producers or there are few who use techniques that are considered "traditional," which according to Slow Food staff and the producers who practice them are precisely why they need to be supported and valued. This was the reason that the Presidia label was considered appropriate for the *Culatello di Zibello*, a sausage made from a part considered valuable of the pig's leg. The Presidia project is a way of promoting the products selected and, in many cases, helping producers improve or enhance certain production methods. But the impact of the project is not simply the way it affects production and producers. From an analytical point of view, there are other interests involved as well.

Places and values of "typicity"

Much like we think of "typical" products, Slow Food describes the "typicity" of a project or object by its specific relationships to space and time. In order to become Presidia, food products must possess a "history" of specific production practices and of the knowledge linked to these practices, this repetition and reproduction over time thus guarantees a product's typicity (Siniscalchi 2010a; Papa 2002). Even though Presidia are seen as "traditional" products with a past, they are like many *produits de terroir*, only partially constructed by projecting them from their past into the present. They are conceived as projects for the future; they are considered to be social connectors and instruments of economic development. At the same time, since typicity is also defined through its link with a specific space, products must be linked to a geographical and cultural area or region (the French word *terroir* synthesizes these links) as well as to a social group of producers.

Slow Food

The literature on "typical" production is abundant and these questions are treated from very different perspectives: from the studies of material culture interested in techniques, knowledge, and their transmission to the research on the construction of typicity. In these studies the local dimension is considered a value in itself that different social actors construct, show, defend, and finally sell. The limiting aspect of this literature—particularly the French literature on *produits de terroir*—was the consensus that typical products and regional labels should be created, although potential conflicts were scarcely addressed (see among others, Bérard and Marchenay 1995). By contrast, typical products are controversial fields, as well as Presidia are.

Other studies take a related, although revisited, approach to the analyses of Mintz (1986), Appadurai (1986) and Kopytoff (1986), who deconstructed the notion of commodity and proposed new ways of interpreting the processes of "commodification." This involved viewing the product transformation process of goods of exchange from a perspective in which the objects have a "social life," and then attempting to reconstruct the social biography of objects and products, their trajectories, and the modes of fixing their value (Terrio 2000; Paxson 2013; Weiss 2016). Studies that now apply this perspective to "typical" products are interested in the different scales of circulation and the changes in meaning attributed to the product, from the moment of production to distribution and consumption, while paying attention to power relations and how global economic processes interact with local dynamics (see Wilk 2006b or more recently Tsing 2015; Besky 2014). Other researches further developed the anthropological approaches to the political economy by looking at values, practices, and products in terms of their circulation and political dynamics (Meneley 2004, 2007). They question the relationship between the local and the global through product trajectory or tourist performance (Abram and Waldren 1997) that allows "local" products to enter economic circuits far wider than the geographical area of production and contributes to the commodification of places (Ulin 1996; Siniscalchi 2000; Papa 2002).[3]

The production of food products by artisans or small agricultural farms using "traditional" techniques and their inclusion in a narrow list selected by Slow Food are elements that make Presidia unique and contribute to their valorization. Therefore, Presidia are located in a regime of singularity. They are defined by a "constellation" of qualities and frequently involve the production of limited quantities as in the *économie des singularités* (economy of singularities) proposed by Karpik (2007), which points to productions like premium wine series or specialty and gourmet foods rather than goods produced on an industrial scale. According to Karpik, the standard evaluation criteria and analytical grids cannot be applied to these products. Their price, higher than that of similar but unlabeled products, contributes to identify them as being different, with superior value that refers to more than simple economic value.

The different types of value embodied in a product and the qualities that contribute to them do not translate directly in a price, and the price is not the translation of an ensemble of valuable qualities (see Graeber 2001; Luetchford and Pratt 2014; Harper and Siniscalchi 2019). Nevertheless, price is actually a crucial issue in typical products as well as in Presidia projects. A higher price implies that quality has a cost; it does singularize products. But the price of food products also has a political dimension. It must be fair in the sense that it must be high enough for the producer to make a living from their production.

At the same time, while the project promotes economic goals for producers, the prices of some Presidia make them inaccessible to a certain segment of the population. This is one of the more sensitive points. West and Domingos (2012) analyze the process of obtaining the Presidia label for Portuguese *Serpa Velho* cheese, comparing the rhetoric used by the association and the effects produced locally by the establishment of the Presidium. Changes induced in the product by Slow Food transform the cheese production process to meet consumers' interests. Today the *Serpa Velho* is more expensive and inaccessible to local people. This type of criticism, pointing to the lack of knowledge of local history and dynamics by Slow Food leaders, is also present in other analyses (among others, Lotti 2010). The high price of some Presidia products is one aspect of the project that makes Slow Food susceptible to the criticism of elitism because of its apparent incoherence with certain elements of the movement's philosophy proclaiming the right of access to good, clean, and fair food for everyone. This principle can appear to be at odds with the other principle that defends the need for producers to make a living from their work and production. In my opinion, this paradox reveals one of Slow Food's internal contradictions and primarily arises from certain positions that staff leaders took with regard to the market, as we will see in the next chapters.

A controversial field

In recent years, several articles have been published on the subject of Presidia cases in various countries (see among others Friedmann and McNair 2008; Leitch 2003; Lotti 2010). A number of these articles highlight the limitations of the project and the degree to which Slow Food is sometimes out of touch with local realities. They criticize the inconsistencies of Slow Food without necessarily taking account of what is really happening between producers and the people in charge of Slow Food projects in a comparative way. Mattioli (2013) even defines the Presidia system as a franchise system. One problem with this literature is that even when the historical and analytical groundwork is extremely deep, as in the case of Leitch or West and Domingos, Slow Food is seen as an actor with a definitive set of politics and goals instead of an association that has a complicated history, internal contradictions, and is composed largely on volunteers and people whose knowledge is based on the projects they have developed. Managing an action like the Presidia project at the local level requires time and availability difficult to keep for volunteers but also for employees based in Italy.

In a similar approach, the implementation of Slow Food projects is analyzed in the light of the gap between what Slow Food claims in its own publications to be or do and what the authors observe on the ground. Some of these authors have been involved as consultants in Presidium projects and the impression one gets from reading their texts is that the criticism is also related in part to the specific interactions they have had, in their

Slow Food

role as experts, with the association and its representatives. Surprisingly the publications produced by the association, and particularly those of Petrini, are treated as scientific publications and criticized as such.

Often these studies miss the internal complexity and heterogeneity of the association which principals and actions are applied differently in the different places where Slow Food is present. Paxson's (2013) work clearly underlines this process. She questions the transformation of Slow Food's European raw milk projects, criticizing the way they have been appropriated and translated for the United States context and pointing to the problem of projects conceived in Italy being translated for implementation in other countries.

Certainly Slow Food does not have the same level of control or proximity with all the projects it launches. And the level of knowledge is not equally shared between the headquarters and the territories where the projects must be managed. This does not mean that conflicts are absent. They are present but in my view they do not indicate the failure of the project. On the contrary, they seem to characterize the lives of many Presidia.

Two examples of Sardinian producers help explain the centripetal and centrifugal tensions characterizing some of the Presidia projects. In one case, the *Zafferano di San Gavino Monreale*, the presidium appears to act like a glue that binds together the producers despite the dissent expressed over their differences in vision. In the second case, *Sa Pompia*, divergences among the producers seem far more important and produce a highly individualized context, despite the fact that they appear united when viewed from the outside. Internal tensions and distance make it difficult for Slow Food staff to intervene in terms of regulation.

The Zafferano, an extra income or a political tool?

The production of Sardinian saffron is centered in the province of Medio Campidano, north of Cagliari, the island's capital. This region is home to both a Presidium, the *Zafferano di San Gavino Monreale*, and a PDO, the *Zafferano di Sardegna*, but the two labels are defined differently, primarily in terms of geography. In the eyes of the Presidio producers, the more geographically limited Zafferano di San Gavino Monreale Presidium was established primarily as a platform for obtaining the PDO. Presidia provide a label for the local actors—elected officials, producers, Slow Food members—signifying the existence of an identifiable geographical and cultural space. Thus, Slow Food becomes an actor in the process of redefining and imagining spaces and places.

San Gavino is at the center of the production area, but when San Gavino's mayor initiated the effort to obtain PDO certification, the towns of Turri and Villanovafranca were added in order to present an area large enough to justify the request. Mario, a saffron producer, thought that the real reasons were primarily political, but regardless of the local politics, the result was a PDO that designates the areas of production surrounding

Gastronomic Biodiversity

these three cities, even though the name, Zafferano di Sardegna, gives the impression of a PDO that would include all of Sardinia.

Over the course of time, the number of producers involved in the Presidium or the PDO has varied, but only a relatively small number adhered to one or both of the labels at the time of my fieldwork. "There were twenty-four of us who were interested in a PDO, then most of them left, and now there are only three of us [from the San Gavino Presidium] in the consortium [of the PDO], and five overall," Mario said to me while showing me his saffron seedlings. A number of producers still conformed to the requirements of the "specification of production" (*disciplinare*) of the PDO even if they did not participate in the consortium, and it is true that all the producers benefited indirectly from the reputation of the labels. The actual effectiveness of the label in terms of sales depends largely on where it is marketed: "If you go to the United States, nobody is familiar with the saffron PDO. But if you say, 'Slow Food,' everyone recognizes it."

Outside of their inner circle of the three Presidium producers, where Presidium issues intermingled with those of the PDO, the situation was distinctly more complicated. Tensions there seemed to be linked to the quantities that each producer was capable of producing. The terrains were small, the production seasons are short, and the work is almost exclusively manual. Slow Food describes the process:

> The crocus flowers are picked by hand in the first hours of the day, when they are still closed or just barely open, then laid gently in baskets. Great care is taken not to crush them. Then comes the meticulous and delicate work of removing the stigmas, which requires skill, time and patience. The petals are opened by hand and the stigmas are removed, moistened with lightly oiled fingers and laid out to dry. They can be set out in the sun or arranged in front of a fire, but it is important that the temperature never exceeds 45°C so that the stigmas can dry slowly. Every hectare planted with the flowers produces an average of 9 to 10 kilos of dried saffron.[4]

"Everything is done manually, the work on the land, the harvest, dissecting the flowers. We're lucky that the price is as high as it is, and that a small quantity of saffron carries a lot of flavor," explained Simona, another producer. In fact, saffron production only represents supplemental income for the majority of producers. Marco was a building manager; Franco taught in a school; Simona worked in a hospital. But some of them hoped to expand production, and in order to do that, they wanted to keep the price a little lower. As justification for lowering the price of saffron, Mario said, "If a person produces very small quantities, he can try to get the highest price, but if I produce a kilogram, there's a risk of never being able to sell it all." For some the price was justified by the work demanded by the harvest and their preparation methods: "We eliminate the white part, our saffron is 100% pure." Others pointed to the principle of accessibility to good food for everyone: "Simona's prices are always higher than mine. But we also need to sell in Sardinia, and everyone should be able to use it, it should be accessible

Slow Food

to everyone." These thoughts are reminiscent of those of West and Domingos (2012) in the Portuguese Presidium cheese case they analyzed, where the rules developed by Slow Food seemed to have made the cheese inaccessible to locals.

Although the economic strategies of producers varied and in spite of these internal tensions, particularly over price, the producers of the Presidium of the Zafferano were able to collaborate and managed to maintain a sense of solidarity at the Slow Food fairs, which operate on a principle of cooperation and shared sales revenue: one of the three producers would go to the show and sell the products of all three, and the expenses and earnings were then divided between the three of them. In that case the internal disagreements over sales were resolved through a form of mediation, but in other cases the producers did not cooperate, and the project looked more like forced cohabitation.

Sa Pompia, cohabitation and competition

> The pompia tree looks like an orange tree, but with strange fruit: as large as or larger than a grapefruit, bright yellow in color and with a thick, ribbed, wrinkled skin. Pompia trees grow wild in the scrub and in citrus groves only in Sardinia, in the Baronia area, which surrounds the town of Siniscola. The citrus has been grown here for at least two centuries, and is an essential ingredient in some traditional sweets, like *sa pompìa intrea*, for which the pith is candied in honey. The rind is also used to flavor spirits.[5]

This unusual, large lemon-like fruit called pompia grows in the area around Siniscola, in Sardinia's northeastern province of Nuoro. Five women producers who all work in the food industry (bakery, patisserie, and restaurant) were involved in the Presidium project supporting this fruit. *Sa Pompia*—as they call it in Sardinia—production is very limited and localized, and these producers market it in sweet preparations sold in their store or offered on the menu of their restaurant. But their businesses are not based specifically on the pompia fruit: *Sa Pompia* acts more as a complementary product which helps attract customers to their primary economic activities. In this case the Slow Food label stepped in to fill an empty space: There was no existing PDO of the pompia, and there were no aspirations (at the time) for the production area to become a PDO.

As a product that is limited and localized in terms of both production and recognition, the pompia seemed to correspond perfectly to the goals of the Presidia project: to instigate actions to save and promote the recognition of products that represent local specificity, "artisanal" products, that can be elevated economically to a level that makes them sustainable over time. Sonia, one producer, said to me:

> We banded together to become a Presidium, because we didn't want others to make it [*la pompia*]. . . . At the beginning there were other [producers], then they left and now they would like to come back. Well, no! Sorry, but we've had the expenses

Gastronomic Biodiversity

[for establishing the Presidium]! We don't want to have too many people, we don't want more people in the Presidium. First of all, you can't make a living like that.

Slow Food envisions the presidium as a means of revitalizing particular local productions, enabling them to achieve economic viability by collectively organizing the producers, but the producers can also appropriate this tool in a more selfish way, creating a sort of "privatized" patent that acts as a mechanism of exclusion rather than inclusion.

The space of typicality represented by the areas of production in this case is a space of tension or conflict that reveals the social dynamics and divergent logics working within it. Although the producers of *Sa Pompia* fixed a common price, there were still forms of competition among them: "[One producer] went to the fair alone and it was a disaster, she only sold her own product. There was a fixed price [for everyone] but everyone lowered their price in secret."

When the Presidium was first created there was an attempt to jointly produce the pompia, but it failed in the face of divergent perspectives: "You don't do it as well as I do." "Mine is better." The standards established with representatives from Slow Food are not always fully respected, "Certain producers use more water and sugar and less honey, to save money," said one producer; "There are some that freeze the fruit and then prepare it later, but that's not right," accused another. Sometimes the liberties assumed by producers concerned the packaging, "It should be put in glass containers, but [they] put it plastic baskets that Slow Food has not agreed to." Other cases stretched the agreement with Slow Food with respect to the attachment of the Presidium label. In this localized context, the Presidium project seemed at times to be an unnecessary accessory that did more to incite conflict than produce agreement. But the interest for these producers lay on a different level, as Marta explained to me:

> I can still sell the product [even without the Presidium label] but Slow Food helps me get outside [of the Siniscola area], to make connections, to get your product out there. . . . You know the same people, so you can meet others. . . . To have references, to be Slow Food is an advantage, because that says there is a difference in the product; Slow Food lets me promote myself and my product.

There are also economic advantages in being a member of the producers' association, as Paola reminded:

> We've been paying for the label [Slow Food Presidium] since 2009. We divide the total into five equal parts that don't depend on how much you produce; you can produce as much as you want with the logo . . . otherwise everyone would have declared less in order to pay less; we are all at the same level. [6]

At first glance, the Presidium seems to be a production space regulated by Slow Food only in appearance, characterized in reality by strong internal deregulation. But the Presidium and its standards do not exclude a certain degree of self-regulation that can

Slow Food

stem from mutual criticism and distrust and the reciprocal control that the producers exercise indirectly on each other's production methods, quantities, and packaging. In the challenging tone of one of the producers, "Ask the same question to the others; I would love to hear what they say! . . . By insisting on certain specifications for *Sa Pompia*, you have to stick to the ancient recipe."

The Presidium also enables relationships to be created at another level. Paola, another *pompia* producer commented:

> In the fairs and exhibitions there are exchanges, you make connections . . . with other Presidia producers [in Sardinia], you become a family. We had exchanges at the Salone [del Gusto]; everyone brings their products, and we exchange. Bucciu [Fiore Sardo cheese producer] brings me his cheese and also ham. He doesn't love sweet stuff, but then he tells me, "Your Pompia is delicious," and that is very flattering; you are proud. It gives you a chance to show off your products, even to other producers who come from Sardinia.

Although associating with Slow Food in the case of pompia didn't relieve all the internal conflicts, and sometimes even seemed to instigate them, being a Presidia producer could take on a positive aspect that is more than simple economics: it provided a sense of membership in a large family, a family of Sardinian Presidia producers, the producers that "are Slow Food." But this positive element can, in turn, harbor its own particular opportunities for discord, much like those found in any family.

Internal dynamics and tensions

At the beginning of my fieldwork, there were around 200 Presidia in Italy and 160 elsewhere. The number of Presidia has remained relatively constant over the long term, particularly in Italy, with a small increase in recent years. Today, there are more than 500 Presidia in the world (more than half of which are in Italy). As the leaders of the movement declare at each public occasion, these numbers seem destined to grow. Once again, numbers are always a central communication tool in Slow Food documents and official speeches. The world of the Presidia is marked by alliances, power dynamics, and different interests, often hidden behind seemingly consensual relationships. When analyzing these dynamics, it is crucial to pay particular attention to the evolution of their processes over time. Beyond the numbers, new Presidia have been designated each year, while others have been declassified for various reasons.

Sometimes, the production levels remain too marginal in spite of Slow Food's intervention, and the product never achieves financial viability. In some cases the product did not manage to move beyond the scale of family production. In still other cases, conflicts between producers who have not managed to work together have drained the Presidium of its "social" relevance, an aspect considered pivotal from the point of view of those who work on Presidia projects. Conflicts can erupt between Slow Food and producers when the element of trust is lacking in their relationships or when the price that producers set becomes too high from Slow Food's point of view. The issue of the price set for a Presidium product does not directly affect Slow Food, but it may influence the decision to close a Presidium. An excessively low price can be a sign of dysfunction in the food chain, but the excessively high price of a product can justify its removal from the Presidia project, because it indicates that the product no longer needs support, such as the *Lardo di Colonnata* (a spiced pork fat) and the *Fagiolo Zolfino* (a navy bean). These products have become well known, production has greatly increased, and Slow Food's intervention is no longer considered necessary.

Tensions also emerge when other actors with diverging interests try to appropriate a project by draining it of its political meaning, for example, concentrating only on its economic advantages. In these cases products might lose a previously granted right to use the Presidia label. Sometimes tensions are about the relationship between money and labeling. The use of the Presidia logo is subject to payment of an annual fee, fixed on the basis of a complicated calculation that takes account of several variables, including the volume of production. During my fieldwork between 2009 and 2014, those payments ranged from 50 to 1,000 euros per year for most producers. Slow Food officers saw these payments as a compensation for the benefit of being associated with the movement's name and notoriety and as a contribution to costs and time invested by the association in helping launch the presidium. Some producers disagreed over the amounts to be paid and believed that Slow Food finally had become a profit-seeking, capitalist machine. From the point of view of those who work in Presidia offices, the royalties were more symbolic and did not begin to cover the association's costs. Indeed, the Presidia office in Bra was one of those that did not generate enough income to support itself and must be financed through other association projects.

In some cases, friction appears simply because Slow Food is too far removed from the actual needs of local producers or fails to understand the specific local dynamics. Therefore, Slow Food Presidia must be understood as the result of unstable political and social agreements, they have an origin, and they can also have an end. They should be considered as a combination of political, economic, and normative characteristics. Indeed, Slow Food's involvement in environmental activism expressed through Presidia is also an engagement with a new kind of economic development. Sometimes, Presidia are seen as an instrument for encouraging certain producers to legalize activities that might be "undeclared or hidden" because the productions involve small quantities. In this respect, Presidia that are developed in European countries often do not have the same status as those created in the Global South. As the president of the Foundation for Biodiversity, Piero, told me:

> There is a shift of meaning between the South and the North. In the Southern world, where there are interesting products, our goal is to activate Presidia, to create commercial outlets, revive producers' confidence, show them the importance of their work, reactivate local networks. . . . In the Northern world the symbolic and

Slow Food

cultural value prevails: Presidia allow us to send strong signals on the theme of domestic biodiversity, in order to guarantee gastronomic excellence vis-à-vis an agriculture that is becoming increasingly quantitative.

Slow Food's activities can, above all, be viewed as investments in the promotion of these products, increasing their visibility through brochures, fairs, and various taste laboratories and training programs offered to members. The Presidia project represents one of the most direct and concrete ways of creating relationships between Slow Food activists—who are in large part consumers and food connoisseurs—and these producers. And even despite the small number of producers involved in some of these presidium projects, the cases observed on the ground, in Italy and France, show the political and economic impact of many of them, although not always in the way staff members had anticipated. Moreover, in the South, these projects allow Slow Food to highlight its interest in small farmers and peasants, to help consolidate Slow Food's image and political legitimacy (at the local and international level), and equally important, to publicize the movement more widely in terms of its ideas and membership. They are political, flexible, and strategic even if they are not always in step with all local contexts. At the same time, Presidia enable Slow Food to exist around the world, and to maintain a presence in regions and countries where the movement is weaker (such as China and countries in the Global South). And the producers become (indirect) participants in this process.

Notes

1. The book was then translated into English with the title *Slow Food Nation: Why Our Food Should Be Good, Clean, and Fair.*

2. Hermitte (2001: 202) defines PDOs as a "paradoxical right"; rather than being totally private, it is an amalgam of intellectual, economic, and regional rights—the region, or local area, being viewed as a co-author—thus a private sector right, belonging to a group or private collective that acts "above all" as a means to transmit to its members the permission to exercise this right.

3. On the production of spaces and places, see Lefebvre (1991); on processes of "localization," see Appadurai (1998), Gupta & Ferguson (1997), Low and Lawrence-Zúñiga (2003).

4. https://www.fondazioneslowfood.com/en/slow-food-presidia/san-gavino-monreale-saffron/

5. https://www.fondazioneslowfood.com/en/slow-food-presidia/pompia/

6. Since 2009, the producers of Italian Presidia (followed by those in Switzerland and now in other countries) can use the specific "Presidio Slow Food" label.

Photo 8 Roberto, a *Fiore Sardo* cheese producer, Ovodda (Italy), 2018. ©Franco Zecchin.

CHAPTER 8
CHEESE REGULATIONS
POLITICAL BATTLES AND ECONOMIC INTERESTS INSIDE THE PRESIDIA PROJECT

In November of 2010, I met with Sandro on the ground floor of one of Slow Food's offices. Usually I would have found him in the Presidium office on the second floor where he worked with the other four staff members. But his functions had temporarily changed, and with the versatility that often characterizes the work inside the Slow Food offices, he was packing cardboard boxes containing cheese to be sent to Italian members who had requested them. For several weeks, the office had witnessed the arrival of unsold rounds of *Fiore Sardo* Sardinian sheep's row milk cheese, along with *Canestrato di Castel del Monte* from Abruzzi and a number of other cheeses labeled Slow Food Presidia, all of which were then stock-piled on the association's premises. That year, *Fiore Sardo* cheese producers (as well as other Presidia cheese producers) still had cheese wheels in their cellars that had been produced some months before and had not yet been sold. The production season began the following December, and producers needed to sell the unsold cheese to free up storage space on their farms and to avoid blocking the capital represented by the cheese. In such cases, wholesalers from other Italian regions often took advantage of the situation, offering extremely low prices (even 6 euros per kilo that year). Slow Food staff and leaders, in agreement with the producers, took an unusual initiative and launched a buying campaign called "*Resistenza casearia*" (Cheese Resistance) among the association's members. *Fiore* and other cheeses were proposed to members for 19 euros per kilo. The campaign was a great success, both from the point of view of the buyers, who were able to buy the cheese "directly" from the producers at a much lower price than that offered by delicatessens (where *Fiore* can reach as much as 40 euros per kg), and from the point of view of the producers, who were able to sell all their stock and to obtain a much higher price. Why had Slow Food officials agreed to take on the role of direct sales when they had always refused to do so in the past? To understand this temporary detour in the functions of the office usually devoted to labels and relationships with producers, in this chapter I will investigate the relationship between regulation, political battles, and economic interests through the Presidia project and actions in the field of cheese production.

Slow Food

Raw milk struggles

Presidia embody Slow Food's battles against the industrialization of food, and one of the most historically important and ongoing battles concerns the defense of raw milk cheeses. In 2001 Slow Food unveiled another manifesto, this time dedicated to milk and cheeses, the *Manifesto in difesa del formaggio a latte crudo* (Manifesto in defense of raw milk cheese). But why have raw milk cheeses occupied such an important place on the movement's political agenda for twenty years?

> Raw milk cheese is more than just an extraordinary delicacy, it is an authentic expression of one of the best gastronomic traditions. It is an art and a lifestyle. It is a culture, a heritage, a beloved countryside. And [it] is threatened with extinction! Threatened, because the values it embodies are the opposite of the sterilization and standardization of mass food production. . . . In addition, non-pasteurization preserves all the organoleptic qualities of the cheese. (*Manifesto in difesa del formaggio a latte crudo*)

Raw milk cheese has been important because it simultaneously combines the historic, landscape, and organoleptic values that the Slow Food movement seeks to defend, not only with valorizing actions but also through the political battles that it undertakes on different scales, using various tools. Large Slow Food events, such as Cheese (see Chapter 11), provide awareness and knowledge for the movement's members. After these events, the members and leaders carry the featured issues into other economic and political spaces: the regions of production, the European Commission, the Agriculture Ministry, the press, and media debates. Slow Food leaders and staff often attempt to reshape European standards—such as those that regulate food safety—or national standards in countries where, for example, the marketing of raw milk cheese is prohibited, as in this case:

> We call for the abolition of all discriminatory laws in the European Union, the World Trade Organization, the United States Food and Drug Administration, and numerous other government organisms worldwide, which arbitrarily limit the freedom of citizens / consumers to choose and consume these cheeses, and which attempt to undermine inexorably the sources of income of the artisans who produce them. (*Manifesto in difesa del formaggio a latte crudo*)

As the focus of this manifesto, raw milk cheeses became the standard of a new way of perceiving food production, one in which this production is the bearer of knowledge and values (social, historical, environmental) and the guardian of important differences typified by the diversity of raw milk cheeses. Slow Food views pasteurization and the use of ferments as synonymous with uniformity and the loss of "agro-food biodiversity" (Paxson 2013).

The field of political policies regulating production operates in a space that includes the dichotomies of diversity (or specificity) versus standardization, which includes the issue of raw milk versus pasteurization. The association has worked to position itself as a legitimate actor in this political context on the national and international levels. With that capacity, it seeks to influence official regulatory bodies such as the Italian Ministry of Agriculture which translates and applies European standards.

Slow Food leaders' objective is to modify the norms in certain countries that either forbid the marketing of raw milk cheeses or require producers to meet conditions of hygiene and food safety that radically constrain the practices and techniques forming the basis of these products and their specificity (Siniscalchi 2013a, 2013b; Siniscalchi and Zecchin 2018). The Presidia become an instrument in these regulatory battles, and Slow Food uses them to support legalizing production of non-pasteurized cheese in countries such as Canada and Ireland, where the standards are threatening raw milk products. The Irish Raw Milk Cheese Presidium was introduced as a tool of rebellion against the legal standards that threatened to eliminate these production methods and their "illegal" products. "The Presidium is made up of eight cheese-producing units working with a variety of styles and techniques but with the common goal of producing high quality cheese using non-pasteurized milk sourced from their own herds" (*Presidia*, Slow Food Foundation for Biodiversity, 2008). In the literature produced by Slow Food, the Irish project, more than others, is presented as a political project that aims to change a normative system:

> The Presidium is represented by a group of cheese dairies seen as ambassadors of Irish cheese production [that can] encourage all non-pasteurized cheese producers of Ireland by promoting consumption of these cheeses. . . . This project aims to raise awareness of the qualities of these cheeses among consumers, retailers and food policy experts. (*Presidia*, Slow Food Foundation for Biodiversity, 2008)

This symbolic battle recalls others in which Slow Food has played a different role: for example, the struggle to ease European rules such as HACCP (Hazard Analysis Control Critical Point)[1], accepted by Italian legislation on food safety, but which Slow Food considered unsuitable for small artisanal activities. Again, in 2012, the movement participated in the mobilization of support for the (failed) California proposition requiring labeling to identify products containing GMO (Genetically Modified Organism) ingredients (see Brundage 2016). These battles to change specific norms are also struggles to establish new normative systems and new legalities. I consider the affirmation of new legalities to be forms of political commitment and one of the most important aspects of Slow Food Presidia at a broader level.

Negotiation and normalization

Presidia are conceived as singular products of high quality and, in some respects, I see Presidia as playing the role of both a prototype and a paradigm. They are considered examples to follow not only for other actors in the same productive network, but more generally, for food producers and livestock farmers who share the desire to change the modes of production and the rules of food distribution. The prototype delimits that change by defining the margins of possible variation. Therefore, in the process of identifying Presidia products, Slow Food defines a range of micro-possibilities of variation characterizing "typical" products that are never reproduced identically. This process is different than that of Europe's labeling structure, the Protected Designation of Origin (PDO, see 1992 European regulation n. 2081). Although part of its intention is to protect the variety of Europe's regional products, the PDO's normalization process results in a sort of oxymoron—un-diversifying the local diversity—as seen in Cristina Papa's analysis of the case of Umbrian olive oil (2002). At the same time, Presidia projects are based upon (or often anticipate) very precise production protocols. They define techniques of production (such as copper boilers instead of polyvalent electronic machines for the preparation of *Fiore Sardo* cheese), breeds, species, areas (such as the space needed for capons in a farmyard), seasons, and places (such as high mountain pasture for cows whose milk is used to produce *Asiago stravecchio* cheese).

Variations aside, the uniqueness and authenticity of Presidia products are still determined by their adherence to the model, but the defining paradigm is always the result of negotiations involving different actors. These can be producers, Slow Food staff and leaders, researcher, members inside convivia or *condotte*, or local institutions supporting the project (such as, a regional or national park, a region, a municipality). Although the process of becoming a Presidium varies by country, the decision to start a Presidia project always involves a mixture of economic, political, and social interests. In many cases, the local leaders of the association are at the center of the process: they often have the first contacts with producers and notify the Slow Food staff of productions they believe are interesting and appropriate candidates for protection and valorization. In others cases the headquarters of the association play the most important role, identifying those "interesting" productions. Staff members in the Slow Food Foundation for biodiversity always visit the producers, taste the products (at the production site and in Slow Food offices), and then discuss their potential with producers (and local Slow Food leaders). During the process of selecting products to be considered as Presidia, the staff negotiates with producers over production techniques, quantities, place of production, ingredients, and taste itself. They acknowledge the need to appreciate tastes that are different from those with which they are familiar, thereby respecting the principle of a subjective palate and a subjective notion of *buono* (goodness), which they introduced as a principle of relativity in their definition of taste as it relates to the triad of "good, clean, and fair." In this phase of the selection process, tasting is not simply a unidirectional step: it is an interactive moment in the negotiations between the producers and the Slow Food representatives at the local and national, or international levels.

On one occasion during my fieldwork in the Slow Food headquarters, I was in the offices in charge of the Italian Presidia. The staff had just received a package of cookies from a region in southern Italy which was sent by the *fiduciario* of the local *condotta*. This *fiduciario* was suggesting the initiation of a Presidium for the production of these cookies and sent a sampling from three different producers. We began to taste them in turn. The comments of the employees and managers of the office, interspersed with the occasional grimace, insisted on the fact that they couldn't find any exceptional element in the taste of these cookies to justify the initiation of a Presidium. These simple results of the tasting seemed to close the door on any possibility of a label: the cookies seemed too dry, too sweet, and the texture too uneven. But in the middle of this chorus of clearly negative comments, one of the staff members continued to taste and began to list the modifications that he would have eventually asked the producers to undertake in order to improve their product, such as reducing sugar or processing the dough differently to make it less grainy and more uniform and pleasant for the palate.

The negotiations for the initiation of a Presidium are often invisible, situated in various places and on various occasions during the labeling process. The taste of a product might be too far from Slow Food's idea of goodness, and the staff may ask for changes in some aspects of the production process. In these cases, taste acts as criteria for including products in the Presidia project: Tasting is a way of selecting and guiding the transformation of products into Presidia and a way of reconfirming a Presidium's status. But it can also be a reason to exclude products and producers, or it might signal that the producers have strayed too far from Slow Food principles. The taste itself is the result of a process that incorporates recognition (a taste that is familiar and can be appreciated, or not), education (such as through taste laboratories, the master's program, and other Slow Food education initiatives), and adjustments to others' tastes—this relative aspect of taste that the movement increasingly advocates. Negotiations do not stop when the label is attributed but may continue over time. Local leaders (volunteers, often a governor, a regional or *condotta* committee member for the Italian Presidia) and staff members visit productions, solicit producers for certain events, and may later intervene on aspects of production.

Slow Food, an intermediate regulatory body

These processes allow us to consider Presidia not only as specific products and places of production but also as specific spaces of action and regulation of production. Slow Food leaders propose new normative models at public events, in manifestos like the one on raw milk, and with product specifications in a project like the Presidia. The standards that are developed or proposed by the movement are not only aimed at modifying certain aspects of legislation, but also at reversing the relationships of power (between industrial and artisan producers or between regional, national, or international institutions and producers) in the field of production and food regulation. Slow Food uses the products labeled Presidia to fix limits, define form, and confirm the content of the object singled out for reproduction and value. Moreover, through these production protocols, Slow Food acts (and presents itself) as an intermediate, regulatory body, operating between the State and the self-regulation of producers.

As some of the people working in the Presidia office remember—with a measure of humor—the early specifications, formulated at the beginning of the project, were often too narrow and failed to take into account the realities of production constraints. The *Cappone di Morozzo*, one of the first Presidia products, is a good example; the constraints that Slow Food officials specified in the first measure were too strict—the number of capons each farmer could have was excessively limited—and not at all compatible with the actual situation confronting the farmers raising capons. Ultimately, the rules had to be changed because no one could follow them.

Over time, the support and utilization of scientists and scientific knowledge has gradually become more important in these processes; however, their role is not directly linked to the actual selection of products. Their presence alongside Slow Food staff provides legitimacy to Slow Food's initiative and the knowledge provided by "scientists" helps officials evaluate the products, vegetable species, and animal races. Benefiting from this combination of support and experience, staff inside Slow Food have honed their knowledge of the world of production and have become legitimate mediators for many producers.

Product specifications are determined in consultation with producers, during visits to sites of production, and in meetings that precede the initiation of a Presidium. Therefore, the protocol is generally produced after long negotiations and several interventions. Producers must respect the set of rules in the determined protocol if they wish to remain in Slow Food's field of action and benefit from its initiatives of promotion. In most cases, the rules that are defined by Slow Food and the producers occupy "empty" spaces in the regulatory system: Presidia are often products that have no other labels or designations because their production and economic impacts are very small. Here, Slow Food seems to play the role of an institute of certification that distinguishes itself not only by its method (the development of the protocol with producers, the links established with partners on the ground who are charged with maintaining relationships with producers) but also by the principles that govern its version of labeling, and the emphasis placed on trust rather than monitoring systems. Slow Food staff and leaders refuse to assume the role of monitor (e.g., through surprise visits or by verifying details like an auditor; see Cavanaugh 2016) and insist that producers exercise this surveillance among themselves. The entire normative record and the relationships—those between Slow Food and the producers that adhere to a Presidium's specifications, and those between Slow Food and the consumers—are understood by staff leaders as an outcome of trust. Trust is also seen and exhibited by most of the producers as a value that allows the construction of these new normative systems.

The regulations elaborated by Slow Food may be considered as a kind of soft law. "Soft law is typically embodied within non-binding legal instruments such as recommendations or declarations, but also 'resolutions,' 'code of conduct,' and 'guidelines'" (Zerilli 2010: 9). As such, "soft law should . . . be explored as an object, an apparatus, in Foucauldian terminology *un dispositif*, namely a political technology which creates, enhances, maintains, perverts and modifies the exercise of power within a given social body" (2010: 11).

But this intermediary role is not neutral; it produces specific tensions. Conflict can materialize when Slow Food Presidia rules intervene in spaces already "occupied" by

European standards. For example, Italian products that have already obtained the PDO (Protected Designation of Origin) may seek to enter the Presidia project as a means of distinguishing themselves from a designation seen as too generic. In this situation, the Presidium often identifies a smaller area of production, or specific preparation and cultivation techniques, or even a particular species involved in a PDO product. For example, in addition to being within the vast territory of the PDO of Parmigiano Reggiano, the Modenese white cow became a Presidium (*Presidio della Vacca Bianca Modenese*) because its milk is used to produce mountain Parmigiano Reggiano cheese, which is considered to be superior in quality compared to the cow's milk used by most Parmigiano producers.

Slow Food norms are often stricter than PDO norms, and as a result, the Italian Ministry of Agricultural Policy in some cases perceived the Slow Food regulations as unconventional and symbolically opposed to the State's regulations. This opposition can have tangible consequences. The Ministry has tried to impose sanctions (later revoked in most cases) on some Presidia cheese producers who choose to use both labeling systems.[2] This happened with the *Bitto* cheese: producers lost their PDO certification when they started to name their cheese as *Bitto storico* (the name of the Presidio). Subsequently, they could not use the name "Bitto" (protected by the PDO) so they replaced it with the Italian word for rebel as a reminder of their struggle against the PDO consortium: *Storico ribelle* (see Corti 2011, 2016; Grasseni 2017).

In refusing to accept both labels on the product, the Ministry has contended that the juxtaposition of the two normative systems could implicitly reduce the value of the PDO label, since it implicitly states that it is a more selective label than the PDO alone. Therefore, the Italian Ministry has opposed organizations like Slow Food that act in much the same manner as the State, in the same fields, and moreover, applying stricter standards for regulation. The possibility that Slow Food could produce another form of regulation has been seen as something unacceptable that opposed and weakened State regulation.

The pragmatism of goat cheese producers

In other cases, such as the *Brousse du Rove* goat cheese in southeastern France, acquiring a Presidium label provided producers with the visibility and legitimacy in the market that enabled them to aspire to a PDO. Even in a country like France where labels certifying origin are quite pervasive, the *Brousse du Rove* had not been recognized or protected by a designation of origins because of the relatively small size of its production and economic relevance. The Slow Food Foundation website describes the case of the Brousse du Rove.

> [Brousse du Rove] is now a victim of its fame and in the last years shops have sold versions of Brousse prepared using milk from other goat breeds and sometimes even cow's milk. . . . The aim of the Presidium is to protect the market from

imitations . . . which are damaging the image of traditional Brousse du Rove. The Presidium would also like to attract new shepherds to the region. This is an important strategy that both defends the image of a local product with unique flavor and also indirectly ensures that the Rove goat and the associated traditional knowledge of pastoral agriculture are protected.[3]

The issue described here is one of defending the "true" Brousse, the original product made with raw Rove goat milk, from imitations produced with other goat breeds, or even cow's milk. This was clearly part of the motivation for producers to join a Slow Food project, but there were still others, as cited by the producers like Magalie:

It started with a goatherd friend who was contacted by Slow Food about being a Presidium product, and we said yes, because that can be a source of help, because communication is important in this history of PDO. A product that is way too unique, you know, it's bound to be unknown, that doesn't work, even if the product is local, it has to represent something, not just in the past, but today, also. So, it's good to have this kind of support.[4]

Over a period of ten years, a dozen producers of *Brousse du Rove* who were part of the Slow Food Presidium, banded together to undertake the process of obtaining a PDO. Magalie defended their candidacy, "The PDO is always on a very precise area, you need consistency in terms of climate, of vegetation, of the origin of the breed, that's the Rove, so it's here, so it's not logical for someone to make Brousse du Rove in Strasbourg." The specifications established for the designation also require that the goats must be pastured in the *garrigues* (rocky scrubland in southern France) around five or six hours per day, ensuring that they consume the vegetation that grows in the region and gives this cheese its unique flavor.

During the years it took to obtain the recognition of a PDO, the Presidium label made it possible to access other spaces and levels of visibility, and in particular the trade shows and fairs organized by Slow Food. "That gives us the opportunity to promote the Brousse, since we are still in the process of the PDO, communication is necessary," reminded Magalie. Every other year Magalie and Luc have attended the Salone del Gusto in Turin or Cheese—the event that Slow Food organizes around milk products—in Bra, where Luc can sport his "Provencal" look as an exhibitor, and together they can follow and participate in the market and debates about food production and food regulation. In 2017, the Brousse du Rove became the forty-sixth and smallest PDO in France.

They sell their cheese on the farm and at farmers' markets, and for several years now, through the AMAP [*Association pour le Maintien de l'Agriculture Paysanne*] association of producers and consumers in France. But their membership in Slow Food is not in evidence when they sell their products through the AMAP. In fact, their association with Slow Food doesn't really affect sales in this particular context. Their customers there are local, already familiar with the Brousse cheese, and appreciate it without relying on reassurances from a label of quality. Still, for these producers, the link with Slow Food remains both political and pragmatic. Even if Slow Food doesn't directly affect their local sales, they see its promotion of the principles of "good, clean, and fair" on an international scale as complementary to the defense of local and/or organic agriculture, which other structures such as the AMAPs implement in their region. Slow Food is also perceived by producers as a source of ideas, a tool to forge connections with other producers as well as consumers, and an internationally recognized political actor capable of influencing political decisions on food production. It is this capacity for action in political arenas and vis-à-vis supra-local lobbies that particularly interests many producers.

From pasture to policy

The case of the Sardinian *Fiore Sardo* seems to me exemplary of the Slow Food intervention inside a PDO area. The Fiore Sardo is an artisanal sheep's milk cheese coming from the Barbagia region, in the center of the island, around the small town of Gavoi. Stefano, one of its producers, describes it:

> The Fiore Sardo is made by people who are very obstinate and stubborn, and particularly because they are so stubborn, don't associate with each other. Outside the Barbagia producers banded together, and formed cooperatives, but they lost their traditional production methods, which today leaves only the large dairies to make cheese, and these cheeses are all the same. But in the Barbagia region, the Fiore Sardo cheese continues to exist because producers are stubborn, arrogant, they didn't want to abandon their know-how.

When I met with Stefano he was living in Gavoi (around 3,000 inhabitants).[5] At the time, he had a herd of 300 sheep and had been producing Fiore Sardo cheese for fifteen years. When he spoke about shepherds like himself, he used the stereotypes and narratives often used to speak about Sardinian shepherds—individualist and stubborn. They have maintained their skills, but they could be seen as "failures" from an economic point of view.

The truth is that Stefano and his confreres, whose activities include both raising livestock and producing cheese, are very familiar with market logics. They are involved in a fight against and within these logics, defending or proposing alternative models of production and distribution of cheese. Joining forces allowed them to fashion their coordinated efforts into a political and economic tool. Stefano was already a member of the governing board of the PDO consortium when I started the fieldwork in 2011 to explore the point of view of Sardinian producers linked to Slow Food through the Presidia project. The PDO consortium is the organism in charge of defending the denomination of origin of Fiore Sardo. It is one of three PDO *pecorini* (sheep milk cheese).[6] The territory of the Fiore Sardo PDO extends all across Sardinia and at the time of my research grouped together approximately twenty shepherd-producers and another ten industrial producers making cheese with milk purchased from various farmers of

Slow Food

"Sardinian" sheep. The farmers who produce Fiore Sardo solely from their own milk production market it under their own name. Obviously, there is a substantial difference in the quantities produced by these shepherds compared to that of the industrial producers. Each of the shepherds produce between 150 and 3,000 wheels of cheese per year each weighing between 3 and 4.5 kg (totaling from 500 kg to 9 tons), depending on the size of their herd.[7]

Initially as part of—and since 2012, outside of—the PDO consortium, Stefano and other shepherds like him have fought a legal and economic battle against the industrial production of Fiore Sardo.[8] Some industrial producers supply the local market with a cheaper cheese that does not respect the designation and has been suspected—by the shepherds, some technical experts and a number of industrials not producing the Fiore Sardo—of being produced with pasteurized milk. The shepherd-producers and some technicians have asserted that the difference in bacterial loads resulting from combining milk from different herds (as in the case of industrial productions) creates reactions in the cheese production process that necessitate controlling the bacterial load through pasteurization.

The Fiore Sardo shepherd-producers have also fought with cheese retailers and traders who don't promote their products and constantly attempt to negotiate ever lower prices. This battle is seen as a struggle against institutions that have elaborated standards and norms that do not protect small producers, do not give them visibility (sometime even reducing it), and do not leave a place for them in a competitive market. As Antonio, another shepherd, explained:

> In 1987, we were not yet a PDO. The producers came together to draw up the Protected Designation of Origin. But then the drafting of the text was delegated to institutions that had other purposes in mind. The result is that today the industrial producers make Fiore Sardo, and the consumer eats industrial cheese without any difference being recognized at the legislative level. That cheese is protected as if it was ours. We make it with raw milk because it is the milk of a single herd. But industrial producers, who buy big quantities of milk from different farms, must pasteurize it—otherwise everything goes bust. . . . The PDO policy is all in their favor.

The text of the PDO standards is the result of political negotiations: experts, health institutions, and agrarian scholars contributed to its codification. In this sense it has "standardized" production and quality of the cheese by rendering invisible the ability to produce certain characteristics that the shepherd-producers consider important to the quality of their production (e.g., the smoking process). The PDO's specifications treat these characteristics as optional, resulting in a degree of imprecision in the certification of origin that is the primary focus of these smaller producers. For them, the issue lies in the definition of a "true" Fiore Sardo, and the possibility to differentiate their cheese from that of the industrial producers, which the Slow Food Presidium label affords them.

Stefano is also a member of Slow Food and participates with other producers in the Slow Food Presidia project; therefore his cheese is not only labeled as Fiore Sardo PDO but also as a Slow Food Presidium. What drives shepherds to participate in both of these projects? And what is their role within them? In this context, the Presidium designation appears to be an instrument that challenges the hegemony by acting against the power of the industrialists who, as the small producers point out, "set the price of milk" and appropriated a cheese that many producers claim they had no right to produce, and against the regional and national political institutions that have elaborated and defended norms that don't protect the artisan producers. Once again, Slow Food acts as a regulatory body, providing an additional set of specifications that supplement the requirements of the State regulation. The Presidia project provides a way for these farmers to distinguish themselves among PDO productions without renouncing their PDO status. Even if that status does not protect them from their internal "enemy," the industrial cheese producers, the PDO designation remains an essential legal instrument that limits the production of this cheese to their region.

The Presidia producers are not situated outside the market or market logics: they are seeking to modify these logics from inside and improve the status of their Sardinian product. They see the Presidia project as one of the possible ways to accomplish this. Slow Food rhetoric complements their strategies: the movement's political positioning (against the bureaucracy or certain imposed standards) is determined with input from producers and thus consistent with the shepherds' representation of adverse regulations. This position provides the shepherds with support in their conflictual relationship with those regulations.

Labeling economies

Through the Presidia project, Slow Food also defends and promotes "non-standard" taste, playing the role of the promoter of a new kind of goodness. The taste of *Fiore Sardo* cheese is considered far stronger, and more piquant than the more standardized taste to which the average consumer is accustomed. Taste can marginalize or exclude a product from some markets and limit its economic viability. Slow Food's intervention is aimed at avoiding that and enhancing consumers' appreciation of diverse flavors. Taste participates in the diffusion of the movement's philosophy, but it is also used in Slow Food's actions and politics to counteract market logic and trends, as we will see in the next chapter.

The *Resistenza casearia* (Cheese Resistance) campaign mentioned at the beginning of the chapter was a way for Slow Food leaders to act economically on behalf of producers who were having trouble selling their product; it was also a way to educate members in the movement and bring them closer to the world of production. For members, it was a way to be involved in one of the movement's actions and buy a quality product at a below-market price. At the same time, the direct sales operation gave producers an opportunity to sell their product at prices that were three times higher than those

Slow Food

offered by retailers and within a time frame that protected their perishable stock of cheese. Although it eliminated the traditional intermediaries this direct sales approach did not appear to create any economic profit for Slow Food; no percentage was taken on the sales price other than that representing packaging and shipping. Slow Food leaders do not ordinarily conduct direct sales of Presidia and refuse to become trailers.

In reality, the profit for Slow Food was in political currency; these raw milk cheeses were tools in the political battles of the movement for "good, clean, and fair" food. The campaign and the accompanying response by a supportive media helped reinforce the political role of Slow Food in the field of food production and regulation as well as its image as a supporter of small producers. Some of these producers see Slow Food's engagement on their behalf as being too focused on political issues, inconsistent and limited to specific campaigns, and weak in terms of economics. But in the eyes of the association's leaders, this is the right way to draw consumers closer to the producers, while at the same time, engaging those producers in the association (as members) and transforming Slow Food's image from a consumer association to a movement acting politically on a global scale in defense of small producers.

Two visions confront each other inside the Presidia system: the producers' perspective centered on Slow Food making a stronger and more concrete commitment in the market, and the perspective of Slow Food itself, which is above all political. From my point of view, once again, it is not possible to separate the politics from the economics: market logics and political aims are always present in the actions of Presidia producers and in the actions and rhetoric of Slow Food. Presidia reflect the contradiction between a utopian market and a real market, or between morality and profit.

Food and food products in general are political objects, objects of negotiation, conflicts, and debates. Lien (2004: 2) emphasizes that "the politics of food takes place both inside and outside the arenas normally designated as political, . . . [and] it also implies drawing attention to how food itself has become a political object." Although the modes of expressing tensions and rhetoric are different from other fields in which food is more explicitly at the heart of conflicts (e.g., the debates over genetically modified maize, see Fitting 2011; Müller 2008), Presidia are the result of more or less explicit power struggles). They are economic objects with a strong economic and political dimension. This dual character of Presidia as an economic market activity and a model of political action allows Slow Food to expand its place in the politics of food and to define political, prescriptive, and economic spaces, where logic and forces, even if sometimes opposing, continuously produce new social configurations (Tsing 2005).[9]

Notes

1. "HACCP has become synonymous with food safety. It is a worldwide-recognized systematic and preventive approach that addresses biological, chemical and physical hazards through anticipation and prevention, rather than through end-product inspection and testing," https://www.fao.org/3/w8088e/w8088e05.htm.

2. The "Presidio Slow Food" label enables buyers to identify the Presidia in the marketplace and makes a visible reference to their association with Slow Food, thus contributing to the appearance of a common space. However, it is not the same logo as the movement's snail emblem, the use of which could lead to abuses or project an unsavory image of Slow Food as a commercial organism. The label is drawn in the form of a colorful spiral which is an abstract reflection of Slow Food's snail emblem without actually being a snail.

3. https://www.fondazioneslowfood.com/en/slow-food-presidia/rove-brousse-goat-cheese/

4. Some of the interviews with producers of *Brousse du Rove* were conducted by Nicoletta Stendardo in the framework of the EqualimTerr project (funded by the Provence-Alpes-Côte d'Azur Region, France), which I directed.

5. I spoke with Stefano and several other shepherds and artisan cheese producers, industrial cheese producers, cooperative responsible, veterinarians, and experts while doing research in Sardinia on local Slow Food dynamics (from 2011 to 2014) and then on the "political and economic life of Sardinia PDO cheeses" (from 2017 and 2020).

6. Before the 1996 European regulation, the *Fiore Sardo* already benefited from a certified origin that was instigated in 1955. This certification was defined by the Stresa international convention of 1951 and integrated into Italian law 125 on April 10, 1954.

7. By comparison, annual industrial production, per company, varies from 18,000 wheels of cheese (60 tons) to 70,000 wheels (270 tons)—data from AGRIS (*Azienda regionale per la ricera in agricoltura, Regione autonoma di Sardegna*, for production in 2014, 2015, and 2016).

8. Not all of the industrial companies actually produce Fiore Sardo. Some of them buy cheese made by shepherds before the label certifying origin has been affixed in order to market them under their own name (see Siniscalchi and Zecchin 2018). The sheep farmers feel that these industrial companies are more respectful of their work and the quality of their product than the industrial companies that actually produce cheese, even if there can still be tension in the relationship between them.

9. Tsing observes "the way people, their ideas and desires collide with each other, producing unpredictable results" (2005: ix). These results may take the form of conflict, collaboration, or (in the Indonesian case study she analyzes) devastation.

Photo 9 Tasting cheese and wine. A *laboratorio del gusto*. Cheese, Bra (Italy), 2017. ©Franco Zecchin.

CHAPTER 9
INCLUSION AND EXCLUSION
THE POLITICAL TASTE OF SLOW FOOD

After their final meeting of 2010, the national board members of Slow Food Italia were invited to dinner in the town of Alba, not far from the association's international headquarters in Bra. Since the beginning of my fieldwork a year earlier, I had attended all of the board's meetings as an observer, and this position landed me an invitation to that dinner. Everyone was asked to bring a bottle of wine, and of course considering they were connoisseurs even if no one worked directly in the wine sector, it would have to be an excellent bottle. I was somewhat bewildered by the task but finally settled on a "natural" French wine (*vin nature*), with an exotic note that I thought might compete with the other wines. As a bonus, the winery's name brought to mind that of a very expensive Piedmont wine which gave me the opportunity for some playful ambiguity when I announced my contribution. My natural wine came from *Les vignes de Gaïa*, and the Piedmont winemaker is *Gaja*. Over the course of the dinner, at least eighteen bottles were opened, their nose savored, and the range of flavors and characteristics analyzed in a multitude of exchanges and commentaries.

Since the creation of the association in the mid-1980s, taste has been one of the elements at the heart of Slow Food. In this chapter, I delve into this unique space created by taste and practices of tasting in order to analyze the political use of taste by Slow Food and the changes that have shaped this use over the years. When I first began to reflect on the role of taste within the movement,[1] I had the impression that different ways of understanding and using taste had followed one another through the different phases of Slow Food's history. It seemed as if what had begun as an element of inclusion had developed into an instrument of exclusion. But today, after years of observation, I believe that these different interpretations coexist. Beginning with taste and tasting, I examine the tension that exists between inclusion and exclusion inside Slow Food.

Inclusion and exclusion through food

Food and the act of eating and drinking together continually define the inside and the outside of the group. But this is not only a Slow Food phenomenon. Anthropologists are very familiar with this mechanism: you don't choose to eat with just anyone (Mintz and Du Bois 2002). Numerous studies (Bloch 1999; Mintz and Du Bois 2002; Korsmeyer 2005; Chee-Beng 2015, among others) have followed elements of Mary Douglas's analysis in "Deciphering a meal" chapter (1979). Although from different theoretical

Slow Food

viewpoints, they portray food and commensality as ways to strengthen bonds (kinship, friendship, filiation, class, gender) and define social boundaries that can exclude others. "If food is treated as a code, the messages it encodes will be found in the pattern of social relations being expressed. The message is about different degrees of hierarchy, inclusion and exclusion, boundaries and transactions across the boundaries" (Douglas 1979: 249). Whether or not people share meals allows them to delineate different spheres of intimacy and distance, from close family to intimate friends, or neighbors, or simple acquaintances. Obviously, as Bloch (1999) points out, the similarities and almost universality of certain practices do not mean that things are the same everywhere. In the French context studied by Bourdieu (1979)—even his approach is rather schematic and rigid—food is an instrument of social distinction between members of different social classes who share the same capital, cultural more than economic. But food can do more than simply confirm existing boundaries; it can also help move those boundaries to include people who were previously excluded from an intimate circle. "Commensality," Chee-Beng writes, "can also be used as a political expression to challenge the rule of social exclusion" (2015: 24). Mintz's classical work on sugar (1986) follows the trajectories of a specific product within a capitalist economy and analyzes the transformations of taste and how they have been used in the processes of building and consolidating social hierarchies over the course of time (see also Mintz 1996).

Other studies have looked more specifically at the question of taste. Korsmeyer and Sutton (2011) analyze the role of memory and the cognitive dimension of taste. Sutton (2010, 2017) is particularly interested in the use of senses in constructing social difference through food. Using what he calls "a gustemological approach," he suggests that "taste takes on the quality of a total social fact, tied to multiple domains of social life" (Korsmeyer and Sutton 2011: 469). Counihan and Højlund's book directly addresses the question of taste, its transformations, and its public role: "taste is a central daily part of people's eating habits, affecting what and how much they consume, what it signifies, and whether it satisfies not just their nutritional but also their emotional and social needs" (2018: 2). Taste, as the two anthropologists underline, is produced "on the palate, in our communication, through our hands and craftsmanship, or in our sharing values and activities" (2018: 3).

Taste and pleasure

As Caroline Korsmeyer points out in *The Taste Culture Reader*, "Tastes are subjective but measurable, relative to culture and to individual, yet shared; fleeting sensations that nonetheless endure over many years in memory; transient experiences freighted with the weight of history. And finally, tastes can provide entertainment and intellectual absorption" (2005: 8). Taste is linked to pleasure, a notion that is central in Slow Food. But what is specific in the case of Slow Food is that taste is openly linked with politics. Risking the inherent wordplay, we could say that Slow Food's leaders and members, with their taste for politics, have made taste political. The political role played by taste and the

Inclusion and Exclusion

taste for politics within the Slow Food community are expressed through projects related to wine, to food and, more generally, to gastronomic and food biodiversity. At the same time, taste continues to be part of an intimate sphere that defines belonging and sharing, or not.

In 1980s Italy, the founders of Slow Food believed that "occupying" the field of food was a way to democratize what previously had been considered a prerogative of the (right-wing) elites. In a similar sense to what Chee-Beng writes, those historical leaders saw the attention to (good) food as a matter of entering a sphere reserved for professionals, such as cooks or sommeliers, or gourmet clubs. The Slow Food community has never been scornful of frequenting gourmet restaurants, such as the *ristoranti stellati* ("starred" restaurants, in guides such as Michelin). Over the years, they have even launched initiatives enabling young people to experience dining in more expensive places at relatively low prices (*cene stellate*, starred dinners). Some of the leaders of the second generation recall this type of initiation to the cuisine of starred chefs and high-quality wines as their introduction to Slow Food and its other tasting and eating initiatives.

But the attention to (good) food also means enhancing the skills and knowledge of cooking, and of food and wine production. A few years after the publication of the first Slow Food Manifesto [Portinari 1987], the Slow Food Dictionary extended the manifesto's perspective by defining taste as "the recognition of flavors, expanded to the rituals of the table, stemming from the artistic and intellectual heritage of a civilization" (Ruffa and Monchiero 2002: 87–8; my translation). In this view, taste is tied to knowledge and the table, and, in a larger sense, to the civilization of which they are a part. On the one hand, (good) food is democratized, but on the other hand it acquires a new status as food produced by local culinary traditions, the result of knowledge that is passed on from generation to generation. The way Slow Food members think about and practice food allows them to create a bridge between these two poles, and taste becomes a part of the ways in which they express their cultural and political commitment.

The pleasures of the table and the rediscovery of the taste of regional cooking became the motor of Slow Food's diffusion into the various Italian regions. Restaurateurs often became ambassadors of good will for the association and the *osterie*—that cook traditional local dishes and serve quality wine—became gathering places for members and followers of the movement. As longtime Slow Food leader and restaurateur Giovanni said: "I operated a restaurant, the Ochina Bianca, for 13 years. One day each month, I closed the restaurant, and it became a place for Slow Food events, and I organized dinners and meetings of the association." As both a restaurateur and *fiduciario* of the local Slow Food *condotta* in the town of Mantova, Giovanni was one of the "elders" or historical leaders of the association. His case illustrates the blend of gastronomy and collectivism and points to certain informal policies inherent in the association. The get-togethers (dinners or tastings) that he organized at his establishment were a means of supporting the existence and visibility of Slow Food and marking territory through a grassroots presence of the association. They also served to enlarge the circle of members and followers in an atmosphere of conviviality imbued in the sharing of wine and local cuisine.

Slow Food

Tasting events, organized around a product or wine and open to nonmembers, transformed tasting into a collective practice, and at the same time, it was a means of inclusion. At the end of each event or get-together, unaffiliated participants were encouraged to become members. But beyond facilitating recruitment, taste and tastings also defined and demarcated membership in Slow Food. The events were opportunities to meet friends, to exchange and share practices and knowledge about food in the atmosphere of an extended family, in essence, characteristic of the Italian *osterie* where they often took place.

Expanding the association and spreading its principles through taste and tastings has not been limited to Italy and the early years of the association. As Slow Food has spread across diverse portions of the globe, the methods have been tailored to blend with local customs in each country. From Sardinia (Counihan 2019) to France, and in social contexts as distinct as Japan and California, the *"classiche cene"* (classic dinners) and tasting sessions characterize Slow Food's evolution and continue to be structuring elements in the life of local chapters. Above all, the tastings are mechanisms for collectively shaping taste, and developing membership through the appreciation of taste. They contribute to the creation of a type of "cultural intimacy" (Herzfeld 1997) of taste that remains a distinctive characteristic of the association's membership.

Playing with taste

The capacity of practices based on taste to define or mark adherence to the group is particularly evident in one specific event organized by the Italian association: the annual olive oil tasting, known as the *Gioco del piacere* (Game of Pleasure). In June of 2010, I joined nine staff members in the Italian association's offices where they would work late into the evening as they coordinated that year's event. Cases of olive oil had previously been shipped to all the condotte that had decided to participate in the game. The cases consisted of a collection of four different olive oils produced in different Italian regions and recommended by the *Guida agli extravergini* (Guide to extra-virgin olive oils). The guide is one that Slow Food has published every year since the early 2000s; it presents and ranks a list of high-quality extra-virgin olive oils produced in various Italian regions. The labels had been covered with a ticket bearing a number. The same four bottles, with their original labels, were placed on the table in the association office: one bottle of olive oil from Puglia, one from Sicily, one from Lazio, and one from Liguria. Two of the employees returned with loaves of bread, and the game began—simultaneously—in all the *condotte* registered to participate. From Sicily to Veneto, in all the participating local groups, the members gathered in the *osterie* for a blind tasting of olive oil. In each *condotta*, the *fiduciario* or a member of the group guided the tasting. The point of the game was to have the members of each participating *condotta* rate and classify the olive oils and then assemble the local results into a national classification.

As each *condotta* finished its tasting, the *fiduciario* telephoned the central office in Bra to report the results. In the Bra office, Alberto, Serena, Fabiana, Marco, and Fabrizio followed the expected protocol that requires contacting each *condotta*'s game manager three times: first to confirm the number of participants and provide final instructions for the game; a second call to obtain the number of points noted for each olive oil during the tasting; and a final call to announce the national ranking after all the resulted had been tabulated. This final call communicated the number of votes obtained by each olive oil and confirmed the evening's winner.

While waiting for the results from the fifty-seven *condotte* involved, the office staff and I began to taste the olive oils and rate color, then nose, then palate, in a similar way to what happens with a wine tasting. The difference here is that instead of sipping the oil directly, you taste it on a slice of bread. Everyone expressed their thoughts and preferences, then tasted again and decided on a rating (on a scale of 1–4). From time to time the telephones rang with demands for clarification from latecomers, and with time to spare, we tasted again, and the conversation turned to stories about various *condotte* or comments about certain *fiduciari* that apparently embody the stereotypes of one or another city or group. As the atmosphere relaxed there were a few jokes between employees. Someone decided to call one of his coworkers secretly from an adjoining room, passing for a *fiduciario* and asking pointed questions about the oils and their organoleptic characteristics that no one could answer. After a brief moment of stress, everybody laughed.

Finally, the real *fiduciari* began to call, and everyone returned to their telephones to note the arriving results. The early results were from *condotte* in the North of Italy, while others were late to finish. With each call and rating, the tension in the office mounted: everybody was caught up in the game and curious to know who would be the winner of the competition. By 11 o'clock in the evening, the last group had reported, and the tasting game ended. Once the ratings were tabulated, the *condotte* were called with the results, identifying the producer of each of the four olive oils and the final national classifications. The *fiduciari* were then able to pass the results and classification to the members participating in the event. Each *condotta* tasting was followed by a dinner, and at the end of the evening everyone who had taken part received a copy of the *Guida agli extravergini*.

At these key moments in the functioning life of the association, tasting is a means of creating conviviality and sharing practices (primarily tasting practices), while promoting Slow Food philosophy. The tasting game both informs and transforms the members. It educates them, and that education creates a preference, an educated taste. As noted by certain organizers, the game presents the opportunity to discover and taste olive oil in a convivial setting where the participants are exposed to high-quality olive oils, learning to appreciate, distinguish, and, ultimately, prefer them.[2] While transmitting values of the movement through taste the *Gioco del piacere* also creates social links and a sense of belonging, not only to the local group but to the larger Slow Food family: for an evening, with the intermediary help of the central service, people are connected and participate simultaneously in a unique, collective tasting. Behind the scenes, the game also reveals the discrepancy between the Slow Food members in the *condotte* who are participating in the tasting and employees in Bra. The young staff members are not necessarily experts in terms of tasting a particular food or wine, but working in the headquarters lends them an aura of expertise, which volunteers in the *condotte* sometimes lack.

Slow Food

Defining borders

Taste and tasting are part of the dynamic which defines the position of members and staff within the association, and simply becoming or being a member of Slow Food does not mean being part of the "inner circle" of the association.

The internal organization of Slow Food is extremely hierarchical, as we have seen. A simple membership is distinct from being an active volunteer member, and volunteers with elected political roles at various local, regional, or national levels (in Italy or other countries) are part of a more exclusive circle which is closer to the upper hierarchy situated in the Bra headquarters. For these leaders, who are often the people organizing tasting workshops, dinners, and Master of Food programs, the ability to teach about taste and its subtleties contributes to an even stronger sense of being on the inside of the movement and an elite member of the Slow Food hierarchy.

When there was still a French national association (Slow Food France), Jacques, its president between 2003 and 2011, would arrive at international meetings with a few "special" bottles of wine in his backpack. The bottles were to be shared with a small circle composed especially of the leaders and founders of Slow Food in Italy. The wines were usually from small French vineyards and were always a testament to his wine-tasting skills. Since the beginning, wine has had an important place inside Slow Food, a place visible in the events and publications but also in the daily practices of its members.[3] As a consequence, the members of Slow Food are often considered and consider themselves wine connoisseurs. So, the bottles of exceptional wines to share with the contingent from Bra did more than just show Jacques's knowledge and taste in wine. They demonstrated his place in the group of historical leaders and Slow Food's internal hierarchy. His sense of belonging is logical when we consider that most leaders at all levels of the association first survived a selection or approval process involving the highest levels of the Slow Food hierarchy. This was the case for Jacques, and it was also the case for the members of the Italian *segreteria nazionale* (national board). They are the closest to the core of power in the association. A significant part of the decisions that concern the functioning of the Italian association and its policies are made or simply validated by this board.

The closing dinner that I refer to at the beginning of this chapter followed the end of those board members' term in office. The exchanges and comments concerning each of the wines presented, and the level of tasting competence exhibited by the members of the board at the table confirmed their place in proximity to the upper echelons of the Slow Food hierarchy. Clearly, one can hardly fathom a leader in the movement who doesn't know and appreciate wine. This informal and intimate tasting session exposes and defines the boundaries of the inner circle of Slow Food and allows me to highlight the specific political and cultural intimacy of that circle.

That evening revealed other types of distinction that reflect the permanent tension between inclusion and exclusion which, in my opinion, characterizes the social dynamics throughout the movement. The board members present were almost exclusively men, some of them long-term leaders in the movement. The only woman

162

Inclusion and Exclusion

present besides myself was the head of the education office, one of the members from the national headquarters. At this extremely masculine dinner-meeting she brought a white sparkling-wine, a choice more often associated with the preferences of women, which accentuated the predominately male composition of the group and the gender distinction prompted by the wine itself.

Still another telling episode took place that evening. At the end of the dinner, after two of the less integrated board members had left, one of the historical leaders from Bra made a tour of the table and asked the guests to each contribute twenty euros without any explanation. We gave him the money without asking anything; no one else seemed surprised, and I kept mine well hidden. He then went off to discuss with the manager and chef of the *osteria*, and came back with a bottle of Barolo Monfortino. He promptly began to expound upon its characteristics in an elaborate initiation to this great, and expensive, wine which we had all just participated in purchasing. It was a 2001 vintage and the winegrower only bottled once every four or five years. We began tasting the wine in typical fashion by observing the color in the glass, then appreciating the nose—an aromatic discussion that took some time—and everyone was ecstatic. Finally, we evaluated its impression on the palate with small sips while listening to an account of its virtues. The tasting continued as various members of the group shared their appreciation of the wine.

During the evening of that final dinner, the sharing and tasting of a renowned bottle of wine was not only an activity of taste; it was also an example of the means and activities used to delimit this inner group of leaders who are historically important in the association. Teil and Hennion suggest that "taste is a performing activity . . . an action, not a fact; it is an experience, not an object" (2004: 35). At the end of this special experience, as we all began to leave, the member of the group responsible for this last tasting approached me, "Spy, do you realize what just happened?! This evening you tasted a bottle of Monfortino!" In truth, I had not only discovered and tasted a particular wine, but I had also participated in an intimate moment among this inner circle at the heart of the movement.

The objectives and ambitions of Slow Food have evolved over time, increasingly demonstrating the metamorphosis of a food and wine association into a social and political movement which encourages members to become more aware of the production process and the need to support small producers, but the role played by wine (and tasting wine) has remained important. Even if the approach to wine has generally followed the movement's philosophical evolution, it has lagged behind other priorities: with a long history as one of the core elements bringing together Slow Food members, it had been resistant to change, at least until the first years of my research, according to the opinion of many leaders and staff members.

Training through taste

Since the 1990s, the *laboratori del gusto* (taste laboratories) have been proposed during Slow Food events organized at the local, national, and international levels (Salone del

Gusto, Cheese, Slow Fish, etc.). They are a type of workshop that enables both members and the general public to discover products and the relationship between products (e.g., wines or artisanal beers and cheeses) through a sensory experience based on taste. A taste laboratory is actually an event within an event: a "device" that can take different forms and can be found in large Slow Food events or in small events organized by the association's local chapters around the world. The laboratories are neither free nor limited to members of the movement—anyone can pay to participate in what is at the same time a learning experience and a commercial device that allows Slow Food to collect money. Tasting events, probably one of the most original inventions of Slow Food, are a means of promoting the association and building membership, but perhaps even more importantly these tasting experiences present an introduction to the philosophy of the movement and enable Slow Food to showcase new themes.

At the end of the 1990s, the leaders of the movement began to focus on the environment—now one of the most important elements of Slow Food philosophy. It has also increasingly included producers and the concern for their living and working conditions, creating projects oriented around "food communities," small producers, and local economies. Along with the changes in Slow Food philosophy and actions expressed by the triad "Good, Clean, and Fair," education has become a central and strategic element for the movement; education in taste acts as a tool for safeguarding products and species but also as a means of focusing attention on producers' perspectives as part of the process of acquiring knowledge about products. In parallel with the movement's ideological evolution, taste laboratories have become more attentive to the aspects of production. Frequently they feature the producers themselves, who come to present their product. A producer may provide a history and explain production methods while the participants taste and savor the flavors and characteristics of his or her product. The learning that takes place during these events thus goes beyond the direct organoleptic experience of the product and encompasses elements such as the conditions of production, the choices of production techniques made by the producer, and the environmental contexts. The tasting practices become rituals in which food is both a means of connection and of communication: these rituals are a form of sociability that links producers and consumers through specific knowledge.

Slow Food leaders and members see initiatives in taste education as opportunities for people to learn to recognize and appreciate "good, clean, and fair" food and to discover less-known but high-quality wines and foods. In some ways this reflects the inclusive sense of democratization that I referred to earlier. It is true that the defense of producers and the notion of access to quality food for all have been integrated into Slow Food's principles and political efforts. Nevertheless, some of the association's concrete actions exemplified by these educational mechanisms are often aimed at gourmets and an economically privileged audience who has the means to access the products that Slow Food defends and the training that it offers. The objectives of these actions are not accessible to everyone, and in that sense they are exclusive. While they are carefully planned in terms of the choice and pairing of products as well as the quality of promotional text for attracting the public, the cost to participante is not negligible.

In larger events such as the Salone del Gusto, Cheese, or Slow Fish, the price of the workshop can be 20 to 50 euros per person. This means that participating in multiple laboratories can become extremely expensive. The contradiction between actions that teach people to recognize, understand, and appreciate quality food and production, while employing methods that financially limit access to the knowledge gained through those actions, is frequently criticized from outside the movement.

The same contradiction can be found in another Slow Food initiative known as the Master of Food program. It consists of training sessions to provide instruction in Slow Food principles by improving knowledge about food and drink. Initiated and managed by the association's education office at the headquarters in Bra, and conducted by Slow Food "trainers," the Master of Food program expounds "*il gusto di saperne di più*" (the "pleasure" and the "taste" of knowing more). The Italian word *gusto* suggests the idea of both the pleasure in and the taste for the knowledge that is addressed in this project. During one or several meetings that can take place on two or three different levels, the Master of Food program offers this training to Slow Food members for a fee. The sessions are organized on a thematic basis and act as a mechanism to pass on the principles of the association to new members or refine the knowledge of experienced members in a particular domain. The more classic programs are organized around products such as cheese or wine, but new programs have been added over time on themes, such as food shopping, garden products, and cooking without waste. Concerns over protection of the environment or reducing waste cohabit with the knowledge and know-how Slow Food has developed in the domain of the senses and seeks to promote.

Il gusto giusto, the right taste

Taste also provides part of the reasoning to include products in the Slow Food list of *Presidia*, as we have seen, which makes them the clearest example of the political and economic use of taste. In most cases these products have a taste (also a smell and sometimes an appearance) that is far removed from the so-called "standard taste" to which most consumers are accustomed. This different taste is one of the elements that make the presence of these products on the market more problematic because it can make them more difficult to appreciate. Learning to recognize and appreciate their particular taste becomes a political goal for Slow Food. But even in this new political dimension, taste can be a tool of exclusion: it can exclude products that do not meet the criteria of the label, or sanction producers who no longer comply with the specifications. It can also create invisible borders within the circle of Slow Food members.

In February 2011, Slow Food organized a three-day training program for people in charge of Presidia in each *condotta*, region, or country. After an initial presentation concerning different aspects of Presidia projects, the training involved some exercises and a comparative blind tasting session. The President of the Slow Food Foundation for biodiversity introduced this session with an explanation: "By tasting, I make a judgment on the quality. Now we must turn that around. The story of the quality needs

Slow Food

to be told . . . but the story cannot be told through the experience of a single producer because it does not provide enough assurance of sustainability." With his reference to a story, he formally introduced a new element: the narrative, the history of the product.[4] "Blind tasting is no longer sufficient; we have to listen to narratives in order to understand . . . the product's characteristic features need to be explained."

When the tasting session started, he asked the participants to taste a series of three cheeses, then to listen to his narration, and taste again. The exercise was repeated with three apples, and three sausages. In each series of products, there was an industrial product, a good product, and a presidium. Participants were asked to identify the best one from the Slow Food perspective. The first series of cheeses was composed of a raw milk *Maccagno* (a Slow Food presidium), followed by a *Maccagno* from a dairy using added ferments (enzymes) that, the President of the Foundation for Biodiversity explained, "render the taste and smell homogenous; recognizing them during a tasting requires experience, but you will begin to perceive them." The third cheese was a tomme made with pasteurized milk, and the President noted, "Here you can smell the sharp acidity of the fermentation enzymes and the lack of balance." He continued by explaining that to qualify a cheese product as a presidium the animals must be fed with field hay in winter as well as summer. He also outlined the specificities of breeds and then summarized, "So, in one cheese, there is the breed and the raw milk, in the other there is the breed but no raw milk, and in the last there is nothing and we have no idea where the milk comes from." After this final explanation, he pointed to each of the three cheeses, one at a time, and asked the participants to raise their hand if they liked it. I remember one of my neighbors at the table where I was sitting, a newer member of Slow Food, being nervous when it came to raising his hand to indicate which was the presidium cheese. These group exercises functioned as a sort of collective control: participants could make mistakes, but they could not say that the industrial product is the presidium. This would have discredited them in the eyes of the other participants and especially the leaders of the movement. Taste, tasting practices, and this kind of collective training in taste are also a way to "test" and shape people, a tool of inclusion and exclusion at the same time.

Tasting as a tool of a moral economy

In today's Slow Food world, taste seems to be increasingly subjected to a moral characterization: "good" food is also "morally" good because it is produced with respect for the environment and animals. This characterization applies to processed foods such as cheeses or sausages, but also all agricultural products, animal breeds, and even the "neglected" fish found in the Slow Fish events. Consuming these "morally" good products signifies not only respect for the environment but also for the work of producers, and it implicitly helps them to make a living from their work. Good food must be accessible to all, but equally fair working conditions must be guaranteed to all producers. In a previous work (Siniscalchi 2014a) I analyzed an article that appeared in the August

18, 2010, edition of *La Repubblica*, one of the most important Italian newspapers. The article, signed by Carlo Petrini, denounced industrial Sardinian cheese and defined it as a "bad (*cattivo*) cheese because it behaves badly." The article called for a revolt against the infringement of moral rules, symbolized by this bad cheese which behaves badly with respect to its own region and the people who care about this land, and "with the Sardinian shepherds who created the reputation of this cheese" (the producers of *Fiore Sardo* that we saw in the previous chapter).

In recent years, the movement's philosophy and actions have evolved toward a redefinition of the limits of human action and the morality of the economy. "Good, clean, and fair" have also become the parameters of a moral economy that is partly an alternative to unbridled free market capitalism, and partly a reform of it. The defense of local economies involving farmers and producers all around the world is aimed at creating "food communities" with performative goals woven around productive activities and imagined economies (Anderson 1991). These goals are directly related to an ideal past that was not subject to the damage from capitalism, industrial production, and the irresponsible exploitation of resources. The more utopian and inclusive dimension of Slow Food's message is aimed at bringing the poles of the food chain closer, connecting all the actors of local economies in different parts of the world to try and change the food system. This posture is similar to Papa Francesco's environmental perspective in his last Encyclical *Laudato sì* that I mentioned in Chapter 2: these proximities contribute to the reinforcement of the moral dimension included in the current message of Slow Food.

Since the beginning, taste and tastings have been at the heart of Slow Food philosophy and political practices. Taste was a new way of expressing political commitment for the first generation of leaders, but it has also been a way to involve new members inside the movement. Through the years, tasting games and trainings have defined and demarcated the membership, hiding internal hierarchies and allowing people to feel a part of the larger Slow Food "family." At the same time, taste is a tool of distinction and exclusion in determining who belongs to the "inner circle" where the sharing of certain taste practices contributes to a sort of "taste intimacy." This intimacy, in turn, reveals aspects of the internal functioning of the movement. But the pleasure and taste inherent in the Italian word *gusto* is not simply about food; it concerns the knowledge of food that is now seen as an integral part of the political commitment of Slow Food members. The evolution of taste in Slow Food is not one from inclusion to exclusion. Those opposing dimensions have been present since the beginning. The change lies in the development of the moral connotation of taste that was not present in the early years of the association. It is this moral dimension that allows Slow Food to weave bridges with the perspectives of (a part of) the Catholic Church as expressed by the current pope.

Becoming a moral political tool, taste once again creates boundaries through exclusion: it becomes the basis for the exclusion of industrial or morally bad food, producers that do not do "good" work, and people that are not able to recognize "good" food. At the same time, this moral shift exercises inclusion by assembling small producers from all over the world and making them feel that they are part of the Slow Food family.

Slow Food

Notes

1. This was when my colleagues Carole Counihan and Susanne Højlund asked me to collaborate on the *Making Taste Public* volume (2018), in which this text, with some differences, was first published.

2. Other scholars analyze similar processes of transformation of taste and preferences; see Mintz (1996), Terrio (2000), Paxson (2013) and some of the writings collected in the volume edited by Counihan and Højlund (2018).

3. The creation of the Libera e Benemerita Associazione degli Amici del Barolo (the Association of Lovers of Piedmont's wine) by the same people who later founded Slow Food is another reflection of this intimate relationship with wine.

4. In the same aim, Slow Food leaders propose new methods of labeling in order to counteract the "mystification" that often accompanies products and the meager amount of information actually required by law. The *etichette narranti* (narrative labels) are conceived as a sort of "counter-label." Slow Food uses these narrative labels to introduce other elements that define the quality: not only the link with the place where products are grown, raised, or transformed but knowledge, a story about these links, an explanation of the product's characteristics, the region and environment of its origins, and the techniques of its production.

Photo 10 Alessio inside his *osteria*, San Marco dei Cavoti (Italy), 2012. ©Franco Zecchin.

CHAPTER 10
POLITICS AT THE DINNER TABLE AND IN THE VINEYARDS

Eating and drinking have been two elements at the heart of Slow Food's philosophy and actions since the very beginning of Arcigola and the Benemerita Associazione degli Amici del Barolo. Wine and small-family restaurants (*osterie*) have been the foundation on which the notions of conviviality and pleasure have been built. But as Slow Food becomes increasingly perceived as a movement in public spaces, what happens to this central dynamic, which is rooted in local activities and central to membership practices and the association's modes of dissemination? This question reflects both a specificity and a weakness. It is precisely this close link with the world of restaurants and the world of wine that is at the origin of the image that Slow Food's leaders have been trying to change for years: it continues to make the members of the association appear as gourmands, more interested in what is on the plate and in the glass (the good) than in production (the clean) and producers (the fair), even if the latter have become more present in the ranks of the association. In reality, the relationships between Slow Food and restaurateurs and winemakers have not always been the same over the years. In this chapter, I will explore how politics "go to the table" and enter the vineyards.

La Guida (the Guide)

The meaning of the Italian word *osteria* has evolved over time. Initially it was used to describe a warm and friendly place where it was possible to have a glass of wine and a quick bite to eat. Sometimes located outside of urban spaces and off the main roads, the *osterie* became places where travelers could stop and have something to eat. Slow Food's use of the term has revitalized and updated it, and today numerous places that serve food present themselves as such even though they have no connection with Slow Food. According to the definition in *Il Dizionario di Slow Food* (Ruffa and Monchiero 2002: 118), the *osteria* is a place synonymous with traditional family-style cuisine, simple service, unpretentious hospitality, and quality wines, all for a reasonable price (see also Capatti 2000).

When members renew their membership, they are given a copy of one of the publishing house's bestsellers, *Osterie d'Italia*. Often simply called "*La Guida*" (the Guide) or "*Osterie*," it is both an instrument of diffusion, for increasing awareness of the association and its principles, and a result of the work of diffusion. Although the

Slow Food

annual editing process of the guide is coordinated and formatted at the association's headquarters in Bra, it is based on collaboration among the association's members. Around 400 members contribute to the redaction of the guide *Osterie d'Italia* pointing out the *osterie* in their area to be included in the guide and writing the information sheets. They discover, report, and monitor the establishments that they feel are worthy of belonging in this "primer of eating and drinking, Italian style" as it is described in the subtitle (*Sussidiario del mangiarbere all'italiana*). Once the restaurant has been included in the guide there is an implicit engagement between Slow Food and the restaurateurs. Even though there is no written contract, the fact remains that a restaurant can be removed from the guide should it be determined that it no longer respects the conditions required for inclusion.

Slow Food members use the *Osterie d'Italia* like a manual for discovering the country. It leads them not only to places where they can eat well but also to places of "cultural intimacy" (Herzfeld 1997). For the members, these *osterie* represent places that are both familial and familiar, and that correspond to similar values in terms of their management and their link with the association. The importance of the *osterie* and of conviviality itself can be seen in the vocabulary of the association. For several years, the group that coordinated the *condotta*, led by the *fiduciario*, was called the *piccola tavola*, the little table, as we have seen in previous chapters.

By providing a direct link between the restaurants and the membership, the guide contributes to the creation and consolidation of Slow Food's associative structure, while at the same time acting as an economic instrument. To be included in the guide is still, today, an ambition for many restaurateurs because it represents added value. Many restaurateurs have profited from their inclusion in the *Osterie d'Italia* by virtue of Slow Food's visibility and legitimacy in terms of knowledge about local regions and eating establishments that are familial and convivial. But beyond economic interest, what kind of involvement with the movement and its philosophy do they have?

Beriss and Sutton (2007: 1) introduced an ethnographic volume on restaurants by noting that "restaurants bring together nearly all the characteristics of economic life, . . . forms of exchange, modes of production, and the symbolism behind consumption— under one roof." And that "political life often takes form in and through restaurants." In the case of *osterie* that are part of the Slow Food network, the political dimension takes a particular form and is never separated from the economic dimension.

Osterie

Number 14 Via della Mendicità Istruita is the site of Slow Food's headquarters in the historic center of Bra. The building itself is ancient, encircling a small interior courtyard lined with balconies that lead to the offices of the association. For tourists and local people, this is the address of *Boccondivino* (in English this translates as a "divine morsel"), one of the renowned *osterie* of the Langhe wine region. But actually, the Boccondivino is more than just a simple *osteria*. Opened in 1984 by the I Tarocchi cooperative, which was established by the founders of Slow Food, this *osteria* preceded the birth of the association and became a place of assembly and experimentation. It is one of two restaurants in which Slow Food maintains a financial interest (the other is in the neighboring city of Alba), and it often functions like a second home for Slow Food personnel and the association's leaders. Many of the headquarters' more or less formal dinners and meetings are held in the second-floor dining rooms or around tables installed in the garden during the summer. The Boccondivino is not only the restaurant where Slow Food leaders and staff members entertain visitors; it also acts as the in-house canteen where the staff go to eat when they don't want, or don't have time, to go further to eat. With access to the *osteria* directly from the balconies of their office, they can go there just to relax, read the paper, and socialize with their coworkers.

Pianetto, Galeata, Emilia Romagna. At the beginning of 2005, Roberto and Alessandra were not restaurateurs, they were just Slow Food members who were passionate about food.[1] Roberto is a land surveyor and Alessandra is an elementary schoolteacher. Like many of the association's members in Italy, they loved trying the *osterie* reviewed in the *Guida* and searching for good products, and they participated in all the Slow Food events and exhibitions. One of their friends who was the *fiduciario* of their *condotta* in the Bidente valley of Emilia Romagna, encouraged them to participate in the activities of the association and passed along his passion for Slow Food, high-quality local products, and for the places where one eats well. "Slow Food ruined us!" said Roberto laughingly. "It was after becoming involved in Slow Food that we opened our restaurant." Their interest in changing professions became a reality when they learned about a country house being put up for sale in the countryside about 40 kilometers, south of Forlì. They decided to buy it and opened their *osteria*, *La Campanara*, in 2005.[2] At the beginning, they kept their respective professional activities, but after several intense and exhausting years they decided to concentrate completely on the restaurant, which today runs at full capacity. In 2009 they obtained the *chiocciola*, the snail symbol representing the art of "slow" and the Slow Food logo, noting it as a favorite in Slow Food's guide, *Osterie d'Italia*. The guide identifies restaurants that respect the principles of the association in terms of the quality of their food and service. Family-style cuisine and management, local dishes, and a reasonable price are necessary[3]—but not the only requirements—for being noted in the guide. The snail logo is attributed to establishments that have several additional characteristics in tune with a commitment to Slow Food's principles.[4]

Via Porta di Rose, San Marco dei Cavoti, Campania.[5] This is the name of a street in the old section of the small town where Alessio, a 42-year-old from a family of artisans and shopkeepers, opened an *osteria-pizzeria* in 2004 and named it *U Magazzeo*.[6] After an education in the hotel business and several years working as a waiter during summers in Rimini and London, he had decided to return to his native city and open a restaurant. His dream was for it to become a "Slow Food restaurant." The expression is used within the association to indicate restaurants that represent the philosophy of Slow Food, host some of the movement's local activities (dinners, tastings, meetings) and are noted in the Guide. And in fact, U Magazzeo has been noted in the *Osterie d'Italia* for several years.

Slow Food

Restaurants are not proposed for inclusion in the guide by the restaurateurs themselves, but by members of the association whose role is to be responsible for the guide in their region, and who visit the establishments following Slow Food recommendations. For his menu, Alessio chose local products (cheeses, cured meats, fresh pasta) and also beers and wines produced within the region. Today, the local Slow Food *condotta* Tammaro-Fortore uses Alessio's *osteria* for dinners with association members and tastings with local producers.

What are the common characteristics that link these three restaurants, one in the north, one in the center, and one in the south of Italy? All three of the *osterie* described above maintain a relationship with the Slow Food movement, but they do so in very different ways. The first, Boccondivino, is centrally located on the actual premises of the association's offices—you could say in the "belly" of Slow Food—which is also the "historical" location of the association's birth, and for some, its cradle and physical connection to the commercial world of serving food. The second, La Campanara, is an *osteria* created by impassioned members of the association and deeply inspired by its philosophy. The third, U Magazzeo, conceived far from Bra, shares the movement principles but does not maintain strong associative links with its national components. *Osterie* can be considered as economic and political spaces where Slow Food philosophy is practiced in very concrete ways. These three places don't just serve food; they are also places that embody different modalities of Slow Food's presence, diffusion, and expression in Italy.[7]

The place of the restaurateurs

Since the beginning of the 2000s, an increasing number of projects were focused on the environment, and local production or economies, as we have seen in the previous chapters.[8] Parallel to the evolution of Slow Food's philosophy, the political organization of the association has become more complex with the creation of new officers and new decision-making bodies. The statutes elaborated in 2010 are also aimed at reducing real, and potential, conflicts of interest. Slow Food's name, the visibility of the movement, and the contacts with producers and institutions have at times been used to benefit personal interests. With a few exceptions, members of certain professional categories, directly involved in the culinary field from a professional point of view, including restaurateurs, were no longer considered for the position of *fiduciario*.

Over the course of these changes, the chefs/restaurateurs, who have long constituted a strong base of support for the movement—especially in the early years—seemed to lose some degree of the importance they once had. The number of projects that concerned restaurants diminished as the association's principal preoccupation turned toward producers. Nevertheless, even though some restaurateurs—like some members—have strayed or been pushed aside, a number of others have stayed and evolved with the association.

In this context, the Boccondivino remains the discreet showcase of the association. The *osteria* doesn't appear to have changed, neither in its style nor in its interior design. Although frequented throughout the year, it hasn't become a simple tourist stop, and it hasn't succumbed to a process of "typicalization." It has evolved along with the association, enabling the testing of new links with the world of production that are now at the heart of Slow Food philosophy. Presidia products are used in the preparation of numerous dishes identified on the menu with the colorful spiral symbol that denotes the Presidia label. But contrary to most other *osterie*, this place doesn't need to post a sign to indicate its relationship with Slow Food, and it is not even the menu that marks this connection: the link is there, in evidence, without needing to be underlined. At the same time, the Boccondivino has remained a sober and intimate place, an extension of the living and working space of the leaders and staff of Slow Food. Many of the association's ideas, political strategies, and projects have first seen the light of day here, as many historical leaders remember. This *osteria* incarnates the historical relationship between Slow Food, politics (in the sense of social engagement), and the restaurant world. It constitutes a sort of icon and tacit model for other *osterie,* whether they were born with the philosophy of Slow Food or assimilated it over the course of time.

The restaurateurs: business people or activists?

Roberto and Alessandra, and Alessio, are among the restaurateurs who opened their *osteria* in the 2000s, when the most radical transformations of Slow Food were taking place. The way that they compare their business with that of other restaurants reflects the engagement and principles of the association. Roberto explained it this way:

> In a sense, we are not really restaurateurs. The restaurateurs are business people, so their approach is based on economics, they try to reduce costs, and to do that they often use technology. For us, it's different, we have been Slow Food members, so we haven't had to make changes, we started out like that, with the spirit of Slow Food . . . and right away we were included in the Guide. Plus, in 2009, we were noted with the *chiocciola.* (the snail rating)[9]

The link with Slow Food is not simply one of passion and engagement. It is also economic: "If you do things well, that also pays from the economic point of view. . . . The 'snail' brings us even more people; it serves as communication, to make sure that people come looking for you, but it also pushes us to always do better," said Roberto, "For us, the Guide is an extraordinary thing, it makes us known." The restaurateurs thus seem to be both activists and economic actors, and this economy passes in part through their political engagement.

Alessio has not been awarded the "snail" rating in the Guide, but the link with Slow Food principles is nevertheless presented as a component of his business. "I know Slow Food. When I opened, I took it as a philosophy for my activity. . . . I don't have many

Slow Food

tables, I have a limited menu, I don't have awful products, like frozen stuff, seed oils, I put out simple dishes. . . . The garden vegetables are my parent's, the pork too," said Alessio.

Alessio's approach, and that of Roberto and Alessandra, constitutes examples of the application of Slow Food's philosophy, certainly from their point of view, but also from the perspective of the movement's leaders and that of consumers. These cases grant legitimacy to Slow Food in terms of local and regional knowledge, and the products and places of family-style cooking that are good but also attentive to production methods. Alessio exhibits the *Osterie d'Italia* guide in his establishment, with extracts of articles and photos that reflect his relationship to the movement (see the image which opens this chapter).

A colorful collection of objects is exhibited in a corner of the dining room of La Campanara. They are all in the form of Slow Food's snail symbol and sit next to several jars of Presidia products. On the wall, carefully framed, hang various certificates that Slow Food has awarded the couple and their restaurant over the years, notably, the certificates awarding the "snail."

> Osterie d'Italia proclama 'La Campanara' interprete esemplare della tradizione del mangiarbere, luogo di accoglienza e di convivialità' (*Osterie d'Italia* declares La Campanara a perfect example of the tradition of eating and drinking in a welcoming and convivial atmosphere).

The iconography contributes to transform these convivial food spaces into political spaces. But sometimes this political dimension also imbues the exterior of the restaurant. For example, Roberto explained that La Campanara added a kitchen garden near the *osteria*:[10]

> We created a kitchen garden, and we hope it can be educational: Our garden provides the basics, we are not able to produce everything we need, but we have our customers visit it and this helps them understand the products that are in our dishes. Our approach . . . to cooking also includes reutilization such as *polpette* (meat or vegetable balls) or dishes that use stale bread, and dishes with less prestigious cuts of meat, like tongue or tripe.

Membership in Slow Food also led Roberto and Alessandra to integrate another aspect of the movement's philosophy, such as education. In addition, the relationship with the direct knowledge of local producers constitutes a fundamental aspect of their activity. "When I bring certain products to the table, I am comfortable, I can explain who made them, the history behind them, how the producers were able to achieve this result," Roberto told me. Two days each week, when the restaurant is closed, Roberto and Alessandra make the rounds of their suppliers: "The producers are not merchants, you call them and they're in the stable with the animals. Sometimes it is difficult, but if you want their products you have to go pick them up directly at their place."

176

Politics at the Dinner Table

When restaurateurs characterize their activities, the word *"commercianti"* (merchants) appears again as a negative aspect ("we are not typical restaurateurs; so we are not merchants"). The producers that "do things well" are not merchants either. In a spirit almost Aristotelian, someone who works well, and who is a good farmer, is not a business person: She or he doesn't concentrate on reducing costs but instead respects the environment, the animals, and the products. And the restaurateurs, those who are answering their "calling" and are "inspired" by Slow Food, are not considered as merchants either. They work toward a form of mutual interest, respecting both the producers and the consumers. Although everyone, in one way or another, is a middleman—including the movement to which they belong—the "good" middleman is thought of as one that doesn't profit from the work of others. The good middleman enables the establishment of links, and makes introductions, in a sort of ideal and virtuous economic model. The moral dimension of the notion of "good" appears again, and here it becomes an economic resource (as well as a political banner) as happens with Presidia. "On my menu, I always indicate the name of the producers where I get the products. That gives them a small economic return," said Roberto. The links that are created help the *osterie* and the local producers to make a living. The place that chefs have had in the Terra Madre event since 2006 too, along with the small producers from around the world, symbolizes this intermediary role, promoting local products and economies (see Chapter 11).

The *osteria* is a "familial" place in the sense of managing the restaurant's activities and arranging the interior space, and a "familiar" place in the sense of its relationship with the movement. It is personalized around the owners like Roberto and Alessandra who perform both the cooking and the table service. The personalized menu contributes to this structure and calls particular attention to the "local" dimension. This is not a concept that reflects an imaginary rurality, unlike what DuPuis and Goodman assert (2005). The products and recipes are not simply "local"; they have real names, faces, and stories.

Contrary to U Magazzeo, often referred to as "da Alessio" (Alessio's place), or La Campanara where the personality of the owners constitutes a major part of the *osteria*'s identity, the image of Boccondivino is not associated with the face of the owner or chef. Although various individuals important in the internal history of the association have spent time in front of the *osteria*'s ovens, or training new generations of chefs, or even serving tables, the Boccondivino does not have an image constructed around a single personality. It is based on the restaurant's fundamental and constituent connection with Slow Food. This trait reflects the movement's style of functioning where, outside of the implicit notability of its president, there are no individual personalities that are displayed or promoted.

Alliances and new economic and political spaces

In 2009 Slow Food developed a project of "alliance" to promote collaboration between the restaurateurs and the producers of Presidia-labeled products. It was called "*L'Alleanza*

Slow Food

tra i cuochi italiani e i Presidi Slow Food" (The Alliance between Italian cooks and Slow Food Presidia) and directed toward Italian chefs. This alliance formally brings together two of the social actors involved in Slow Food's philosophy and actions: the restaurants, represented by the chefs; and the producers, represented by the Presidia project. As we have seen, the Presidia project is an "old" project in an association that needs to constantly invest in new actions in order to maintain its visibility and legitimacy in the conflictual field of food policies. At the same time it is a project that continues to be important for the movement even if its place among Slow Food actions is periodically questioned in informal discussions and in the association's places of decision-making. Is it a project that still merits investment? As we have seen, the producers of some Presidia are unable to sell all their production. What position and what strategies should the association adopt? From the viewpoint of a number of producers, Slow Food uses the project primarily as a political project and doesn't pay enough attention to the economic dimension. But the association refuses to become the middleman, a "wholesaler" of Presidia products except on extremely rare occasions (see Chapters 7 and 8). Even though the economy is at the heart of Slow Food and its functioning, its leaders often repeat, "we are not merchants and we do not want to become merchants."

Slow Food's engagement vis-à-vis the producers (small producers in general, not only those of the Presidia) is considered to be eminently political, in the sense of a bridge between the world of production and the consumers. This link can stimulate the local economy, but in principle it should not constitute a specific means for making money, even if some projects also serve to fund the association or its actions when they are not financially self-sustaining. Slow Food's project of Alliance was meant to further confront this commercial issue and help small producers of Presidia products to compete in a market dominated by the agro-industrial food system.

The Slow Food Presidia label that producers can place on their packaging allows them to call attention to their connection with Slow Food in a material way, showing that the product belongs to an exclusive list, selected by the movement. The project of Alliance between the chefs and the producers of Presidia takes another step in the direction of addressing the economic needs of these producers. It does this by responding to the question of finding more sustainable outlets for Presidia products—one answer being the restaurants. And the positive effects of the Presidia label extend to the restaurateurs as well. At the base of the Alliance, there is a written contract, established between the restaurateurs, the Presidia producers, and Slow Food. The restaurateurs that join, either spontaneously or through the recommendation of a local Slow Food leader, accept to follow the principles of Slow Food and commit to use at least three Presidia products from their region. They also agree to organize a yearly dinner, *"la cena dell'Alleanza"* (the Alliance's dinner), where a small charge (amounting to 5 euros in the 2010s when the project was initiated) added to each cover sold during the evening is transferred to Slow Food to finance new Presidia projects. In exchange, the association furnishes the wine, donated by the wine producers who sponsor the event as a way of gaining visibility. Behind this complex mix of exchanges among different actors, we can see the meeting of diverse interests.

Politics at the Dinner Table

Some restaurateurs use the Alliance project to expand their resources. "We threw ourselves into the project because, in my opinion, it's the real strength of a place, it makes it possible to create networks within the [Slow Food] network," said Roberto supportively. He organized the evening event with four other restaurateurs in his region, all of whom were also in the Guide: "We cook together, in one place, to demonstrate the alliance within the Alliance." But the project is not only aimed at those who are already in the Slow Food network (through the Guide). It seeks to expand the network by including those who, for various reasons, are not included in the Guide but nevertheless reflect the principles of the association. There are the *stellati* (restaurants with Michelin stars) for example, that have prices too high for the Guide's limits, and some restaurants that were simply not well known in the Slow Food network. Teresa, a Slow Food staff member, said,

> The project was also interesting for this reason: the *fiduciari* have been able to include [in the Alliance project] these other restaurants that deserve to be in the Guide but can't be included among the [guide] *Osterie,* for example, because of the price. . . . We have been able to please the restaurateurs that would never have been included in the Guide, and also help them get to know Slow Food better.

This comment is typical of the project's staff and reveals the pragmatism that is one of the hallmarks of the association. Every project, in addition to its own unique objectives, has the fundamental goal of extending the network, not only in terms of memberships but also in order to expand the diffusion of Slow Food's principles.

Then there are other restaurateurs who, like Alessio, were noted in the guide but decided not to participate in the project: "I don't want to be a slave to Slow Food, I only use one Presidia product, and drinks made from other Presidia products. The project is more adapted to those who are in town, who have the possibility to shop around. . . . I use products close by, from good producers." In fact, only half of the restaurateurs (out of a total of about 220) who participate in the project are also included in the Guide. This describes a different set of restaurants that operate close to the principles of Slow Food and are thus able to benefit from the association's image through a sort of *à la carte* engagement. For the same reason, it lends itself to being manipulated by some restaurateurs, and occasionally even by the *fiduciari*. "The Alliance helps those who do good work, giving them visibility, but some rather crafty ones make it onto the wagon as well," said Antonio, a Slow Food staff member. "There are some chefs who make their dishes totally based on Presidia products, which isn't right. If you are going to do it right, you need to use the local, regional products, even if they aren't Presidia. You shouldn't make the entire menu with Presidia products," explained Anna, a local Slow Food volunteer in charge of Presidia in her region.

Sometimes Slow Food appears to be too far out of touch with what has happened with Presidia projects and doesn't notice how some projects' intention has been subverted by certain participants. But the association's leaders are aware of this: "It is impossible to monitor everything, that would be too complicated, the circuit is too large and there are

Slow Food

always things that escape our attention," said Federica, another Slow Food staff member. Nevertheless, some participants have been expelled from the list. Showing me the list, Teresa commented:

> This one, for example, said that he uses multiple Presidia products, but there are only three on the menu; that's not too serious. But the *fiduciario* visited and saw that his meat was imported from Argentina, that he uses endangered bluefin tuna, and no local wines. . . . If you want to be included in the project, you have to show that you are committed.

With its focus on trust, the Alliance project reflects the relational mode that is at the heart of principles expressed by Slow Food. This confidence is awarded from the top, from the leaders of the movement to a restaurateur and his establishment, and it characterizes the ensemble of actions and relationships that are established through the project: relationships with producers, customers, and the movement members. Even if there is a written form, which the restaurateur uses to formalize his commitment to respect a certain number of details, participation in the project is first of all seen as a "moral" commitment. The restaurateur himself describes the characteristics of his establishment and the Presidia products that he uses in his bill of fare. In this agreement—as with the Presidia project in general—Slow Food is not defined as a monitoring body. Verifications are performed by local leaders—*fiduciari* or representatives of the Guide for example— that are tasked with ensuring the establishment's conformity to the criteria of Slow Food and the commitments defined by the Aliance project—particularly when the establishment is not listed in the Guide. When these commitments are not met and the moral contract is broken, the relationship ends, and the restaurant is no longer included in the list of establishments participating in the project.[11] Occasionally there are restaurateurs who manage to escape this type of verification, so the list is not infallible and generally works as a way to show the strength of the project a whole rather than the consistency of each participant.

Even though the project is considered to be a means of ensuring commercial outlets for Presidia producers, the "contractual" obligations for participating are not particularly demanding. The project has helped some producers solidify their ties with restaurateurs in their region, but for others it has not changed their economic situation and the difficulty they have accessing the market. The Alliance also has another objective, that of creating new relationships between Slow Food and the restaurateurs under the heading of "good, clean, and fair" while sensitizing both restaurateurs and consumers about the small producers and local economies that are now at the heart of Slow Food's preoccupations. Indeed, Slow Food does not invest in the Alliance project simply to create new economic spaces for the producers. The project also creates new political spaces for the movement[12]; it constitutes one of the attempts to re-establish the connection between restaurants and activism, and acts as a means of enlarging the movement's base by consolidating and preserving ties with the restaurant world, which remains an important source of support for Slow Food.

Where does wine go?

During the same period that the Alliance between restaurateurs and Presidia producers was created, another project was launched by Slow Food which was also conceived as a space to re-connect the association to the world of production, in this case, wine production. In December 2009, in Montecatini Terme (Italy), Slow Food organized the second Vignerons d'Europa, a wine event in Tuscany that brought together a thousand small wine producers from Italy and other European countries. The first edition had taken place two years earlier in Montpellier, France. The aim of this event was to unite small wine producers around the defense and valorization of their profession. The final meeting's objective was to draft a manifesto, not a Slow Food Manifesto but a *Manifesto dei Vignerons d'Europa*[13] (Manifesto of European Winegrowers). Where did this initiative come from, and what was its relationship with other Slow Food actions related to the wine world?

During the first months of my fieldwork, many Slow Food leaders and staff talked to me about wine as one of the areas where Slow Food was still lagging behind. The steps forward that the association showed in the other fields of action had not been made. Wine seemed to be the sector most resistant to change in evolution of Slow Food, but why? Wine is one of the first products in which Slow Food's founders and leaders invested and mobilized, not only through interventions in favor of quality wine production (since the methanol wine scandal, mentioned in Chapter 2) but also through initiatives to valorize the Langhe wine region and production.[14]

Italian wine "conventions" (*le conventions del vino*), among which Vinitaly is one of the highest and most visible expressions, have been a testing ground and an opportunity to acquire skills for Slow Food leaders and staff. For example, Ilario, who was responsible for the fundraising office, joined Slow Food after helping his friends during the Piedmont wine *conventions*, serving wine in the taste laboratories. Angelo, responsible for fifteen years of the *laboratori del gusto* (taste laboratories) inside the big international events organized by Slow Food, as the Salone del Gusto, Cheese and Slow Fish, started his relationship with Slow Food collaborating to the redaction of another "historical" guide *Vini d'Italia* (Italian wines), published by Slow Food and Gambero Rosso. Wine runs through the entire history of Slow Food and was constantly present during my research: from tastings to dinners, during official meetings or winery visits, and in evenings after work.

Although wine has always been a central object in the association, over the years, it seems to have followed its own path, parallel and not always compatible with Slow Food's other initiatives. "Carlin no longer thinks about wine, now he's only interested in Terra Madre," a staff person told me, "and since he is no longer interested in the wine world, he has abandoned it." The same criticism, that the old themes have become less important and are not among Carlo's priorities anymore, and therefore not among Slow Food's either, is also expressed, discretely, by some of the older generation. A historical employee told me, "Wine represented the territory and the farmer who produced it. The *Atlante dei vini di Langa* is the only book that Carlin claims describes a first image of

Slow Food

Terra Madre. From there, we went around and around and then went back [to producers, making Terra Madre]." From that perspective, the relationship with producers which was presented as a novelty and had taken up so much space through the development of Terra Madre was present from the beginning in the focus on wine producers.

Wine's legacy

The "*Liquidi*" office, as we saw in Chapter 5, is an office that many describe as separate, functioning on its own. The office was marked by the fact that only three of the six employees were permanently in Bra; the others were based in their region, and above, all some of them were essentially tasters, mainly interested in tastings, rather than in the new issues that the association was developing. Gianfranco told me about his work in the publishing house and then in the "*Liquidi*" office:

> The themes of wine had remained asleep. We did the [taste] laboratories, we did the Presidia, but I felt that here, inside [the headquarters] we were considered as the office of the "prostitutes," the office that was useful but that from an ideal and ethical point of view did not maintain the pace, on the contrary, was far behind.

The *Vini d'Italia* guide is published every year and was for a long time a sign of the past bond that Slow Food had with *Gambero Rosso*, which was first a supplement of the daily newspaper *il Manifesto* and then an autonomous magazine and editorial group. The story surrounding this guide and its relationship with Gambero Rosso probably contributed to and certainly reflects the loss of the importance of wine within the association. The director of Gambero Rosso had been one of the signatories of the Slow Food Manifesto and an Arcigola member, although over time the two structures had grown apart. The collaboration for the wine guide, which was a great editorial success, a reference point in the world of enology, and a source of important profits for the two publishing houses, remained in place. But it was also an element of weakness for Slow Food. "We were living this marriage [with Gambero Rosso] with great difficulty," said Gianfranco, who was responsible for the wine office. During a meeting of the *segreteria nazionale* (the Italian national board), he intervened in the discussion around *Vini d'Italia* guide: "The guide had become a game for the prize, and many of Slow Food's interests outside of the [wine] glass lost their value." In reality, the set of principles that guided the visits, tastings, and choices presented other problems. They were left further and further removed from the principles that Slow Food was trying to promote. They remained *degustazioni a catena* (perfunctory chain tastings), without really taking the time to meet the producers or to properly visit the wineries. They partitioned Italian regions (to present wines in the guide) and emphasized mostly the wines and their taste with little consideration for production and vineyards. Moreover, the preparation and editing of the guide, victims of its success, were in fact very distant from the principles of "good, clean, and fair" which the association now defended. This was a criticism evoked by many emerging

Politics at the Dinner Table

voices inside the association, from both the staff and the leaders and even the tasters. Periodically, conflicts of interest appeared in the Gambero Rosso proceedings that could also damage the image of Slow Food, and the guide increasingly came to be seen as an "Achilles heel" in the change of image that the association was trying to achieve. The guide carried on Slow Food's strong and important heritage of wine, but also its contradictions. The cessation of this publishing success was often discussed inside the Italian association offices and inside its political bodies, but it presented multiple risks. Editorial enterprises like the wine guide are in fact economic and communication enterprises at the same time, both important for an association like Slow Food which diffuses ideas and promotes projects but needs to make alliances—political and economic—in order to survive and have a role in the debates about food and wine.

The event organized with small wine producers was part of this context of political and economic reflection regarding the future of the guide and more generally the relationship with the world of wine. The first edition of *Vignerons d'Europa* in 2007 was born as a project of almost secondary importance, and it seemed that nobody was interested in the "*Liquidi*" office, except Gianfranco, as he himself later claimed. The idea of organizing the event in France and linking it to another event that Slow Food France was organizing at the time seemed to give importance to both events. Between the first and second editions, more groups of independent winemakers began to see Slow Food as a possible intermediary to create a network. Gianfranco described the context:

> The practical and utilitarian spirit of Slow Food prevailed: [with Vignerons d'Europa] you create an association of 400 people. External recognition in the field of wine was important, especially at a time when [Slow Food's relationship with] the guide was heading towards a slow death. Since 2004, it had been said every year that this was the last year that the guide would be done together [with Gambero Rosso]: it was a marriage of interests, and there was a danger for Slow Food that this would bring considerable risk, economically, financially, and in relation to wine producers.

Small producers, vignerons, could be allies in Slow Food's change of direction on wine. The meetings with vignerons, according to Gianfranco, helped to take the decision to develop a new guide: "[With Vignerons d'Europa] Slow Food had the opportunity to do something about wine that was not as commercial as the guide." In fact, the meetings were not intended for economic purposes, unlike the guide *Vini d'Italia*, whose focus was now primarily economic and media visibility. Gianfranco continued:

> Wine moves an important amount of money. Living the world of wine from inside [the association] allows us to create events in which we have authority: we can create the Salone [del gusto], the *Banca del vino* (Wine Bank), publish a magazine in which we talk about wine and in which we have advertising/publicity inside. If Slow Food didn't come out with a wine guide it would have lost authority on wine, and Slow Food was born on wine. We feel this role inside the office: we are

Slow Food

probably no longer central to Slow Food, but we have behind us what Carlin and the others started to do; we have the responsibility to continue.

Wine had been and continued to be important within Slow Food beyond the meeting of independent vignerons, and many on the staff felt it is an important legacy to preserve.[15] In the first months of 2009, despite the economic risks involved, Slow Food leaders decided to abandon the collaboration with Gambero Rosso, leaving the guide *Vini d'Italia* to their former partner. Actually, the income Slow Food received from the wine guide *Vini d'Italia* was important but what was most important was the legitimacy and notoriety that the guide provided, the relationship with producers, and the possibility of sponsorships. In the separation, some of the staff members of the *"Liquidi"* office left Slow Food for Gambero Rosso: "They didn't believe in the project [of a new guide] nor in the Vignerons: they were pure tasters and not really political promoters of a movement," another staff member told me. Some months later, I participated in the meeting of the *segreteria nazionale*, in which the Vignerons d'Europa meeting was presented. Gianfranco introduced the progress of his office's first year of work on creating a new wine guide:

> There was a need to break free from the slavery of judgment, making judgments, but more importantly a need to describe the complexities of wine production in order to guide companies toward sustainable, clean agriculture. . . . The idea [now] is that all wineries are visited, with meticulous description and simple judgments, . . . a guide that is not exclusive but inclusive: the idea is to highlight the positive aspects of each vineyard (the 50-year-old vine for example, or the dry-stone wall) so others will try to do better if they see that these things are valued.

The members of the board did not discuss the problems of the previous guide, nor the economic difficulties; they talked about how to build a guide that follows the principles that Slow Food defends today. For example, the criteria for the attribution of the *"chiocciola"* (snail) in the new wine guide should not be the same as the criteria for the attribution of *"bicchieri"* (glasses: 3 glasses were the highest score) in the *Vini d'Italia*. The balance between the terms of the triad "good, clean, and fair" was an object of criticism among the members who disapproved of the weight given to "clean" and "fair," as compared to "good," particularly in the field of wine: they often pointed to the risk that Slow Food's new themes, which were making it a global movement, could completely eliminate the early interests in good food and wine. But Gianfranco reassured the board members that the *"chiocciola"* would not be given to producers simply for being *"clean"*: "they must also make good wine," he told them.

The new guide had to take account of the winery's ecological posture (not adding chemical products), even when not directly related to wine production. The board members examined the kind information that would be included in the file of each producer, discussing the necessary training for the people who would visit the wineries and meet the producers. They animatedly discussed what now counted more, the list of

Politics at the Dinner Table

wines (like in *Vini d'Italia*) or the wineries. Finally a proposal for a title with the future cover was presented: *Uomini, Vigne e Vini* (Men, Vineyards and Wines). No one, in this *segreteria nazionale* composed of 95 percent men, seemed to notice that the title refers only to men. But other titles did emerge from the discussion: "Vineyards and Wineries," and "Winemakers of Italy." The first edition of the Guide was eventually more soberly titled, *Slow Wine. Storie di vita, vigne, vini in Italia* (Slow Wine. Life histories, Vineyards, Wines in Italy), and was published the following year, in 2010 (guide for the year 2011). The preface signed by the president of Slow Food and by the director of the publishing house, affirmed:

> We arrive at [the guide] *Slow Wine* after three, almost four editions of Terra Madre, with the construction of a network that has taken Slow Food's thinking and action much further than in 1987 [the year of the first edition of *Vini d'Italia*].... The Terra Madre network has helped us to understand even better the importance of work in the fields and vineyards, it has made us understand how, in a critical situation for the planet, these producers are able to provide a wealth of knowledge and work in harmony with their territory.... From these experiences is born a guide which does not have at its center just the goodness of wines but it also talks about who makes them and how they are produced, about vineyards and soils, about naturalness and agronomy, about grapes and cultivation methods, about a sustainable future. (C. Petrini and G. Piumatti, in *Slow Wine*, 2010: 7, my translation)

Alongside restaurateurs, winemakers also represent an important support for Slow Food from the early years. The new guide allowed wine to keep up with the rest of the projects carried out by Slow Food in more recent years, projects that are more and more attentive to the environment and to small producers.

The governance of wine

From the point of view of the leaders, the new guide allowed Slow Food to reconnect these worlds with the association's interests, but it remains an associative tool, and around its preparation, the tensions that characterize the relationship between "Bra" and the "territory" re-emerged. One of the first items on the agenda of the *consiglio dei governatori* (governors committee) meeting in Benevento in November 2009 was the presentation of changes inside the publishing house, Slow Food Editore. Among these changes was a new director who came from Gambero Rosso and was a past regional Slow Food governor. This was followed by Riccardo, the President of Slow Food Italia, announcing the decision to publish a new winery guide and a description of the training that the headquarters staff was preparing for the wine collaborators in the various regions. He underlined the importance of the relationship with the "territory" in the compilation of the guides. Like the other Slow Food guides, such as *Osterie d'Italia*, this guide would be compiled with contributions from about two hundred members in the various Italian *condotte*.

Slow Food

But immediately one of the governors intervened, reminding everyone that "the association is the backbone [of Slow Food initiatives]," meaning that local leaders would have to be more involved. Other guides had been perceived as "top-down impositions" with very rigid criteria and "overly tight timelines." "The *fiduciari* felt dispossessed," he said. The governor of another region recalled: "We are people who also work, and we can't keep up with everything. The people from the national should organize a training instead of sending us all these documents to read."

This debate highlighted the contradiction in the communication tools, such as the guides, which need to represent the association being an instrument of dialogue with the *condotte* and membership, and at the same time, follow the professional criteria needed to be credible outside the association. "We will create groups of fiduciaries and managers in the territory," said one of the staff leaders in order to reassure the governors, "the collaboration with the territory and the groups of [local] leaders will be very close." The president specified that no regional president nor any governor will be in charge of the guide: "collaborators must be approved by the editorial staff: the political [bodies] will not 'stick their noses' inside the work of the editorial staff, neither I, nor the regional presidents. We discuss the general approach, but if the '*chiocciola*' does not go to the winery that has been our friend for a long time, patience." A historical leader and president of a major wine-producing region added, "But when the head of the guide comes to my region, I want to be informed. Experts must take into account that their behaviors also reflect on the association." A governor brought the discussion back to the emotional dimension: "If we put our heart and soul into it, we can't fail. Producers are waiting for a breakthrough to regain a focus on their work. It takes good faith, a good attitude, and a personal pact with the project." The discussion became increasingly animated around the question of whether or not fiduciaries or governors could be locally responsible for the guide. The *fiduciari* were said to be too tied to their local networks, the regional presidents, too absorbed in the governance of the association. In the end, the assembly decided to keep a "soft position" without fixing any rigid rule.

Although projects like this one, and the *Guida Osterie*, add work to the local leaders and volunteers, they are important ways to create or maintain contacts with producers in their own areas and maintain the local legitimacy that Slow Food allows them to have. The new guide would not only have an effect on the image of the association as a whole but also on the local leaders who contribute to the existence of the association in the regions and *condotte*. "Some people in the territory still reason according to the criterion of companies that are friends of Slow Food and companies that are not friends, which is to say they do not support (economically) the association," a member of the staff from the "*Liquidi*" office told me during the governors' meeting. A few months after working on the new guide, he made these comments:

> Wine guide should only be done by professionals. It is very difficult for our work if the guide ends up in the hands of the *fiduciari*: you turn into a compiler and you lose all the decision-making power. But wine is not an *osteria* you go to visit: you must have much more important skills, tasting is a much more important

experience. We might taste 120 wines a day, you have to be trained, you have to be prepared, you have to be at a higher level than a normal *fiduciario* or member. The choice of the regional manager has been complicated but we succeeded. They had to be legitimate referents from the point of view of the association but not necessarily referents of the association.

The professionalism of the staff has developed through their work in Slow Food. The association's projects and events shape the image of Slow Food and, at the same time, the skills and practices of the staff. But once again, the results of this professionalism can appear in opposition to the volunteerism of local leaders, who are not professionals, but whom Bra needs to supervise. Finding a balance in terms of power, legitimacy, and who has the right to do what, is the result of long negotiations involving all levels of the association.

What happens, when Slow Food's messaging regarding wine leaves the confines of its offices and the *condotte* takes on the mantle of a movement and ventures into the world of producers on an international level? The *Vignerons d'Europa* is a good example.

Vignerons translations

The staff of the "*Liquidi*" office think of *Vignerons d'Europa* as an event that is similar to Terra Madre but smaller, with a very limited number of interventions from Slow Food staff and leaders. "So the producers feel that it is their own event," said Gianfranco, the head of the office, when speaking to the members of the national board in October 2009. At the opening of the meeting, in Montecatini, Tuscany, he presented the event and suggested that one of the goals should be a document discussed and written by the producers themselves: the vineyard owners and small wine producers should feel personally involved and see the manifesto as something of their own creation.

After two days of exchanges and debates, some thirty delegates, selected from the assembly of winegrowers present at *Vigneron d'Europa*, drew up a list of key points around which to structure the Manifesto, striving to account for the diversity of situations represented by the participants in the meeting. The discussion started and organic production was at the heart of the debates: "Let's not make the mistake of setting rules for ourselves; let's not build cages for ourselves," said one of the producers, "Organic and biodynamic will come; we must not be set against each other" added another. One of the French winegrowers insisted on the need to find a consensus on organic: "We must at least say that sustainability means not using synthetic molecules or chemicals." Another winegrower warned his colleagues about the risks that such a decision would entail: "It would mean cutting ourselves off from three quarters of the assembly [of winegrowers]." Another answered, "We have to accompany them, to give time to the others to grow."

The participating Slow Food staff and staff leaders listened to the discussion, suggesting key words and trying to find common points among the opinion. Finally, the delegates met in four small groups to translate the Manifesto from the Italian draft into each of the official languages of the meeting: Spanish, French, and German. However,

Slow Food

these groups did not produce strict translations of the drafted Italian text: without having planned it explicitly before the translation, each group slightly adapted the initial text so that the winegrowers of each country could recognize themselves in it and the political authorities could understand it. The French group was by far the most animated: the winemakers tried repeatedly to modify the content of the Manifesto, and Slow Food staff tried to control the process, which sometimes got out of hand.

What was happening with the vignerons was not very different from what I had observed for months among the Slow Food France board of directors. This episode provides an insight also into the heterogeneous world of small wine producers. Some were more avant-garde (natural wine, biodynamic, organically farmed vineyards), and others were resisting for fear of excluding their confreres or being themselves excluded. Typical of the Slow Food world, the final text in four languages was the result of negotiations and confrontations between different cultural, political, and social contexts and practices. Despite the fact that the association seemed to lag behind on biodynamic, natural, and organic wine issues, this initiative allowed Slow Food leaders to create new alliances, even including the "rebellious" natural wine producers. These independent vignerons contributed to the consolidation of Slow Food's (new) legitimacy in the field of wine and its image of an international movement acting politically in the wine sector.

Notes

1. Except for the restaurateurs cited as examples, the names are pseudonyms (see the question of confidentiality in Chapter 1).

2. The "campanaro" is the church bell-ringer. The name is a reference to the fact that the *osteria* is located in the courtyard and ancient presbytery of a sixteenth-century church.

3. Until 2014 the price was not to exceed around 35 euros. During the years prices have increased slowly. After the health crisis in 2020 and 2021 and the prolonged closure of dining establishments in Italy, prices have increased, and the guide's information has been adapted to the context.

4. The *Osterie d'Italia* guide reports on about 1,700 establishments, presenting them by region. Approximately 200 *osterie* are noted with the chiocciola in each edition.

5. San Marco dei Cavoti was my fieldwork throughout the 1990s. At the time, I was interested in the agricultural and industrial economy, the links between local politics and the economy, and networks of social and economic exchange. U Magazzeo had not yet opened. The area where the *osteria* is located was an old area of the town, first abandoned and then renovated beginning in the mid-1990s.

6. In the local dialect, "u magazzeo" is in Italian "il magazzino," meaning the warehouse or storehouse, which was the previous function of the building where the restaurant is located.

7. As geographers Miele and Murdoch have analyzed the aesthetic dimension of attention to food and food quality in some *osterie* linked to Slow Food in Tuscany (2002, 2004).

8. For an analysis of activism among restaurateurs in another Italian region (Sardinia), see Counihan (2019). On the subject of consumer engagement and ethical dimensions of

economic practices, see among others Dubuisson-Quellier (2009), Carrier, Luetchford (2012).

9. They are still noted with the *chiocciola* in the *Guida Osterie* 2022.

10. Since 2014, the presence of a kitchen garden is indicated in the guide along with other criteria that have been added over time such as vegetarian cuisine.

11. Up until 2012, a restaurant's participation in the Alliance project was only noted on the Slow Food website. At the end of 2012, it also began to be noted in the new *Presidia* guide.

12. Over the years, the project has expanded to include Ark of Taste products, and from Italy it has been extended to other countries that have Presidia projects.

13. The French word *vignerons* was used, even in Italian.

14. Folco Portinari, writer and essayist, author of the *Manifesto dello Slow Food* came from the wine world and culture (he was the son of an enologist). Among the anthropological studies on the wine world, see Ulin (1996), Garcia-Parpet (2009), Black and Ulin (2013), Demossier (2018).

15. In 2003, for example, in the Agenzia di Pollenzo, the same buildings that host the University of Gastronomic Sciences, Slow Food promoted the creation of the *Banca del Vino*, a cooperative society devoted to conservation, promotion, and education in the wine sector. In these wine bank cellars people can visit the reserves where producers "deposit" high-quality bottles of wine, to be stored. The visitors can taste wines and attend trainings: wines can be purchased, but the museum and the dimension of learning seem equally important.

Photo 11 Visitors and Presidia exhibitors in the "Via dei Presidi," Cheese, Bra (Italy), 2017. ©Franco Zecchin.

CHAPTER 11
REAL AND IMAGINED ECONOMIES AND POLITICS IN ACTION
TERRA MADRE, SALONE DEL GUSTO, AND CHEESE

The entire economic system is experiencing an historic crisis. Many of us are worried, but at the same time, there is a sense of liberty. It is time for this shameful system to come to an end, for the speculative bubble to collapse. . . . An economy based on subsistence and respectful of nature will save the planet from an insane market economy.

Foreshadowing the spirit of the days to come, Carlo Petrini used these words to open the 2008 Terra Madre. He often crafts his speeches in a context of current events, and this one was no exception, being situated in the middle of the emerging financial crisis of the time. Terra Madre is one of the occasions that allows the Slow Food President to explain his vision of the economy and of the economic role to be played by the world's small producers that gather in the city of Turin to participate in the event. Terra Madre is one of the largest international meetings organized by Slow Food, along with the Salone del Gusto, also in Turin, Slow Fish in Genoa, and Cheese in the city of Bra.[1] Like the relationship with restaurants and the Presidia, or the relationship with small wine producers, these events are designed to be both political and economic. But what kind of economy do the movement's leaders and members defend through these events? In this chapter I examine the economic stakes, practices, and imaginaries that emerge within Slow Food events and also examine their links to the political objectives of the movement.

"Fare Terra Madre," doing Terra Madre

Terra Madre was created in 2004 from one of the numerous ideas of Carlo Petrini. The principle was to invite small farmers and producers to Turin—ten thousand was the initial objective of the project—to share their experiences and encourage them to create a worldwide network. Although it was initially seen as a crazy idea, even by Carlo's closest collaborators, the idea gradually came together and took form.

During several days at the end of October in Turin, a flood of buses and people descend upon the Oval, a sports structure built for the 2006 Olympics.[2] At each edition, this space has welcomed roughly four thousand producers from throughout the world to discuss food policy, the future of the food system, and the modes of sustainable production.

Over time, Terra Madre has evolved from a biennial meeting bringing together farmers, fishermen, cooks, researchers, and all the actors of the agro-food supply defending sustainable practices and food biodiversity to become a point of reference that links the movement's diverse events in various places and reflects important changes inside Slow Food. In a book using the event's name as its title,[3] Carlo Petrini described it thusly:

> Terra Madre is a network of communities, hence of people, real people who work with food and for food. . . . Terra Madre is participatory democracy and real, local, natural, economy. . . . Terra Madre is a political subject. . . . Above all, Terra Madre is a project with long-term, maybe limitless goals. It is a series of short but decisive steps toward a new humanitarianism, a renaissance, which like the Renaissance, begins with beauty. By beauty I mean good, clean, and fair food, our villages and landscapes, not to mention our relationship with nature, which generates beauty and teaches us how to enjoy it. Terra Madre is a project with boundless capacity to build and to create. . . . Terra Madre has to be free from ties with politics and economics, with the system of power that govern the world today. (Petrini 2010: 149–50)

The notions of slow and pleasure as espoused by the leader of the movement have taken on a different connotation than the one found at the beginning of Slow Food's history. It is no longer, or less, about the conviviality and pleasure of dining together, of good wine and good food. It has evolved into the pleasure of a relationship with "nature," the pleasure of food that respects the environment and the producers. This pleasure associates itself with the idea of "responsibility." Terms like "community networks," "political subjects," and "innovative projects" are used in Petrini's book and more largely by leaders and staff in their communications to define Terra Madre. The semantic shift from the image of an association to that of a movement accompanies and stimulates the transformations in Slow Food and has become more obvious in the association's recent history. Terra Madre is both a result of this phenomenon and a participant in it. At the core of this firmly structured association with memberships and reports and complex political issues, Terra Madre represents the other, non-structured side of the movement, the network that appears to have neither a president nor a guiding system of statutes. Although this new network is orchestrated and promoted by Slow Food International and its president, and managed by volunteers and members from various *convivia*, the association's founders maintain that it must remain independent from the hierarchies of the Slow Food machine. For several years now, Slow Food members have affirmed the message imparted by the movement's leaders, "Slow Food is what we are, and Terra Madre is what we do; Terra Madre is our project."

"*Chi semina utopia raccoglie realtà*" (Those who sow utopia harvest reality), said Carlo at the first Terra Madre in 2004. In the words of the president of Slow Food, Terra Madre and the meeting of small producers from around the world represent the concretization of the utopian vision that the leaders of the movement promote. Terra Madre is considered as Slow Food's political front line, serving to legitimize Slow Food as a political movement and an actor in the field of food politics. It projects that political image even more than the initiatives analyzed in the previous chapters and could be described as a synthesis of them. In any case, Terra Madre undoubtedly has a concrete effect on the people who participate in it. It is imagined and performed as a meeting space, creating a network of exchange and experience between worlds that have neither had the habit nor even the possibility of communicating with each other. In the five days following Terra Madre's opening, the spaces created in the interior of the Oval become the site of dozens of meetings, round tables, and workshops—eminently political—where agriculture and livestock farmers, and fishermen, invited as delegates from countries around the world participate in debates and discussions. Attending the event does not leave participants indifferent, even mere observers.

A political performance

The opening evening, with some variations from one year to another, sets the tone of the event. Usually, the general secretary of Slow Food International starts the meeting with the power of numbers attesting to the expansion and importance of Slow Food: in 2008, for example, there were 4,783 delegates (including producers, cooks, academics) representing 153 countries and 1,652 food communities. These statistics have increased with each Terra Madre and add to the list of numbers that Slow Food staff and leaders use in their communication tools, in their public speeches, and at meetings of political bodies within the association. At the rostrum of the Palaisozaki, a succession of political representatives rise to proclaim their support for the event. During the event, both Italian and international politicians communicate their positions and declare their relationship with the movement or certain initiatives it promotes. In 2004, Prince Charles of Wales intervened in the closing ceremony. In 2006, before Vandhana Shiva, one of Slow Food's vice presidents, the President of the Italian Republic Giorgio Napolitano gave an opening address outlining the association's new principles:

> Only a grand and fascinating objective, like the one you present with Terra Madre can put together peasants and farmers, chefs and gourmets, workers and university researchers. You are right to remind us of the value of "food communities" that represent a concrete response to the risks exacerbated by forms of intensive agriculture and by a food system inattentive to the specificities of local productions and the quality of products. A new perspective of agriculture can lead us to improved values and models of consumption, respect for the environment, and working conditions, for all of society.

In the same year (2006), the president of the Italian Chamber of Deputies, Fausto Bertinotti (*Partito della rifondazione comunista*, Communist Refoundation Party), and the Minister of Foreign Affairs at the time, Massimo D'Alema (*Partito democratico di sinistra,* Democratic Left Party), added to the parade of participating politicians when

Slow Food

they gave closing speeches that followed the five days of Terra Madre. The presence of these left-wing politicians was a reflection of the fact that the center left had just won the elections against Silvio Berlusconi's *Forza Italia* Party and Romano Prodi was Prime Minister. Two years later, Berlusconi was elected again and the Minister of Agriculture passed to the *Lega Nord* (Northern League, a right-wing party). Adjustments to the political current meant that that year's opening address went to the Minister of Agriculture and Environmental Policy, Luca Zaia (*Lega Nord*), followed by the President of the Piedmont Region, Mercedes Besso, and by the mayor of Turin, Sergio Chiamparino, both belonging to the Democratic Left Party. Describing the same edition of Terra Madre 2006, Adrian Peace (2008) uses the expression "political theater." Even if not as radical as the perspectives presented by the international president of Slow Food, the politicians, particularly in respect to links with global problems such as the financial crisis or food insecurity, all reiterated the principles and contributions of Slow Food in the domains of agriculture, product quality and biodiversity, and specific positions against genetically modified organisms (GMO) or in favor of organic agriculture.

What were all these politicians and institutional representatives with diverse political affiliations doing at Terra Madre? Why did politicians with such different sensibilities speak out in favor of agriculture, biodiversity, and small producers on the planet? Terra Madre seems to be a must-attend event to which few politicians dare to ignore an invitation, and their support of the event has not been limited to their presence. In the years described, the Italian Ministry of Agriculture and the Ministry of Foreign Affairs, along with the Piedmont Region and the Turin Municipality, were among the public funders of the event. Politicians are also well aware that Terra Madre, like any major event organized by Slow Food, constitutes a political platform and presents an occasion for high visibility in the media. Slow Food leaders see the political interchange at the rostrum of this large event as necessary to the economic and political support for these events and the movement itself. The success of the event allows Slow Food to amplify and spread its philosophy.

At the same time, the critical press sometimes portrays this proximity to political parties—judged to be far removed from Slow Food sensibilities, and above all, from the sensibilities of most of the "historical" leaders—as an example of opportunism or a departure from the movement's principles. Nevertheless, having observed this succession of politicians on the stage of events organized by Slow Food for several years, one gets the impression that the lifespan of governments and political alliances in Italy is very short, while that of Slow Food as a political actor outside of political parties, is more enduring and growing, at least in those years. The movement's actions were reinforced year after year and Slow Food leaders continually refined their speeches with elements from other movements or other intellectuals, enlarging their audience and influence among a diverse array of political and intellectual actors.

Slow Food's political connections do not stop at the borders of Italy. In 2010 Dacian Ciolos, the European Commissioner of Agriculture (from 2010 to 2014), took a turn at the podium of Terra Madre. The Commissioner also spoke at the opening of the movement's International Congress, which occurred in 2012 at the same time and in the same exhibition center (Lingotto Fiere) as Terra Madre and the Salone del Gusto. The presence of the European Commissioner was a sign of the importance that Slow Food attaches to the European political arena. Slow Food leaders considered Dacian Ciolos to be the first commissioner to take an interest in small producers and therefore present him as a privileged interlocutor in view of the CAP (Common Agricultural Politics of European Union) reform that was preparing for 2013.

Diversity's oxymoron

Terra Madre unfolds between two poles: one, the representatives of politics and institutions and the other, the representatives of small producers from all over the world. The Terra Madre spaces are progressively invaded by a colorful and cosmopolitan throng, many producers dress in native garb, the place comes alive with diverse sounds and faces. The president of Slow Food, in some of his public speeches, suggests that the Terra Madre network is like a "karstic river," slowly flowing underground and surfacing every couple of years. Each edition, during the opening evening, after the official speeches, it becomes the turn of representatives from the "food communities" who briefly take the stand in their native languages to share their experiences and the reason for their participation in the meeting. At most of the Terra Madre editions that I attended, there was a well-known Italian TV presenter who took the microphone, to introduce the succeeding groups and speakers at the podium. The delegations then marched by the hundreds with their native flags and "traditional" costumes in a grand display of human diversity. It was a veritable parade of languages, music, and folklore, that highlights groups from the Global South representing small producers from Asia, Africa, Oceania, and America, but also including those from the European countries in which Slow Food is active. Surrounding them, thousands of people equipped with multilingual headphones listened to the solemn speeches and announcements.

The spectacular effect of this opening with the music and parade of traditional costumes produces moments of shared emotion. I remember the typical ovations following speeches by Carlo or examples of disapproval like the booing and backs turned against the video sent by the center-right Berlusconi government's Minister of Foreign Affairs, Franco Frattini, in 2008.[4] The Italian participants wouldn't pass up an opportunity to express their disagreement (the dominant political sensibility of the participants remains decidedly to the left wing). According to Peace, the event produced "a sense of intercontinental unity" and "many present were emotionally and deeply immersed in this collective happening, which gave real substance to the claims of global interconnectedness that had circulated previously" (2008: 33).

Kindled by the speeches and the sensation of participating in a unique moment, the emotion seemed to touch not only the thousands of delegates and hundreds of volunteers but also the event's coordinating team from Bra whose members, phone in hand, stood discreetly in the wings of the stage. Each time I was there, I observed the staff members from headquarters, moving from space to space, following a script they may have repeated many times but one that always remained dense with unexpected events and problems to be solved at the last moment. After weeks of growing stress, the tension was released: the show had begun. The occasionally strange demands—like one to quickly find fifty megaphones for directing groups of delegates to buses waiting to transport them to their lodging—had almost all been met. The department charged with organizing events up until a few days before the opening had done its job. Everything seemed to be functioning and under control.

From one year's event to another, the network of Terra Madre grows with new actors. In 2006, the second edition, two new categories were added: one for cooks working with products from agriculture and fishing, and another for researchers who work on food issues. The presence of cooks marked the renewed effort by Slow Food to highlight links between the world of production and that of restaurants. And their addition put even more emphasis on the aspect of a political alliance rather than a simple economic alliance. Taking advantage of a highly visible, mediatized setting, it exposed the links between Slow Food and restaurateurs outside of the familial space of the *osterie*. The sight of chef's white hats, joyfully tossed in the air in various short films about Terra Madre produced by the association or in the images that documented the event, seems to proclaim the strength of these links.

Adding a different element, the presence of academic researchers is related to the "research" and "teaching" dimensions that Slow Food began developing through the University of Gastronomic Sciences created by the association (in concert with a number of academics, intellectuals, and business personalities) in 2004.[5] These dimensions corresponded to the growing importance that education was taking among Slow Food's objectives and engagements, and also reflected the important role of students and graduates in spreading Slow Food's message. The presence of academic researchers can be interpreted both as a way of forging links and of showing that the movement is expanding a dialogue with the world of research, but also that this dialogue takes place under the umbrella of Slow Food and on the themes that the movement already defends. But this presence can also be seen under the light of the occasionally ambiguous relationship that the association has had with the intellectual community. From the beginning, numerous intellectual figures and journalists made up the circle of Slow Food friends.

In 2008 the Terra Madre circle expanded further to include invitations to still other actors: There were the producers of textile fibers and musicians who at first glance did not seem to be directly related to food issues but added other dimensions of the local cultures first represented by the small producers. There was also the effort to include "young" people and students that represent the future in Slow Food's vision. Then in 2010, the attention turned to local populations, women, the elderly, and all the minorities that the movement claims to defend. The representatives from all over the world, along with their "ethnicity" (which was highlighted in the theatrical setting and native costumes), allowed Slow Food leaders to draw attention to other categories of "forgotten" people— women, elders, indigenous populations, and youth—that are not accounted for (or listened to) by the lobbyists and decision-makers who act in international arenas. These "peasants" and minorities of the Southern and Northern hemispheres are conceived as actors in a new "humanism" as well as drivers of change in the economic imbalances that govern food production and distribution.

What struck me, from the very first edition I attended, was the melting pot of people from different worlds, from Finland to Kenya, Japan to Brazil, people who were really exchanging ideas and discussing where they came from and what they were doing. These discussions ranged from global political issues to minute professional techniques: the weight of multinational corporations or land grabbing, prolonged drought and other visible consequences of climate change, fishing techniques or solutions to protect a crop from certain insects. A myriad of discussions took place not only in the dozens of conference rooms organized inside the Oval but simply standing in the huge lunch line, or seated at large tables set up for impromptu encounters, or while relaxing in a corner waiting for the next meeting. People exchanged addresses, information, and pieces of knowledge. Even from one edition to the next, people who had met two years earlier would meet again at the next Terra Madre. In individual rooms created for the event, there were meetings that resembled other forums in which speeches followed one after another and were translated simultaneously into four or five other languages, but what was most interesting was the swarm of people moving from one space to another, conversing with strangers and exchanging experiences as they circulated between the Oval and the adjacent spaces where the Salone del Gusto takes place.

More than six hundred volunteers, predominantly Slow Food members, come from all over Italy to help organize and offer assistance to delegates during each Terra Madre biennial event. Some of the members from the Piedmont region open their homes as accommodations for delegates. Each evening, after the exchanges of personal, political, and economic ideas and experiences, the area surrounding the Oval is invaded by crowds of delegates. Megaphones fill the air with the tired voices of Slow Food staff—those from the *Centro Studi*, or from the offices of the International Foundation—working to assemble groups of delegates. The cars are packed with delegates and head for Turin's surrounding towns and villages where the delegates are housed. Joseph, member of the national board of Slow Food France and one of the biggest critics of the policies of Slow Food international as well as those of his own national association, often recalled the warm reception the French delegates received among the families of Fossano, a small town 70 kilometers from Turin. In his opinion, the bonds established during those convivial evenings spent together represented the best part of the Slow Food network.

Food communities and food economies

The event functions as a collective ritual that serves to create and secure links between delegates themselves, between Slow Food members and producers worldwide, and also between the members and the headquarters. But the event is also a moment that makes it possible to showcase evolutions in Slow Food philosophy, to announce new objectives and promote initiatives—such as the one that financed a thousand vegetable gardens in Africa, "*1000 orti in Africa*," an objective that was increased to ten thousand in 2014—that benefit from Slow Food's investments. Terra Madre is at the heart of the changes that the movement has undergone in recent years, especially the changes oriented toward environmental and ecological themes and portraying a more utopian dimension in the ideals expressed by Slow Food: bringing the producers and consumers of the food chain closer together and putting together a network of all the actors in local economies around the world to better understand how to improve the food supply system.

From the perspective of the movement's leaders, this relationship with the producers must be nourished in both directions. Members should provide an example by changing their habits and redirecting their attention. They are actors in food choices, and also active actors in the network; rather than remaining simple consumers, they must become "co-producers." This word has a performative value: it reflects the movement's new interests, and it encourages the members to move in the same direction, even if the "co" prefix itself is not enough to make the objectives and actual practices fuse and operate as one.

Organizers want Terra Madre to show that the movement has reoriented, that it no longer reflects the elitist image that Slow Food continues to hold in certain circles—that of an association composed of people seeking only to buy and consume expensive, high-quality food. It is not an accident that Terra Madre is the event most frequently cited by Slow Food members: the event has changed the way many of the long-term members and historical leaders see the world of food and changed their sense of membership, the network, and the exchange. For those who subscribe primarily to the ideals and objectives that Slow Food represents, participating in Terra Madre has given real sense to previously abstract ideas. For members who are far removed from the "center" of Slow Food, this gathering provides an occasion to appreciate all the dimensions of the movement, and be involved at the heart of current issues.

Along with Terra Madre, a new term appeared in the Slow Food vocabulary: "food communities," defined on the website as a "group of small-scale producers and others, united by the production of a particular food, and closely linked to a geographic area. Food community members are involved in small-scale and sustainable production of quality products."[6] The term is difficult to grasp, even for those who work within the central core of the association at the headquarters in Bra. For some it is too vague, although it makes it possible to speak about actors from diverse local economies by putting the accent on the dimension of a social "community" involved in food. This perspective recognizes "communities" of objectives woven around the productive activities and "imagined" economies directly related to an ideal past that never experienced the damage seen in the present (see in this regard the "imagined communities" of Anderson 1991). Slow Food leaders see this damage as being caused by the anomalies of capitalism, of industrial production, and the irresponsible exploitation of resources. The concept of "food communities" allows Slow Food members to imagine coherent entities, living and working in a harmonious relationship with "Mother Earth"—peasants and small producers all over the world, directly linked to this idealized past free from the damage of capitalism and industrial production, and the irresponsible exploitation of natural resources. In this slightly mythologized image of peasant culture, working the land often appears as superior to other modes of resource use, such as those of nomadic populations, which are often overlooked or interpreted as belonging to a past without agriculture. The increasingly assertive use of the term "peasant" ("contadino" in Italian) is part of this transformation of the Slow Food's philosophy and the emphasis that the association leaders put on the "movement" dimension. They have used the term from the beginning, but today it has taken on a new political nuance in the initiatives promoting small producers and in the agricultural mobilizations and networks such as AMAP (Lamine 2008; Siniscalchi 2019b), the *Réseau semences paysannes* (Peasant Seed Network, Demeulenaere 2013), and the union confederation, *Confédération paysanne*, in France (Heller 2013), or the international network of *La Via Campesina* (see Thivet 2014, 2019; Narotzky 2016). Slow Food leaders have defined small producers and peasants from the Global South (and Europe) as a potential force for change in the world, even if it is slow in coming.

Parkins and Craig (2009) participated in Terra Madre 2004 and analyzed the event in light of convention theory:

> [Terra Madre] is not only an opportunity for marginalized producers to meet and share information but it also represents an explicit attempt to lengthen alternative food networks, strengthening them through a process of articulating alternative food producers with new markets and consumers as well as attempting to establish supportive political and policy contexts.... [thus enabling] sometimes very isolated food communities to participate in global flows of information and knowledge, as well as commodity exchange. (2009: 84)

In their view, Terra Madre gives great visibility to small producers who are overlooked in international agendas and political arenas. They also point out that the originality of these events lies not so much in the clarity of the political project that Slow Food formulates as in the very fact that it creates an open space for the elaboration of "possible new political imaginaries" (2009: 85).

The moral economy

The term "food community," as an ideal, also has performative value: the peasants and artisans of food production who make up these "food communities" around the world emerge every two years in Turin, helping to legitimize and put a human face on the expanding network and themes launched by Slow Food. Peace (2008: 38) underlines the process of "mystification" in the notion of "community" as well as that of the small-scale independent producer who has a direct relationship with the soil and seeds.

While both mystification and reification are certainly present, the term "food community" functions as an elastic term. Its malleability makes it possible to use less restrictive standards (less restrictive than the Presidia, for example) to identify individuals and groups who participate in the same production system, or who produce the same product, such as *Cappero Selargino* (Selargius' caper) producers in Sardinia or the women who produce Argan oil in Morocco. At the core of an association still perceived as an association of consumers, it became necessary to include producers, according to the Slow Food leaders. But they cannot be considered simply as protagonists in an "exotic exhibition," as the Terra Madre event is sometimes described by critics. As part of this expansion into the world of producers, the "food communities" are more than just participants in the network and the Terra Madre event; they are also granted a specific Slow Food membership—a collective membership for all the producers within a particular food community.

Terra Madre represents the evolution of the movement's philosophy toward a redefinition of the limits of human action and the morality of the economy. "Good, clean, and fair" become the parameters of this moral economy, a new imagined economy, rooted in the past but endowed with an ability to navigate new and evolving political fields. Slow Food leaders' image of a "moral economy" is not so far removed from the meaning some scholars have given this notion (Thompson 1971; Scott 1976; Edelman 2005; Fassin 2009).[7] It should guarantee fair working conditions to all producers and at the same time, good food accessible to all. More than good products, Terra Madre defends "good" economies which are "moral" economies that represent a utopian perspective of the future (as in the case of the "human economy" envisioned by Hart, Laville, and Cattani 2010).[8] "The moral economy is one which creates value by respecting the environment and humans," the Slow Food president often declares. This notion is transformed by Slow Food leaders into a political goal. In this sense "moral" synthesizes "good, clean, and fair" and the economy presents an ideal and moral order. Defending legality against fraud, corruption, and mafias in order to avoid the exploitation of workers is part of the same framework. During another event, the Italian Slow Food Congress in 2010, Diana, a governor from Lombardia, drew members' attention to the links between legality and prices:

> What does food have to do with legality? When we speak of food we are speaking of the mafia. In this field, our choices mark the beginning of the anti mafia struggle. I should know that the lowest price is too high because it has already been paid for by others. . . . If I buy tomatoes and I know that they carry the taste of the blood of Senegalese workers killed in Calabria, I no longer want them. . . . Eating local is eliminating illegality from the field. We can do it.

Camillo, a Sicilian Slow Food governor, took up the idea, declaring: "I like this portrait of saving the planet joyfully. . . . But I wish to speak here of the pleasure of legality. . . . Dealing with legality and the anti mafia struggle is part of our approach. . . . We are anti-mafia, and we are gourmets at the same time."

In this new context, the notion of "slow" has become more and more complex with new significations: the sense of slow allowing the discovery of taste and pleasure in dining that was the early mark of the movement combines with an imagined slow economy respectful of the earth and rhythms of the seasons. From behind the relatively inoffensive notion of slow appears a more aggressive approach which alludes to the fight against the forms of liberalism—in the European sense of the word—represented by seed patents, land grabbing, the privatization of common goods, nuclear power, and nonrenewable energy. Nevertheless, even though the message of Slow Food leaders now reflects a political ecology common to other ecological movements, it maintains the specificities claimed by its leaders. The focus on food in particular, la *centralità del cibo* ("the centrality of food," the title of the international congress document in 2012), remains the means of establishing the link between the environment, the products, and the producers.

Terre Madre's accent on the world of producers in its current form and with the voices it now embraces, however, is also at the origin of a certain distancing among some of the oldest members. In their eyes Terra Madre symbolizes a radical transformation of the movement that has abandoned familiar modes of action. "Before, we worked with local farmers; we could evaluate the positive effects. Now, that is part of the past. The areas where we were productive have been abandoned, and we've headed into a vague, unknown realm," Thomas, a former local leader in France said to me. Of course, among the hundreds of small producers, there are also small farmers from Italy and European countries, but statements like this show one of the movement's contradictions. This dichotomy is seen in the different motivations for membership: there are members who are interested in food and good meals, and there are others who talk about the food system and politics; members who primarily organize diners, and others who undertake less traditional responsibilities; the more nostalgic and the more militant. Louis, another French former leader, explained it to me this way: "In Slow Food, there is an accumulation of objectives that do not make the previous ones disappear. Members come from all walks of life, from friends who come to eat to those who are there because of their activism." These complex worlds, often distant and in tension with each other, reflect the internal contradictions of the association. And trying to hold these worlds together is a challenge for Slow Food staff leaders.

The Salone del Gusto, a political space or an economic space?

Even if commercial elements are never far away, Terra Madre appears very different from Slow Food's other organized events, where the commercial and promotional dimensions occupy a dominant place. The Salone del Gusto is the oldest of Slow Food's organized events and probably the one that the media and general public most associate with the movement. Today it has the appearance of an enormous food fair. It attracts roughly 250,000 visitors over the course of five days and is the subject of numerous articles in the national and international press. During those five days, hundreds of producers, mostly from Italy but not exclusively, set up booths to promote and sell their products, considered by the Salone organizers to be emblems of quality food. Installations representing the association's activities, such as education, tasting games for children, encounters with

Slow Food

writers, the Slow Food publishing house, and Slow Food University, are located in the buildings occupied by the fair.

Between 1996 and 2014, the Salone del Gusto took place just next door to the Oval, in the Lingotto Fiere pavilions which before 1982 had housed the Fiat factory. On Saturday afternoon the crowds are so large that it can be difficult to navigate any of the three pavilions from one end to the other. "The Salone is the many faceted mirror of the complex association that is Slow Food. The Salone is Slow Food's, and for this reason the Salone contains everything: it is linked to the associative networks, to the [national and international] structure, to the publishing house, to the Presidia," said a member of the staff working in the office organizing the event.

Thousands of wines are consumed in the large wine pavilion where the *laboratori del gusto* (tasting laboratories) initiate wine and food lovers in the art of tasting and in pairings (between wine and cheese for example, or beers and salami). The titles of many of the workshops show that the staff in charge of their elaboration also consider them to be "workshops of ideas"; and the irony of some titles harkens back to experiments with this formula at the first edition of the Salone in 1996. Giuliano, a historical leader and past vice president, reminisced about the Salone of 1994, considered the "year zero," which was held in Milan before being moved to Turin. At that first event, they had to invent the name and content of about fifty taste workshops:

> We locked ourselves in a house, me, Carlo, Gianni and a journalist, and we shared the task by each inventing 10 titles with ten lines explaining them. That's where we invented the first titles: *culatello se non è bello* [culatello ham, if it's not beautiful], *porci con le ali* [pigs with wings, from the title of a novel of the same name]. It was the first time that food was communicated in this way. Language was a very important thing. . . . In the workshop there had to be not only the expert who tells, but also the producer, the artisan. We had sensed a reasoning: the idea of exchange and communication [on food] didn't exist before. It was highly innovative and made a difference.

The first Terra Madre in 2004 took place in a building located further away, the Lingotto Fiere. Then in the following three editions (2006, 2008, and 2010), Terra Madre and the Salone del Gusto were held in two adjacent, if distinct, spaces. This proximity exposed the contrast between the two events, which explicitly or implicitly, and each in its own manner, embodied the otherness and variety (of food and people) in a microcosm of diversity. Food was at the heart of both events, but their approaches to the world of food, and access to it, seemed almost contradictory and left them vulnerable to a dose of criticism along with the praise they received from the national and international press. On one side were those who buy and taste, who have the means to buy entry tickets and pay for the *laboratori del gusto* (taste laboratories) or the glasses of wine[9]; on the other side were the small producers, mostly from the Global South, that are at the heart of the debates on food sovereignty, the environment, and local economies: The commercial dimension, the market and exchange of goods versus the commitment, the debate, and the exchange of ideas. Two places and two worlds, separate but with a common border. This sensation was accentuated by the fact that, prior to 2010, the delegates of Terra Madre could explore the more commercial alleys of the Salone del Gusto, but the visitors of the latter did not have access to the Oval of Terra Madre, where producers and "food communities" from all over the world discussed the future of food politics.

Within Slow Food offices and political bodies, the debates and discussions about these issues have continued with each edition of the events. The Salone del Gusto grew larger and its formula has been modified so that each edition could harmonize with evolving Slow Food principles: a shift to the use of recyclable materials, more attention paid to "good, clean, and fair" producers and consequently an increasingly selective choice of exhibitors. In 2010, the Salone shifted from an organization of exhibitors' stalls by product category to one by producer "territories" where stalls of producers from the same region or country were grouped together to recreate the impression of a local market that exhibits the various products of that territory. The political message, from the Slow Food leaders' point of view, was that food is linked to a territory and its social, geographical, and climatic dimensions as well as that of economics. The *laboratori del gusto* also changed focus: rather than simply savoring the wines, the organizers tried to place them in a context of production and place. Products considered in danger of disappearing were very much present in each edition, and there was increasingly more emphasis on the theme of "local production."

In October 2012, Terra Madre and the Salone del Gusto became one single event: the market invaded the Oval, and part of the conferences and debates were moved to the interior spaces of the Lingotto. In 2016, experimentation continued with the eleventh Salone del Gusto taking place in the streets of the center of Turin. The move was based on the model of Cheese, the Slow Food event held in the streets of Bra, but the logistics were simpler to manage in the case of Bra, the "home turf" of the staff from Slow Food's headquarters. Those logistics became very complicated in the center of a large town like Turin, and the experiment was abandoned for the following Salone del Gusto in 2018.[10] Once again the event was held in the Lingotto Fiere pavilions where the integration between the Salon and Terra Madre was re-established.

Although the initial spatial separation and the obvious differences in the roles of each of these events would seem to illustrate a profound contradiction, in reality, it is possible to interpret Terra Madre and the Salone del Gusto as the two poles of a continuum. This was the case even well before their fusion into the same space. These two events express the intertwining of politics and economics and the tensions between the market and the community, between competition and mutuality, as discussed by Stephen Gudeman (2008). On the one hand, the "food communities," the banner of the movement since the creation of the Terra Madre network, and on the other hand the merchants, restaurateurs, and the world of wine and food promotion, linked to Slow Food, and even, in some cases, constitutive of the association since the beginning. The two dimensions embodied in these events may be partially contradictory, but they are not in total opposition. In spite of the contrasting elements, they are actually complementary and constitutive of today's Slow Food movement. Slow Food leaders

Slow Food

do not propose a radical rejection of the liberal economy. The association has been the recipient of important public funds, although the amounts have been greatly reduced in recent years. And the leaders believe the support of private donors, although present in the past, has become more necessary. At each event, the stands of the major sponsors such as Lavazza coffee or the consortium of Reggiano Parmesan cheese producers hold prominent places at the Salon's entry. The impression of these stands and especially their visibility at the entrance to the show constantly elicit criticism, both from journalists in the press and from members more attentive to the militant dimension of Slow Food. The defense of small producers and the presence of agribusiness giants seem irreconcilable in the eyes of many. But by using classical, economic logic and modalities while simultaneously imagining new economic forms, Slow Food's leaders theorize an ideal and moral economic system, conceived in one sense as an alternative to unrestricted liberalism and in another as "reform" of it. In this framework the Salon del Gusto and Terra Madre become complementary spaces presenting ways to create new economic forms, to imagine a new economic order, and to determine new food policies.

Although the Salone del Gusto seems to be simply a huge exhibition and commercialization of food products, it enables the communication of Slow Food messages to visitors who are not members of the movement, and on a larger scale, to the media. In this sense, it is a powerful venue providing visibility and dialogue, where new forms of economy are staged, and politically charged economic messages are diffused.

Cheese at home

In odd-numbered years, when the salon is not held, another event, much smaller in size than the Salone del Gusto, takes center stage in the work of the events office. Since 1997, every two years in September, the Cheese exhibition is held in Bra. This event seems to me particularly significant for several reasons. For four days, around 350 producers from all over the world exhibit their "high-quality" cheeses; dozens of taste workshops, as well as conferences, debates, and round tables punctuate the event's dense program. When compared to the larger events, I think it is noteworthy that this smaller event in the streets of Bra provides a condensed and even clearer image of the relationship between the economic dimension and the political dimension that is championed by Slow Food leaders and members. But it also has an "affective" and "intimate" dimension: for the movement's leaders and members, this event is the most "familial" because it takes place in the streets and squares of the historic center of the city where Slow Food was founded and where its headquarters remain; it is also special because cheese production is one of the movement's oldest interests. During the times that I observed the preparation of the event and attending it, the staff always behaved as if they were receiving visitors and guests at home, even if they were tired from the accelerated preparations that preceded the event. They were all as busy as they are at any event, and at the end of Cheese they would merit a vacation for a few days, but there was no sense of the stress and fatigue that

I witnessed at the Salone del Gusto, where most of the staff also spent hours commuting to and from Turin by car or in a minibus rented for the occasion.

Like other events promoted and organized by Slow Food, Cheese is both a marketplace and a political space where quality is defined and regulated. The selection of exhibitors by the movement's leaders is the first level and establishes the profile of quality according to Slow Food: local production, mostly by small producers or *affineurs*, expressing diversity in the field of cheese production. The structure and type of meetings held during Cheese are not unique. Similar meetings are found both in the Salone and in other even smaller and "younger" events such as Slow Fish: *laboratori del gusto*, lectures, stands with street food, stands with Presidia products, and cultural meetings. The *laboratori del gusto* accompany the participants in the discovery of specific productions, through the practice of tasting, and introduce them to the principles of the association.

Meetings and debates involving producers, Slow Food leaders, representatives of other associations, and scientists allow for discussion and affirmation of the association's principles on a political level. Many of the campaigns and battles in which the members are involved emerge from informal encounters or at these meetings. Cheese functions for Slow Food members and staff as an incubator and a place for experimentation: in this homey space, issues related to production, biodiversity, and the economy of producers are discussed or tested.

During the 2009 and 2011 Cheese editions, the courtyard of Slow Food Editore was the setting for a morning recap. Carlo, the international president, or Riccardo, the president of Slow Food Italia would read and analyze the press, discussing issues linked to food and food politics. Then, in the same space, book presentations and tastings with other staff members alternated. In the Church of San Rocco, a few streets from Via Mendicità Istruita, the new cheese Presidia were presented and the meetings with producers were organized. Between one meeting and another, there were informal exchanges and the occasional animated discussion. In 2009, for example, the head of the international office in charge of France introduced a cheese producer to the president of the Biodiversity Foundation and they discussed the possibility of the Provence-Alpes-Côtes-d'Azur region financing the Presidium project. In the meantime, at another location, the education office organized a meeting with some *fiduciari* to present the new master of food on horticulture, a new program focused on combining the dimensions of "good" for the eater and for the environment. Participants discussed possible target audiences, the costs, and the "personalization" of the master in order to adapt it to the specificities of each region. That same year, a meeting was organized to celebrate the tenth anniversary of the Presidia. During the meeting, a debate began between some producers and the president of the Foundation for biodiversity on the use of ferments (added enzymes) and the real possibility of not using them. It touched on the subject of who were the real artisans, those who used ferments or those who did not use them. Four editions later, in 2017, the question of added enzymes moved to the heart of the debates that the Foundation for biodiversity promotes.

The impression I had, attending Cheese between 2009 and 2017 and observing the preparations during the months leading up to it, was that the market dimension was less

Slow Food

"invasive" than in the Salone del gusto. This impression held even if not very far from Slow Food's headquarters, the debates, and the *Via dei Presidi* lined with the Presidia cheese producers, we would find the great extension of the event's cheese market. In reality, even though this market is located in a separate space from that of the principal Presidia producers, this cohabitation elicited criticism from some producers and the members who advocated for them. Like the other events, Cheese also provides evidence of the divergence and convergence of purpose between Slow Food's interventions in the world of production and the visions of producers, or between Slow Food's philosophy and the practices of cheese makers. The street showcasing the Presidia was lined with the stands of small cheese producers, the Italians and the Presidia from other countries. At the stands, the small pieces of cheese that producers cut to allow visitors to taste them were stormed at certain times of the day, but tasting is not a practice that is always followed by exchange, interest in the story of the product, and purchase. Added to this aspect, the cost of the stand (€1,000 for a small stand during my fieldwork), that is free for the producers of the Presidia only the first years after the establishment of the Presidium, makes some producers consider their participation at the event too expensive. Other producers have the impression that their presence is decorative and serves to justify the "real" market that takes place a few hundred meters away, where large productions (such as parmesan cheese) have big and visible stands. Even at this smaller event, the political and market dimensions are often in tension. Small Presidia producers seem to be both the bridge between these two dimensions and the critical voice, although the criticism is often mixed with the benefits and pride that a good portion of these producers express in the association and in being part of the Presidia project.

As intermediaries the Presidia absorb and synthesize this tension that exists between Slow Food's ideals and its concrete actions, between the market and utopia. In this dual nature involving commercial goods and models of action they become the "go between" of the movement's two facets.

The producers' economy

Going back to the Salone del Gusto, here too the products, their commercialization, and the specific rituals that mark the exhibition's rhythms allow the organization to talk about itself and the new themes at the heart of its philosophy.[11] The economy which is displayed and practiced informs people about ideal perspectives on food and about new ways of producing and consuming. However, the economic aspect expressed by the Salone is precisely what reveals Slow Food's weaknesses and exposes it to the strongest criticisms. The Salone del Gusto is the movement's Achilles heel. The commercialization of products in the Salone is directly linked to the dimension of classic consumerism that Slow Food attempts to rethink, thus seeming to create a conflict with the notion of a moral economy.

And here too Presidia are the intermediaries between these dimensions, exemplified by their moves from one year to another between spaces in the Salone or Terra Madre, as well as the conflicts that have accompanied these changes. In 2006, the Salone's exhibitors were displayed in rows according to a product category (processed meat, cheese, oil, cereals, etc.): "*via degli olii*," "*via dei formaggi*" (the street of olive oil, the street of cheese). The Presidia found themselves grouped together in the middle of the exhibitor's market, a strategically advantageous position and one that allowed them to underline their difference from other products. In the following 2008 edition, the Presidia producers were shifted from the Salone del gusto to the Oval of Terra Madre, where representatives of the food communities debated over local economies and food policies. The aim of this move was to valorize the political dimension of the Presidia project. However, the producers of Presidia scarcely appreciated this new organization because it disassociated them from one of the reasons for their label: economic survival. During the 2010 edition, the Salone's arrangement was completely transformed, and the rows of product categories disappeared because it was decided to emphasize that products are above all linked to a particular territory. The Italian exhibitors, being more numerous, were grouped according to their region of origin; exhibitors coming from abroad were grouped by country or continent depending on their numbers (the Southern hemisphere having fewer participants than the North). With this new logic, the Presidia symbolically reintegrated their "places of origin" within the spatial organization of the exhibition (Figure 11.1).

But once again, the producers did not appreciate the organizational plan. Although they were back in the heart of the marketplace, many of the producers felt the new plan deprived them of the symbolic character they acquired from the collective dimension of being grouped with others in their category. They felt that they were lost among the different products and producers, which were sometimes less good, less clean, and less fair, or required less visibility in the market. In some cases, the Presidia producers found

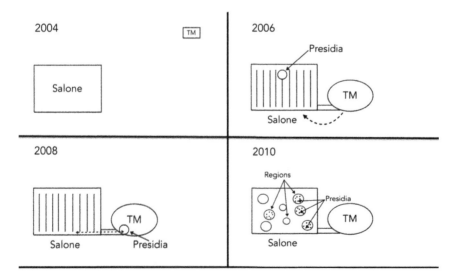

Figure 11.1 Terra Madre and the Salone del Gusto localization from 2004 to 2010 and the different places of the Presidia stands. Created by Adriano Zecchin (from a drawing by the author).

Slow Food

themselves next to industrial competitors from their own region or country, or next to the stands of regional institutions with which they had problems.

Meanwhile, behind the scenes and in a way not expected by the organizers, something else happened. Although the first edition of Terra Madre had been held in a building farther away from the venues of the Salone, the proximity that the two events would have in 2006 inspired a certain pragmatism among some of the small producers representing food communities around the world. In addition to their food-related products, they arrived in Turin with textiles, sandals, and jewelry that they displayed in small, improvised market spaces on the floor of the Oval. Some of them then quickly realized that consumers did not have ready access to this space, which was restricted to Terra Madre delegates. So they moved to the "real" market spaces in the Salone, where there were far more consumers and not just conference attendees. In 2008, when the Presidia stands moved into the Oval, it meant that the general public would have access to this space. The same enterprising producers returned with their improvised market, but this time I had the impression that the staff was less surprised and tolerated it more. In 2010, when the Presidia were moved back to the Salone, the Oval was reorganized, and the staff installed a series of cubicles in the central space to allow this parallel market to set itself up in a more "orderly" fashion (Figure 11.2).

These cases reveal contradictions that often seem like an oxymoron illustrating the poles of a continuum. Even if they are in some sense contradictory, they are not entirely in opposition. They can also be complementary, and they are representative of the range of dimensions in Slow Food today: market, morality, and politics, the dimensions through which producers too must navigate.

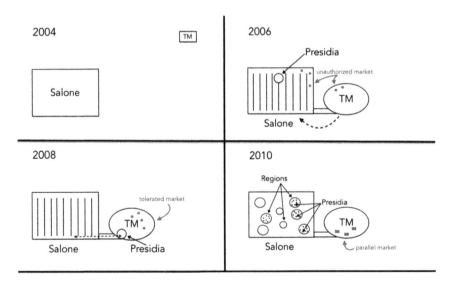

Figure 11.2 The changing places and status of the makeshift market by small Terra Madre producers. Created by Adriano Zecchin (from a drawing by the author).

Notes

1. Terra Madre and the Salone del Gusto are held in Turin during even-numbered years; the Slow Fish event held in Genoa in spring is dedicated to fishing and takes place in odd-numbered years, as does the Cheese event which is held in Bra in autumn.

2. During my research on the Slow Food movement, I participated in five editions of Terra Madre: in 2006 and 2008 as simply an observer, attending the event as an academic with other French delegates; and in 2010, 2012, and 2014, during my fieldwork in Bra as a participant observer together with the staff from the headquarters behind the stage of the event. The descriptions in these pages refer to the event in these years.

3. The Italian version was published in 2009 with the title *Terra Madre. Come non farci mangiare dal cibo.* The translation of the subtitle is How to avoid to be eaten by food, but the English version of book, published one year later, was titled *Terra Madre. Forging a New Global Network of Sustainable Food Communities* (2010).

4. Frattini was member of the coalition *Il popolo della libertà*, composed of *Forza Italia*, Berlusconi's party, and *Alleanza Nazionale*, the "rebranded" name of the *Movimento Sociale Italiano*, which had been created by the extreme right after the Second World War.

5. The University of Gastronomic Sciences was certainly created as training space in the field of food (and to train the next generation of Slow Food leaders, as Carlo often repeated it) but its creation can also be interpreted as a way of gaining legitimacy in the intellectual and academic world.

6. https://www.slowfood.com/about-us/slow-food-terminology/

7. The notion of a moral economy is increasingly present in scientific debates: Palomera and Vetta propose an interesting critical reading of this notion as a constitutive element of economies and capital accumulation: "the structural inequalities generated by particular forms of capital accumulation—mediated by particular kinds of state regulation—are always metabolized through particular fields constituted by dynamic combinations of norms, meanings and practices. It is these fields that we call moral economies" (2016: 416).

8. "We urgently need to make a world where all people can live together. Small may be beautiful and a preference for initiatives grounded in local social realities is unchallengeable, but large-scale bureaucracies, whether governments or business corporations, are also essential if our aspirations for economic democracy are to embrace the movement of the world we live in" maintains Hart (http://thememorybank.co.uk/2013/01/20/object-methods -and-principles-of-human-economy/)

9. The event's entrance ticket was extremely cheap at the beginning but gradually increased with each edition. By 2014 entry tickets were 20 euros for nonmembers and 10 euros for members. In 2018, after an outdoor edition (2016), Slow Food leaders decided to lower the cost of tickets (5 euros online and 10 euros at the ticket office). Taste workshop tickets ranged from 10 to 20 euros in 2014, 25–40 euros in 2018.

10. But as this book was nearing completion, the leaders decided to try the 2016 experience again and hold the 2022 event in the streets of Turin. This is related to the fact that the 2020 edition was largely an online edition due to the pandemic, and even in the current health conditions, an outdoor event was deemed preferable to one held in closed spaces.

11. On links between economic domain and ritual, see the collective book edited by Gudeman and Hann (2015).

Photo 12 Poster illustrating the Slow Food Network, the association's components, the key words of the movement, and the main projects. Bra (Italy), 2013. ©Franco Zecchin.

CHAPTER 12
THE PRAGMATIC UTOPIA OF FOOD ACTIVISM
COPING WITH AMBIGUITY

"Everything we do is economy in the authentic and noble meaning of 'stewardship of the home,' understood as 'stewardship of the common good,'" said the president of Slow Food Italia during a "restricted" meeting he organized to rethink the budget of the Italian association. The economy, as we have seen, has been at the heart of Slow Food projects and actions since the beginning of the association's history. In the previous chapter, I examined the way in which a specific rhetoric of moral economy is elaborated and expressed through the events that Slow Food organizes. In part it serves the economy of the producers who adhere to the association's projects and in part it comes into tension with them. The two registers of economy (the moral economy and the producers economy) cohabit within the spaces of the salons, which are also political spaces. The economy of salons is tied to the economics of budgets, which I will examine in this chapter. The budgets are no less political than the other Slow Food elements, as I will try to show.

In economic alternatives and food activism, a number of notions—such as ethics (Carrier and Luetchford 2012; Jung, Klein and Caldwell 2014), food sovereignty (Edelman 2001; Thivet 2014, 2019), solidarity (Rakopoulos 2015; Siniscalchi 2019a), morality (Palomera and Vetta 2016), and common goods (Nonini 2007; Quarta and Spanò 2016)—are used to rethink production, consumption, and exchange. By studying different cases of food activism, we can see that these notions migrate from one context to another to be appropriated, re-elaborated, and used by other movements. Their meanings shift, and they become a filter through which to rethink economic relations. In Slow Food these notions are incorporated and constantly reformulated in order to define the economic and political spaces of action of the association and the possibilities to intervene on some parts of the food system.

Economy and money flows are often neglected in the analysis of political mobilizations. But in fact, money is often at the center of reflections and experiments that challenge the neoliberal economic system; it becomes an instrument of action, and the vector of political and social values. Through the notions of fair price (Zerilli and Pitzalis 2019; Luetchford 2008), sustainable price (Martinez Alvarez 2019), and fair remuneration of producers, money is the object of claims. The role of money is often reimagined, even if the market relationships are never completely eliminated (Siniscalchi 2019a). In some cases, as in the systems of vegetable baskets in the South of France—part of the AMAP—money circulates in non-visible channels and prices are not discussed during the transaction in order to create an alternative space to the classic market places, where social relations and "economic solidarity" are prevalent (Siniscalchi 2019b, 2021).[1] In other cases, as the project of Slow Food Presidia, the association's interventions valorize small productions that risk disappearing because they no longer have an economic viability: the valorization and labeling, and often the higher price, do not aim to create an alternative market; they aim to make these products thrive in the classic market places (salons, supermarkets, shops).

The changing relationship to money seems to retrace that continuum discussed by Parry and Bloch (1989) and is strongly influenced by the dichotomous view of money that has dominated Western thought, where money is either considered capable of subverting the moral order of society and destroying social bonds, or it becomes an instrument of freedom. Rather than modifying society, the opposite is the case, as the two anthropologists reminded us: the meaning of money is in fact constantly negotiated and redefined according to social contexts and specific worldviews. Inside Slow Food, money is at the heart of the political battles in which members and leaders engage: a fair price for producers, and good and affordable (accessible) food for all. Money becomes a political tool that allows investment in certain projects and a presence in political arenas, but it also funds the reproduction of the machine itself.

The economy of budgets

In the days preceding a national or international council, a meeting of the association's board, or a congress, the administration offices on the top floor of Slow Food's historical building on Via Mendicità Istruita are the last to turn off the lights. The staff stays late, working to prepare the documents and the budgets that will be presented and discussed the next day. An association is also shaped by its budgets. They represent the real economy, the expenses and revenues that are often seen as being removed from the political idea of a moral economy, and their preparation is often an ongoing process and not simply a report prepared in the days and hours before a major official meeting.

The budgets reveal the political priorities represented by the projects that the association decides to invest in, such as the Presidia project or the publishing house. They can show that a project may be undertaken or pursued even if it is not directly profitable in terms of the economic balance between costs and benefits. Slow Food budgets are proposed to the councilors in the movement's political bodies, discussed, and then presented— often in a slightly different form to convey political ideas and strategic choices. Budgets allow Slow Food leaders to imagine and expand the association over the course of time (ensuring its reproduction) and in space (through its local implantations). These impacts are directly linked to the political and future choices made by these leaders. Budgets can also help us understand the relations among Slow Food's various components: Slow Food Promozione, Slow Food Editore, Slow Food Foundation for Biodiversity, the Italian association, and the International one. At the same time, the budgets reveal Slow Food's political choices in the international context and the "genealogical" and power relations between the Italian association and the national associations in other countries, as we have seen in the complicated relations with Slow Food France. During the crisis

The Pragmatic Utopia of Food Activism

experienced by the French association, which ended with the closing of the national structure, budgets were a central element in the negotiations involving the leaders from both sides.

At the beginning of this chapter, I described an August 2011 meeting that was organized to discuss the budget of the Italian association. During the meeting, the president said:

> Up until today, many of the resources generated by Slow Food have been invested to develop the global network of our association, including the funding of projects of the Slow Food Foundation for Biodiversity. Obviously we cannot imagine that the commitment of Slow Food Italy will decrease, because we [Slow Food Italia leaders] created these realities; nonetheless it is essential to redefine the terms and the limits of the Italian association's commitment.

The transfer of funds, in the form of annual contributions from the national associations existing around the world—including Slow Food Italia—to the international, is economic and political at the same time: it is conceived as a contribution to the functioning of the international offices to develop projects in the Global South. But transfers of funds, such us the contribution given by the Italian association to the international to cover nonpayment by other national associations or international project expenses reflect internal hierarchies and the balance of power inside the Slow Food constellation.

In the Slow Food political meetings that I attended, budget presentations and discussions were regular. Budgets were not yet "consolidated" and each structure (Slow Food Italia, the two companies, and the other components) had their own budgets. Income came from a combination of annual membership subscriptions, donations from private companies, and public sponsors (municipalities and parks for specific projects such as the Presidia; public institutions such as the Piedmont region, the Ministry of Agriculture, and, until recently, the Ministry of Foreign Affairs for the Salone del Gusto and Terra Madre events). During the 2010s, national public funds have decreased, but funding for projects has increased from other institutions such as the European Commission. Most expenses consisted of project funding and headquarters expenses for staff salaries and physical resources (the office buildings) and their maintenance.

In July 2010, the meeting of the newly elected Italian *segreteria nazionale* took place. Carlo, the president of Slow Food, attended the opening to welcome the new members. In his speech he announced that the four years ahead would be very tough. "There is a very strong financial regression happening, and a loss of sensitivity to ethical issues is a new characteristic in the world of associations . . . we will have to think about extra-institutional fund raising, about more widespread support in order to live with dignity. . . . The period of the fat cows (*vacche grasse*) is definitely over and the period of lean cows (*vacche magre*) is going to last a long time," he said, using a common Italian expression that originated in the Bible (Genesis) and refers to abundance (fat cows) followed by famine (thin cows).

213

He told board members that the University of Gastronomic Sciences had also gone through a financial crisis, but that thanks to donations from Oscar Farinetti (a well-known Italian businessman, and owner of the food supermarket chain Eataly) and other financially strong partners, the crisis was almost over. He then reminded them that the Italian association must continue to pursue its core issues: "Farmers are only 3 or 4 percent of the membership. We need to get to 20 percent, but not like the unions. We're different. . . . We need to bring in the Macedonian workers from the Langhe (Piedmont), those from Rosarno (Calabria), and the Indians; they are our peasants." He then greeted the members of the board and left the meeting.

These motivational words had to do with the leadership's growing effort to extend the membership to farmers and producers. But in Carlo's words, this should not lead to a local retreat: those he hoped would join the ranks of the association were not (only) Italian farmers. He would include all the peasants who come from other countries for agricultural work in Italy, the vineyards of the Piedmont as well as in the fields of southern Italy. It seemed that the financial issue was unrelated to the need to increase the number of members from the agricultural world. In reality, behind this vision, there is a precise idea of the association and the role of money: Slow Food needed to continue with fewer resources, but without abandoning the production-related projects that now constituted the core of its activities. It would consolidate its image and show consistency as a political movement. The inclusion of migrant farm workers was essential in this framework: By reconfiguring the association and including new membership profiles, its credibility and legitimacy could be increased, with both political and economic consequences.

After Carlo's brief speech, the discussion of the *segreteria nazionale* opened with the items on the agenda: one of the first, as usual, was the budget. Riccardo, the president of Slow Food Italy, introduced it by explaining that the years between 2002 and 2006 were the "most enterprising years in our history." The University, Terra Madre, and the Foundation for Biodiversity were inaugurated in those years. "Today advertising revenue has gone down, our publishing house is small, and there has been a decline in sponsorship of association projects (masters, school gardens, Presidia). Sponsors complain that some of these projects do not give them visibility, that some are now old." But he immediately reassured those present by explaining that the political interest of the projects had to be maintained separate from the aleatory nature of sponsorships and the market.

The administrative director, Fausto, followed with a presentation of the budgets. Without going into detail about the numbers, he quickly noted that the expenses of the headquarters and personnel were stable. He then explained how the two societies (Slow Food Promozione and Slow Food Editore) contribute to the functioning of the association. The new members of the board seemed to want to go into more detail about the budgets than their predecessors, but the discussion was postponed by the president and the administrative director. The president outlined the logic of funding in even-numbered and odd-numbered years, where public contributions for events, and in particular for Salone del Gusto, allow the structure to be sustained in the years without Salone. Then they discussed an invitation received by Slow Food to participate in an event organized by other partners. It was an event where the "enemy" companies were to have a large space. Some members, perplexed, evoked the risk of finding themselves in a segregated "ghetto" talking about the future of food. Others suggested "going on a collision course with these large companies and major economic actors" in order to counter their communication skills seeking to purify their image through their proximity to Slow Food. They discussed the way the presence of Slow Food in these events could be conceived differently: "we can contaminate them." A new member of the board asked, "But how much do we get out of it?" Even when funds and budgets are not directly discussed, the relationship with the market and economic actors, as embodied in this case by agro-industrial actors, occupies an important part of the reflections: from one perspective they needed to refuse to share the same spaces in order to protect the image of the association and avoid being pushed into a corner as if they were a exotic alternative; from another perspective, the best way was to confront the enemy directly and try to contaminate it instead of being contaminated.

Dealing with the market

The *segreteria nazionale*'s discussions described an economy that was still dependent on public funding, in spite of its decline, and sponsors, and needed to increase private support. For years, Slow Food staff and leaders showed a great ability to attract support and funding from public bodies as well as from private businesses. Giuliano, who had previously been vice president of Slow Food, reminded that the first edition of the book *Il piacere del vino. Manuale per imparare a bere meglio* (The pleasure of wine. Handbook for learning to drink better) by G. Ruffa and P. Gho (1992) was presented in a restaurant in Trento. He was at a table with Carlin, another staff member, and the administrator of a large wine company in the region.

> We didn't yet understand that we should be asking for money. We chatted at the table and said we had to have a governors' meeting, "There are 40 of us, it would be nice to come visit with you," and the guy said, "Well, come on over, we'll be your host for three days." We left like three excited children, we felt like we'd won the world.

"Slow Food was in constant financial difficulty," Edoardo, another former staff leader, told me, "until an almost casual and trivial check from the president of the Piedmont region arrived in 1996 for a billion liras." That check was the first funding of the Salone del Gusto, and the beginning of a new system to keep the structure alive: the salons could support the association economically, and simultaneously become a political platform for the association. The budget was financed with income from renting exhibition space and, above all, the funding provided by the city, the region, and the Ministry of Agriculture, plus additional funds that the Ministry of Foreign Affairs provided later for the first three or four editions of the Terra Madre event. Slow Food was and continued to be a militant and nonprofit association, but it secured support from sponsors as well as large subventions from institutions (at least in the past) which meant that it remained tied to more classic modes of funding.

Over the time, fundraising developed and became a vital sector of the association. But the commercial side was increasingly pushed to adapt to the needs of Slow Food's messages and philosophy. The Salone, at the heart of the economic functioning of the association, was gradually transformed into a "sustainable" event, with attention to the materials used as well as to recycling, but above all, the exhibitors were increasingly selected using the criteria of "good, clean, and fair." Although they are not classically measurable or calculable, the requirements suggested by these notions make it possible to include even the smallest producers who are unlikely or unable to meet the requirements of standard certification systems. The ethical or sustainable practices of large companies often seem questionable even if they are more complicated to evaluate. Nevertheless, some of them gain access to the events organized by Slow Food through sponsoring. Sponsors are still necessary, and large companies like Lavazza and Parmigiano Reggiano have been sponsors of the Salone del Gusto since the 1998 edition, but as Slow Food's image and actions evolved, the larger sponsors became cumbersome and intrusive elements at the salons, in terms of image.

The need for private funding led Slow Food leaders to discuss the consequences of cohabitation (like the above discussion at the meeting of the *segreteria nazionale*) and at each Salone edition the staff struggled to find the most suitable place to satisfy the sponsors' desire for visibility, while keeping them as far away as possible from the small producers of quality food that Slow Food promotes. This fraternizing with private sponsors is one of the visible contradictions appearing in Slow Food's economic system. Certainly, it can be read internally as an attempt to broaden the sphere of influence of the movement, to also address its messages to the "bad guys," as some people told me, and not simply to those who are already convinced. But undoubtedly this also has a negative impact on the image of Slow Food. How does an association navigate between militant action and economic issues? How can it defend itself from criticism while making the choices necessary to survive, reproduce itself, and expand its sphere of influence? Can Slow Food be considered a very particular kind of food activism? Or do mobilizations and movements in the field of food production and consumption always have to deal with the ambiguity of their relationship to the market? This relationship is particularly important inside Slow Food, and when we consider the size of the structure, the quantity of projects carried out, and its notoriety, it becomes a matter for the association's survival. The budgets reveal the political relationships with the institutions and the market, which show Slow Food's ability to deal with various political powers. But in turn, this ability also attracts criticism from more militant groups.

During the years of my research, the "Guidelines for Slow Food's fundraising policy" had been drawn up and diffused within the headquarters and local units. The text aimed to establish some parameters to prevent individual local leaders or offices within the structure from acting autonomously and inconsistently with political decisions. The guidelines precisely indicated the criteria and the maximum percentages for economic support that Slow Food could receive. The leadership knew that there are always

The Pragmatic Utopia of Food Activism

companies or industrial producers willing to pay to take advantage of Slow Food's notoriety and image.

> The two fundamental principles ... must be considered binding everywhere in the world and at every level of the Association's structure. ... No Slow Food supporter can influence, from any perspective, the decisions of the Association, its activities, and its independence; Slow Food maintains total autonomy from its supporters [and] subjects or entities whose operations are in clear conflict with Slow Food's philosophy and activities cannot be supporters of Slow Food [my translation]. (white paper, *Linee guida delle politiche di fundraising in Slow Food*)

Although some economic actors, such as Monsanto, raised no doubts and were placed on the list of "bad guys" not to be dealt with, there were other cases where the choices were more complex. How do large producers like the Parmigiano Reggiano cheese consortium or Lavazza fit into this scheme? "In evaluating a potential supporter, it is not necessary that they operate in total agreement with Slow Food's philosophy: such an analysis would eliminate almost all potential sponsors," said the Italian document, "what is fundamental is that the activity of the supporter is not inconsistent with the philosophy and activity of Slow Food." In a pragmatic sense, the staff leaders who wrote these lines knew very well that no one is completely "good, clean, and fair." But this did not prevent them from excluding multinational corporations and

> entities whose principal or exclusive activity is strongly criticized ... with respect to environmental or social impacts ... [or] all those companies that have produced products or supported projects that are inconsistent with the activities of Slow Food [such as providing bad information on food issues, supporting GMO productions, fighting raw cheese productions, or fighting small-scale production] [my translation]. (white paper, *Linee guida delle politiche di fundraising in Slow Food*)

This list, which was updated in later reformulations, provided a concise, perhaps a little too concise, snapshot of the main battlefields in which Slow Food has engaged.[2] The mesh of the net was still too wide, and the decisions about potential sponsors required continuous adjustments and negotiations on the ground.

In some cases, relations with the business world are more complex, as for example, in the case of Eataly[3] a well-known chain of food stores present in a number of major cities in Italy and other countries around the world. Eataly's founder, Oscar Farinetti, is a successful entrepreneur who is originally from Alba, only a few kilometers from Bra. He is sometimes the object of fierce criticism (see among others Bukowski 2015) but at the same time often praised by the press and the business world. He "sells" messages and formulas directly inspired by Slow Food philosophy, adapting them in a series of publishing initiatives (see Farinetti 2015) or in commercial operations that often turn them into decorative slogans that adorn his food centers. In fact, when opening the first store, in Turin, Eataly benefited from the consulting services provided by one of the

217

Slow Food

offices in the Italian structure of Slow Food. Consulting is one of the activities developed by the Slow Food Promozione company, and in this case, beyond the compensation for services, it gave Slow Food the opportunity to "touch a wider audience," as some staff members told me. They felt that these supermarkets are frequented by people who the association's communications would otherwise have difficulty reaching. "The problem with Slow Food," other staff members said, "is that everything is always done through friendship." In fact, in this case it is quite true that the economic and political reasons are not separated from the personal and longstanding ties between Carlo Petrini and Oscar Farinetti, which also happen to be at the origin of the important economic support that the latter has regularly given to the University of Gastronomic Sciences. Farinetti presides over the Association of Friends of the University, which is responsible for raising funds for the University itself.[4]

This interweaving of economic relationships, interests, and other types of solidarity undoubtedly has advantages for the owner of Eataly, but they are less advantageous for the image of Slow Food. The consulting activity did not continue after the opening of the first store, and most of the producers recommended by Slow Food could not maintain the pace of large-scale distribution, so their products are no longer on the shelves of the commercial chain. Nevertheless, many of the chain's customers, as well as its critics, see Eataly as a commercial branch of Slow Food. Farinetti's company has certainly been able to make good use of its relationship with Carlo Petrini and deftly integrated and appropriated Slow Food's messages as its own, but it has often been difficult for the association's leaders to distance themselves from the image of the well-known entrepreneur[5] and his shopping centers, which are perceived as luxury food places where the idea of "good, clean, and fair" food serves to generate profits for the company rather than save the planet.[6] These types of complex market relationships continue to be an issue for Slow Food's position as a nonprofit association.

Budget base zero

When I attended meetings of the political bodies (the *segreteria nazionale*, the *consiglio dei governatori* which later became the *consiglio nazionale*, the international presidency or international council) two voices usually alternated: one was Carlo, who announced periods of economic distress on a large scale requiring everyone to make efforts to maintain the autonomy of the association, and the other was the voice various staff leaders who illustrated the steps that successfully covered the budgets. The positive view of budgets allowed the work of the headquarters to be valued, not just that of the administrative offices. The internal perception of budgets and the way to approach them differed from one part of the structure to another. Administrators would cut the expenses of various offices in order to keep the machine running when public funding was cut back or arrived late, when advertising revenue dropped in the publishing house, or when sponsors who supported the projects disappeared. And from the perspective of institutions and companies it was more interesting to sustain the expenses of Slow

The Pragmatic Utopia of Food Activism

Food political events, which provided a return in terms of image, than it was to finance African vegetable gardens or Master of food programs.

During the analysis of the budgets at a February 2011 meeting of the *segreteria nazionale*, the head of the education office, Valentina, lamented the fact that in the past the projects of her office were not questioned, even if there were fewer sponsors. But she had come to the realization that it was no longer possible to continue projects without sponsors, that the economic dimension was becoming increasingly important.

> When I first came to Slow Food, publishing projects produced revenue from profit margins. Then we said that educational projects were central, even if they aren't economically profitable. Now I see that is the case, they don't produce profit margins, and eventually there will be more and more efforts to reduce expenses. The taste education project has been exhausting . . . [and] our morale has been battered by these cost reductions.

The logic of financing projects (and offices) that operate at a loss as compared to those with activities that produce surpluses has its limits, and this dilemma produces internal tensions that create hierarchies among projects or the different offices of the headquarters. Some projects can be re-launched but others need to be abandoned, because "with fewer we can do better," concluded the president.

A few months later, in August of 2011, the meeting that I referenced at the opening of this chapter was seen as the beginning of a reflection on the theme of "*budget base zero*" (zero-based budgeting), a way to reduce and optimize expenses, rethink fundraising strategies, and, at the same time, reassess the relationship between the headquarters and the regions. I joined the meeting where the Italian president, the general secretary, the director of the administrative office, the presidents of two regions, and a regional councilor (three staff leaders and three volunteer leaders) sat around the table. The Italian president reminded the other participants of a central issue:

> We are a non-profit organization. The profits of our business—if and when there are any—are entirely reinvested in the institution. The allocation of any profits must be determined by the governing bodies and shared ever more fully with the membership. We are an economic entity, which is to say that this entity "moves money:" it generates and spends resources—it's essential to maintain this order—, and it also produces economic activity. We are in some cases a business entity, such as in the sale of publications, or organizing major events. However, at every level the objective of implementing projects that contribute to the development of associative mission must prevail.

The participants then began to discuss how the structure of the association might be improved. One staff leader said: "Over time, you drift away from the reasons that lead you to build a certain kind of structure," meaning the general organization of the association. A local leader shifted the focus to concerns about the headquarters: "Our structure is too rigid: we need flexibility, with virtuous, or horizontal mobility, no more than five years in an office." Another local leader suggested more staff flexibility linked to specific projects: a system of "consultancies that you activate only when you need them." Despite being an association that advocates for small producers against the challenges of capitalism, the neo-capitalist work logic seemed to advance more overtly: they began to imagine a lighter machine made up of project contracts with, basically, fewer staffing requirements.

The discussion then shifted to the future of the association, and different points of view emerged. A regional president said that every regional hub should feel like it belongs to the whole association: "[the regional centers] are also Slow Food headquarters, [like Bra]." Then he added that "the new direction" of the association indicated priorities "in which the economic aspects make what we do effective." But the regional councilor, who had a previous experience inside the WWF, emphasized, "without abandoning our vision." The national president answered, "We can't lose it: like Obelix, we fell into it when we were children." He was comparing Slow Food leaders to Obelix, the protagonist of the Asterix comics, who fell into a magic potion as a child which made him invincible for life. Then he added,

> The WWF has a political structure and a managerial structure, here [in Slow Food] they are mixed together. And this has been our good fortune because it has allowed us to govern the machine in moments of crisis, but there are risks in shaping the political aspect along with the economics because you have to keep the two reins together.

The governor, with experience in the WWF, took up the negative example to say,

> No, this model, ours, has been successful, unlike that of the WWF in which [the people occupying] political positions are elected by the members, and according to the statutes, the staff has no political role. . . . That led to a national board with no management authority [because the staff had it], and that in turn brought WWF to the brink of bankruptcy.

The WWF was a negative example for some of those present because its structure, where political power and staff management were separated, resulted in a leadership that was disconnected from economic and management issues and a staff incapable of dealing with political issues who tried to transform them into administrative issues. The discussion continued with the two regional presidents envisioning a future including employees at the regional level. "We need structures that you commit to because you believe in them, but only for the length of a term," otherwise, there is a risk of demotivating volunteers and discouraging new members, who are both vital for Slow Food's survival.

Revenues and budgets were directly related to the future association that leaders tried to imagine. They were navigating between different models, but neoliberal logics were becoming more apparent. The existing structure in which political offices were occupied by staff members made it possible to keep together the two souls of Slow Food leadership: political power and association management. However, for many of those present, particularly the regional leaders, the model needed to be adjusted in order to reduce administrative expenses and the inefficient structural complexity of the machine while continuing to fund projects. The movement's philosophy and capacity for political imagination was not part of the discussions, probably because those elements remained firmly in the realm of Carlo Petrini.

Controversial elections

In May 2014, something totally unexpected happened within Slow Food. The 8th Slow Food Italy congress was held in Riva del Garda, and for the first time in the history of the association the president had not been chosen in advance or, to be more precise, the internal politics of the association was divided on the question of which candidate to support as president. During his eight years of his presidency, the outgoing national president had initiated and carried out a process of "democratization" of the association, changing its way of functioning to accompany the philosophical changes the movement was experiencing. This process, as we saw in Chapters 3 and 4, changed some of the association's leadership, but the process had created tensions: many had criticized the progressive bureaucratization, others the risk of losing the historical memory of the association and the knowledge and expertise that existing leaders provided. Regions and *condotte* had been given new responsibilities and tasks, including helping to support headquarters through fundraising.

But the elections for the new president of Slow Food Italy presented many other completely unexpected novelties. For the first time in Slow Food history there were two candidates and two lists. Moreover, one of these two candidates was a woman, a radically new element for an association that remained extremely masculine in its leadership. And finally, the other candidate was not a staff leader from Bra, but a regional leader coming from southern Italy. Both candidates presented themselves with a pre-selected board of directors, a sort of collegial presidency (rather than a single candidacy). The choice of having a leadership group had been extensively discussed in the months leading up to the congress, with the aim of giving the regions a larger place in association's leadership. The staff was not, however, absent: even the candidate from the "*territorio*" had a member from the national headquarters on his board.

At first sight, this unexpected situation seemed the sign of a positive evolution of the association in terms of democracy: the end of the "Bulgarian" elections, a woman or a regional member to be chosen as president, a collegial presidency. But in reality these elections were a very difficult moment for the cohesion of the association because they produced a real division among the members from Italian regions and those from within the headquarters, and overall, a great sense of frustration in the two camps. Moreover, they constituted a real caesura in the process of the association's transformation. Why did this happen? In my opinion, the reason stems from the fact that this election (with two opposite candidates and programs) was actually the result of changes that had little to do with democracy.

Slow Food

A document intended for the future electors was presented as an interview with the two candidates. Pino, who had been president of a large Southern region, summarized his program with three words: "Concreteness, Sharing, and Participation." Chiara, director of one of the headquarters' offices and a teacher at the University of Gastronomic Sciences, chose three different words: "Openness, Politics, and Training." When asked to choose a point in the program that each candidate considered a priority, Pino replied, "Without a doubt, strengthening and expanding the Terra Madre network with its food communities. There are still many farmers, breeders, fishermen, and artisans to involve among our own." In her response, Chiara said, "The growth of awareness, skills, and knowledge, at all levels of the association, including staff." Then she underlined the diversity of priorities between the two candidatures, which "depend on political sensitivities, associative histories, and skills that are very different between the two teams." Pino's team had gone into great detail about the organizational and operational dimension, listing the concrete goals to be achieved. Chiara's team, on the other hand, had chosen to focus on the political visions of the future, imagining a future association that would be "Light, but strong, and even more influential; cheerful, welcoming, transparent, and supportive. With many members . . . and thousands of versions around the world: differently defined identities that recognize themselves as a single association. In this system, Slow Food Italy is a *hub*, a bridge of ideas, experiences, and skills."

Behind these official presentations, two visions of the association's future were facing each other: the elections were a confrontation (and a conflict) between two models of governance and two visions with different approaches to the social reproduction of the movement. The different models of networking that Slow Food has practiced over the years allow me to explain my hypothesis, showing the contradictions that each of these models obscures. The first model is represented by the way in which the association was built and developed over time. Its history is the history of a headquarters born before the base: the creators of Slow Food imagined an association spread on the Italian territory, then in the world, and they built it through their personal ties and networks. Local leaders were chosen for their personal networks that they put to work for Slow Food and for their capacity to promote the association (with dinners, meetings, presentations of wine or products), to "make" members and to motivate them. They were linked to the head of the association by a relationship of trust and fidelity. This inclusive model, based on networks, relationships of trust, and personal ties, created a varied and heterogeneous association, an association with a *de facto* center (the headquarters in Bra), some peripheries, and in the middle, semi-peripheries (regions in Italy and other northern countries such as France). The governance model of this complex machine, in which the countries of the Global South are the true peripheries, is based on relationships of dependence (also from an economic point of view) and recalls the model of world system and world economy elaborated by Wallerstein (1974). The Italian *condotte* and regions, but also the national Slow Food association outside Italy, are part of this world organized according to spatial and power hierarchies.

A second kind of networking is represented by the current inclusive policy which has increasingly involved producers, the production world, and new forms of membership.

The Pragmatic Utopia of Food Activism

These are also often strategic alliances for people (restaurateurs, producers) who join the association because Slow Food's public image can be used in commercial or political terms. Alliances like these make it possible to design new local political spaces and broaden the base of the movement. Although past ties were primarily aimed at building the association, these more current alliances are aimed at spreading Slow Food's philosophy to renew its membership and objectives as well as stronger commitments and, as always, new projects. Also included in this type of networking are the ties established with political representatives of indigenous peoples, such as the Sami in Sweden.[7]

A third kind of networking is one that Slow Food has practiced in the last fifteen years, lobbying with private economic and institutional actors as well as agricultural unions (such as Coldiretti) and other movements. These national and international alliances are strategic and allow Slow Food to exist as a political actor. In order to participate in the arena where the future of the food system is discussed or will be decided, it is also necessary to weave alliances and networks with other groups, associations, or movements acting not only in the field of food politics but also in other spaces of contestation (e.g., against nuclear power, land grabbing, or the privatization of common goods). These links with institutional actors and other movements allow Slow Food to consolidate its political legitimacy in conflicting and transversal arenas of food production and consumption, thus reproducing itself as a movement. But they do not absolve Slow Food leaders of the ongoing need to elaborate new visions and renovate the movement philosophy.

Coming back to the elections, each candidate proposed different kinds of alliances corresponding to a different model of governance and reproduction of Slow Food. One candidate underlined the relationships with the "territorio" (producers, cooks, and particularly members). The other insisted on an imagination of the future and on the importance of policy actions at a higher level. One invested in the association, to connect the semi-periphery with the center and to reconnect membership and regions to the headquarters. The other wished to consolidate the movement and its political dimension through lobbying and its presence in the international political arenas. For many of the association's earlier years these models were compatible perspectives inside the same leadership group. Looking back at documents from the 1988 Terrasini congress, for example, the pragmatic and visionary dimensions coexisted. Then, during the 2000s the two dimensions were separated but remained complementary, both embodied by staff leaders: one more visionary and idealist, represented by Carlo, the international president, spreading Slow Food as a movement around the world; and the other embodied by Riccardo, the Italian president, attentive to the internal dynamics of the association and rethinking its internal structure and governance. During the 2014 elections, the two souls of the association seemed to oppose each other through the two candidates. This episode was the symptom of a crisis inside Slow Food linked to its progressive transformation from an association managed by a large group of friends, to an international association with a professional staff, and finally to a movement, which was about to embark on the third step of his story. This progression allows us to reflect more generally on the evolutions of food activism.

Slow Food

At the beginning of the congress, Riccardo, the outgoing Italian president's speech employed metaphors to summarize the meaning that the election should have for the association:

> With this stage we should choose new helmsmen. . . . One of the strengths [of the association] has always been to be able to sail together . . . Our Christopher Columbus is Carlin. Our way to the Indies 28 years ago was the right to pleasure, today it is the right to food. . . . We had faith in his dreams that have become our dreams. . . . We have to figure out if this complex and articulated structure will still be useful. . . . The foundations on which we have to build [the future association] are the territories, the women, and men who are in the territories and most of all the farmers.

Then, the Slow Food (international) president, Carlo, shifted the metaphor of the ship to another scale: "Our ship is a small ship, but we are actually in a much larger vessel that has no course." He continued by evoking the class struggle of the past compared to the struggle of the rich against the poor in the current neoliberal context. Then, to describe the election, he drew on the metaphor of Don Quixote and Sancho Panza, who were one and the same, visionaries and pragmatists at the same time. "Pragmatists alone cannot change the world."

The conflict within this Slow Food election can be read as a conflict between the necessity of the association to be structurally governed (and economically viable) and the necessity for it to be flexible enough to adapt itself to new political fields. At one end of this continuum is the need to link the base to the head and continue to motivate volunteer members, at the other end is the need to claim a place in a field increasingly full of actors, organizations, and social movements while remaining imaginative and original.

Conclusion

What comes next?

The different economic forms that Slow Food leadership elaborates and practices are connected to each other, mutually reinforcing and legitimizing. But tensions and contradictions characterize the development and the life of the association: between gourmets and producers, between political messages and the real economy, and between the budgets of the association and the flexibility of a social movement.

Mobilizations that propose "alternative" ways of production, consumption, and distribution need to be flexible enough to react and interact with the institutions and lobbies that dominate the food sector. As it negotiates a wide spectrum of widely divergent powers and diversifies its fields of intervention and its allies, Slow Food must also cope with ambiguity. Ambiguity and contradictions are probably constitutive of this kind of activism. As June Nash (2005a: 3) points out, social movements must be as flexible as

The Pragmatic Utopia of Food Activism

the global institutions they challenge. Slow Food displays this capacity for adaptation in its projects, alliances, and political strategies. But the association is sometimes myopic about the daily problems of peasants, conflicts among producers, and local political dynamics at the regional or international levels, which are too far from Bra. Sometimes it has a very good distance vision, but it can be presbyopic about the internal realities of the groups that compose it, including inside the black box, failing to pay attention to the reasons that some people leave while continuing to be affectively attached to Slow Food. External and internal constraints force Slow Food leaders and staff to adapt and compromise. At the same time, it continues to convey "critical" messages about consumption and responsible production. Local projects and political issues that are disseminated through salons and international meetings generate concrete effects both in economic and political scenarios.

What has happened in the meantime? Just as Slow Food's philosophy continues to absorb and impregnate notions and battles promoted by others, so in turn it nourishes or is appropriated for very different purposes. The slow movement continues to spread, and the term "slow" is appropriated by other organizations, associations, and movements, as well as businesses and companies. There are structures or groups that have integrated the message of Slow Food, translating it into other battles (such as Slow Science, Slow Money) or that in some cases, grew out of it directly, such as Slow Medicine or CittàSlow. Then there are companies that use the term slow to sell "high-quality" goods or services that last over time (slow wear, slow garden, slow cosmetics) but have little to do with the issues that concern Slow Food. As a term, the word "slow," which Slow Food first helped popularize in the Italian and international associational and political landscape, is a multipurpose term that can be used in different contexts, thanks to the fact that it can be associated with a set of positive values.

But what happened inside Slow Food? The 2014 elections were won by the team that carried the voice of "territory": for the first time in Slow Food's history, the president was not a person from Bra. This choice made the association take the risk, which some people evoked in one of the many meetings that took place during the years of my research, of having a staff that has no political power and a presidency that has no hand in the management of the machine. In reality, the complexity of the machine and the interconnectedness of the internal components probably prevented the two souls from becoming completely detached from each other, and the previous staff leaders have maintained important positions in some strategic nodes of the association such as communication, the publishing house, event organization, and fundraising.

As I was closing the manuscript of this book, the tenth congress of Slow Food Italy had just taken place in 2021, and the presidency team changed again. The team had already changed in 2018 but this time there was no one from the headquarters on the board, and for the first time a woman has become president of the Italian association. Perhaps it is no coincidence that she comes from the rebellious and always avant-garde region of Tuscany: word has it, a woman linked to the world of the countryside and production like others on her presidential team but attentive to the headquarters' way of working, according to some staff leaders, and mindful of relationships often mired in

225

Slow Food

opposition and criticism. The fact that she is a woman might indicate that major changes have taken place within the machine, but I am not sure if that is really what it is about. The fact that she comes from "the territory" and that it is a collective presidency makes the change in leadership less radical in terms of gender relations.

Meanwhile, Carlo Petrini has published two more books, and the one which collects his conversations with Pope Francis (2020) on the future of the planet and integral ecology has been translated in English, German, Spanish, and French. During the last International congress held in Pollenzo, June 2022, he ceded the International presidency to a leader from Uganda and to a team composed of leaders from different countries, sanctioning the transformation of the international Slow Food governance in accordance with the governance model already tested by the Italian association. Nevertheless, he continues to be the most visible voice and face of Slow Food, pursuing his role as a charismatic leader.

Notes

1. Rather than choosing and buying individual products members pay for a predetermined contract that entitles them to receive a certain number of weekly "baskets" containing fresh seasonal products.

2. Later, the guidelines were reformulated, translated, and uploaded on the association's website https://www.slowfood.com/filemanager/official_docs/SFFundraisingGuidelines.pdf

3. The first Eataly store opened in Turin in 2007, at Lingotto Fiere, right in front of the spaces where the Salone del Gusto was organized from 1996 to 2020. Today Eataly has eleven stores in Italy, seven in the United States (from New York to Los Angeles), and stores in France, Canada, Brazil, Turkey, Germany, Japan, South Korea, the United Kingdom, and Sweden. The bigger Eataly stores harbor a supermarket, specialty markets, restaurants, sandwich shops, and spaces dedicated to cooking classes, all oriented toward good quality food.

4. Although recognized by the Italian Ministry of Universities, it did not receive support from this ministry during my fieldwork and until just a few years ago.

5. In 2014, Farinetti was criticized for precarious labor contracts of the staff employed in the Eataly store in Florence. In 2015, he was at the center of an investigation in the context of the Milan Expo "Nutrire Milano."

6. For an analysis from the perspective of the social geography of Eataly stores and their use of Slow Food messages, see Colombino (2018).

7. The interest for the Sami to join Slow Food, as some Sami leaders explained to me during an international meeting held in northern Sweden at the Slow Food Sami group, was to not only be associated with indigenous networks perceived as minorities, but to also be associated with an international movement that enjoys a positive image and legitimacy in many political arenas.

BIBLIOGRAPHY

Abram, S. and J. Waldren, eds. (1997), *Tourists and Tourism: Identifying with People and Places*, Oxford: Berg.

Adam, B. (1998), *Timescapes of Modernity: The Environment and Invisible Hazards*, London, New York: Routledge.

Alkon, A. and J. Guthman, eds. (2017), *The New Food Activism Opposition, Cooperation, and Collective Action*, Berkeley, CA: University of California Press.

Anderson, B. (1991), *Imagined Communities: Reflections on the Origin and Spread of Nationalism*, London, New York: Verso.

Andrews, G., (2008), *The Slow Food Story: Politics and Pleasure*, London: Pluto Press.

Appadurai, A. (1998), *Modernity at Large: Cultural Dimensions of Globalisation*, Minneapolis, MN: University of Minnesota Press.

Appadurai, A., ed. (1986), *The Social Life of Things: Commodities in Cultural Perspective*. Cambridge, London: Cambridge University Press.

Assmann, S. (2010), "Food Action Nippon and Slow Food Japan: The Role of Two Citizen Movements in the Rediscovery of Local Foodways," in J. Farrer (ed.), *Globalization, Food and Social Identities in the Asia Pacific Region*, Tokyo: Sophia University Institute of Comparative Culture. http://icc.fla.sophia.ac.jp/global%20food%20papers/html/assmann.html.

Avanza, M. (2008), "Comment faire de l'ethnographie quand on n'aime pas 'ses indigènes' ? Une enquête au sein d'un mouvement xénophobe," in D. Fassin and A. Bensa (eds.), *Les politiques de l'enquête: épreuves ethnographiques*, 41–58, Paris: La Découverte.

Battaglino, C., S. Ceriani, E. Giannini and S. Milano (2012), *Social Report 2011*, Bra: Slow Food Foundation for Biodiversity.

Battaglino, C., E. Giannini and S. Milano (2010), *Social Report 2009*, Bra: Slow Food Foundation for Biodiversity.

Bérard, L. and P. Marchenay, (1995), "Lieux, temps et preuves. La construction sociale des produits de terroir," *Terrain*, 24: 153–64.

Beriss, D. and D. Sutton, eds. (2007), *The Restaurants Book: Ethnographies of Where We Eat*, Oxford, New York: Berg.

Besky, S. (2014), *The Darjeeling Distinction: Labor and Justice on Fair-Trade Tea Plantations in India*, Berkeley, CA: University of California Press.

Black, R. and R. Ulin, eds. (2013), *Wine and Culture. Vineyard to the Glass*, New York, London: Bloomsbury.

Bloch, M. (1999), "Commensality and Poisoning," *Social Research*, 66 (1): 133–49.

Boissevain, J. (1974), *Friends of Friends. Networks, Manipulators and Coalitions*, Oxford: Basil Blackwell.

Bommel, K. van and A. Spicer (2011), "Hail the Snail: Hegemonic Struggles in the Slow Food Movement," *Organization Studies*, 32: 1717–44.

Bourdieu, P. (1979), *La distinction. Critique sociale du jugement*, Paris: Les Éditions de Minuit.

Borras, Jr. S. M., M. Edelman and C. Kay, eds. (2008), *Transnational agrarian movements confronting globalization*, Chichester: Wiley Blackwell.

Brillat-Savarin, A. (1982), *Pysiologie du goût*, Paris: Flammarion [1825].

Bibliography

Brundage, D. (2016), *Snatching Defeat from the Jaws of Victory: The Curious Case [Study] of California's Proposition 37*. Master's Theses. 722. https://scholarworks.wmich.edu/masters_theses/722.

Buechler, S. M. (2000), *Social Movements in Advanced Capitalism. The Political Economy and Cultural Construction of Social Activism*, New York, Oxford: Oxford University Press.

Buechler, S. M. (2011), *Understanding Social Movements: Theories from the Classical Era to the Present*, Boulder, London: Paradigm Publishers.

Bukowski, W. (2015), *La danza delle mozzarelle: Slow Food, Eataly, Coop e la loro narrazione*, Roma: Edizioni Allegre.

Capatti, A. (2000), *L'osteria nuova. Una storia italiana del XX secolo*, Bra: Slow Food Editore.

Carrier, J. G., ed. (1997), *Meanings of the Market. The Free Market in Western Culture*, Oxford, New York: Berg.

Carrier, J. G. and P. G Luetchford, eds. (2012), *Ethical Consumption. Social Value and Economic Practice*, New York, Oxford: Berghahn.

Cavanaugh, J. (2016), "Documenting Subjects: Performativity and Audit Culture in Food Production in Northern Italy," *American Ethnologist*, 43 (4): 691–703.

Cefaï, D. (2007), *Pourquoi se mobilise-t-on? Les théories de l'action collective*, Paris: La Découverte.

Chee-Beng, T. (2015), "Commensality and the Organization of Social Relations," in S. Kerner, C. Chou and M. Warmind (eds.), *Commensality: From Everyday Food to Feast*, 13–30, New York, London: Bloomsbury.

Chrzan, J. (2004), "Slow Food: What, Why, and to Where?," *Food, Culture & Society*, 7 (2): 117–32.

Colombino, A. (2018), "Becoming Eataly: The Magic of the Mall and the Magic of the Brand," in U. Ermann and K. J. Hermanik (eds.), *Branding the Nation, the Place, the Product*, 67–90, London, New York: Routledge.

Corti, M. (2011), *I ribelli del bitto. Quando una tradizione casearia diventa eversiva*, Bra: Slow Food Editore.

Corti, M. (2016), "Tra Resistenza Casearia e Innovazione: il Caso del (Formaggio) 'Storico Ribelle," *Quaderno SOZOOALP*, 9: 71–80.

Counihan, C. (1999), *The Anthropology of Food and Body: Gender, Meaning, and Power*, London, New York: Routledge.

Counihan, C. (2004), *Around the Tuscan Table: Food, Family and Gender in Twentieth Century Florence*, New York, London: Routledge.

Counihan, C. (2014), "Women, Gender, and Agency in Italian Food Activism," in C. Counihan and V. Siniscalchi (eds.), *Food Activism: Agency, Democracy and Economy*, 61–75, New York, London: Bloomsbury.

Counihan, C. (2019), *Italian Food Activism in Urban Sardinia: Place, Taste, and Community*, London, New York: Bloomsbury.

Counihan, C. (2021), "Food Activism and Language in a Slow Food Italy Restaurant Menu," *Gastronomica*, 21 (4): 76–87.

Counihan, C. and S. Højlund, eds. (2018), *Making Taste Public: Ethnographies of Food and the Senses*, New York, London: Bloomsbury.

Counihan, C. and V. Siniscalchi, eds. (2014), *Food Activism: Agency, Democracy and Economy*, New York, London: Bloomsbury.

Crozier, M. and E. Friedberg (1977), *L'acteur et le systéme: les contraintes de l'action collective*, Paris: Éd. du Seuil.

Deléage, E. (2014), "Le mouvement *Slow Food*: contretemps de l'accélération temporelle?," *Écologie & politique*, 48 (1): 49–59.

Demeulenaere, E. (2013), "Les semences entre critique et expérience: les ressorts pratiques d'une contestation paysanne," *Revue d'Etudes en Agriculture et Environnement*, 94 (4): 421–41.

Bibliography

Demossier, M. (2018), *Burgundy. A Global Anthropology of Place and Taste*, New York, Oxford: Berghahn.

Douglas, M. (1979), *Implicit Meanings*, London: Routledge and Kegan Paul.

Douglas, M. and B. Isherwood (1979), *The World of Goods: Towards an Anthropology of Consumption*, New York: Basic Books.

Dubuisson-Quellier, S. (2009), *La consommation engagée*, Paris: Les Presses de Sciences Po.

DuPuis, E. M. and D. Goodman (2005), "Should We Go 'Home' to Eat? Toward a Réflexive Politics of Localism," *Journal of Rural Studies*, 21: 359–71.

Durand, S. (2021), "Délibérer et enregistrer. Des pratiques politiques locales en contexte monarchique (Bas Languedoc, XVIIe-XVIIIe siècle)," in F. Otchakovsky-Laurens and L. Verdon (eds.), *La voix des assemblées. Quelle démocratie urbaine au regard des registres de délibérations? Méditerranée-Europe XIIIe-XVIIIe siècle*, 83–94, Aix-en-Provence: Presses universitaires de Provence.

Edelman, M. (2001), "Social Movements: Changing Paradigms and Forms of Politics," *Annual Review of Anthropology*, 30: 285–317.

Edelman, M. (2005), "Bringing the Moral Economy Back in to the Study of 21st-Century Transnational Peasant Movements," *American Anthropologist*, 107 (3): 331–45.

Evans-Pritchard, E. E. (1940), *The Nuer: A Description of the Modes of Livelihood and Political Institutions of a Nilotic People*, London: Oxford University Press.

Farinetti, O. ed. (2015), *Nel blu. La biodiversità italiana, figlia dei venti*, Milano: Feltrinelli.

Fassin, D. (2009), "Les économies morales revisitée," *Annales. Histoire, Sciences Sociales*, 6: 1237–66.

Firth, R. (1965), *Primitive Polinesian Economy*, London: Routledge [1939].

Fitting, E. (2011), *The Struggle for Maize: Campesinos, Workers, and Transgenic Corn in the Mexican Countryside*, Durham, London: Duke University Press.

Fontefrancesco, M. F. and P. Corvo (2019), "Slow Food: History and Activity of a Global Food Movement," in W. Leal Filho, A. Azul, L. Brandli, P. Özuyar and T. Wall (eds.), *Zero Hunger. Encyclopedia of the UN Sustainable Development Goals*, 766–74, Cham: Springer.

Friedmann, H. (2005), "From Colonialism to Green Capitalism: Social Movements and the Emergence of Food Regimes," *New Directions in the Sociology of Global Development Research in Rural Sociology and Development*, 11: 227–64.

Friedmann, H. and A. McNair (2008), "Whose Rules Rule? Contested Projects to Certify 'Local Production for Distant Consumers,'" *Journal of Agrarian Change*, 8 (2/3): 408–34.

Garcia-Parpet, M. F. (2009), *Le Marché de l'excellence: Les Grands Crus à l'épreuve de La Mondialisation*, Paris: Seuil.

Garsten, C. (2015), "Flexibility Frictions: Economies of Connection in Contemporary Forms of Work," in J. Kjaerulff (ed.), *Flexible Capitalism: Exchange and Ambiguity at Work*, 93–115, London: Berghahan.

Garsten, C. and A. Nyqvist (2013), "Entries: Engaging Organisational Worlds," in C. Garsten and A. Nyqvist (eds.), *Organisational Anthropology: Doing Ethnography in and among Complex Organisations*, 1–25, London, New York: Pluto Press.

Gaytan, M. S. (2004), "Globalizing Resistance," *Food, Culture & Society*, 7 (2): 97–116,

Geertz, C. (1973), *The Interpretation of Cultures*, New York: Basic Books.

Gottlieb R. and A. Joshi (2010), *Food Justice*, Cambridge and London: The MIT Press.

Graeber, D. (2001), *Toward an Anthropological Theory of Value: The False Coin of Our Own Dreams*, New York: Palgrave-Macmillan.

Graeber, D. (2009), *Direct Action: An Ethnography*, Oakland: AK Press.

Grasseni, C. (2013), *Beyond Alternative Food: Italy's Solidarity Purchase Groups*, New York, London: Bloomsbury.

Grasseni, C. (2017), *The Heritage Arena: Reinventing Cheese in the Italian Alps*, New York: Berghahn.

Bibliography

Grimes, K. M. (2005), "Changing the Rules of Trade with Global Partnership: The Fair Trade Movement," in J. Nash (ed.), *Social Movements. An Anthropological Reader*, 237–48, Oxford: Blackwell.

Green, A. (2018), "Reindeer Fat and the Taste of Place in Sami Food Activism," in C. Counihan and S. Højlund (eds.), *Making Taste Public: Ethnographies of Food and the Senses*, 169–84, New York, London: Bloomsbury.

Gross, J. E. (2014), "Food Activism in Western Oregon," in C. Counihan and V. Siniscalchi (eds.), *Food Activism: Agency, Democracy and Economy*, 15–30, New York, London: Bloomsbury.

Gudeman, S. (2001), *The Anthropology of Economy: Community, Market, and Culture*, Oxford: Blackwell.

Gudeman, S. (2008), *Economy's Tension. The Dialectics of Community and Market*, Oxford: Berghahn.

Gudeman, S. and C. Hann, eds. (2015), *Economy and Ritual. Studies of Postsocialist Transformations*, Oxford: Berghahn.

Gupta, A. and J. Ferguson, eds. (1997), *Culture, Power, Place: Explorations in Critical Anthropology*, Durham, London: Duke University Press.

Harper, K. and V. Siniscalchi (2019), "Value and Values in Food Projects in Europe," in V. Siniscalchi and K. Harper (eds.), *Food Values in Europe*, 1–14 New York, London: Bloomsbury.

Hart, K., J. L. Laville and A. D. Cattani, eds. (2010), *The Human Economy: A Citizen's Guide*, Cambridge: Polity.

Harvey, M., A. McMeekin and A. Warde, eds. (2000), *Qualities of Food*, Manchester, New York: Manchester University Press.

Heller, C. (2013), *Food, Farms and Solidarity. French Farmers Challenge Industrial Agriculture and Genetically Modified Crops*, Durham, London: Duke University Press.

Hermitte, M. A. (2001), "Les appellations d'origine dans la genèse des droits de propriété intellectuelle," *Etudes, recherches, systèmes agraires, développement*, 32: 195–207.

Herzfeld, M. (1992), *The Social Production of Indifference: Exploring the Symbolic Roots of Western Bureaucracy*, Chicago: University of Chicago Press.

Herzfeld, M. (1997), *Cultural Intimacy: Social Poetics in the Nation-State*, London, New York: Routledge.

Holt-Giménez, E. and R. Patel (2009), *Food Rebellions! Crisis and the Hunger for Justice*, Cape Town, Dakar, Nairoby, Oxford: Fahamo Books & Pambazuka Press.

Hsu, E. L. (2014), "The Slow Food Movement and Time Shortage: Beyond the Dichotomy of Fast or Slow," *Journal of Sociology*, 1–15.

Illich, I. (1973), *Tools for Conviviality*, London, New York: Marion Boyars.

Jung, Y., J. Klein and M. L. Caldwell, eds. (2014), *Ethical Eating in the Postsocialist and Socialist World*, Berkeley, CA: California.

Juris, S. J. (2008), *Networking Futures: The Movements Against Corporate Globalization*, Durham: Duke University Press.

Juris, S. J. and A. Khasnabish, eds. (2013), *Insurgent Encounters. Transnational Activism, Ethnography, and the Political*, Durham, London: Duke University Press.

Karpik, L. (2007), *L'économie des singularités*, Paris: Gallimard.

Kilani, M. (1992), *L'invention de l'Autre. Essais sur le discours anthropologique*, Lausanne: Payot.

Kjaerulff, J., ed. (2015), *Flexible Capitalism: Exchange and Ambiguity at Work*, EASA Series, 25. New York: Berghahn Books.

Koensler, A. and A. Rossi, eds. (2012), *Comprendere il dissenso: Etnografia e antropologia dei movimenti sociali*, 13–32, Perugia: Morlacchi Editore.

Kopytoff, I. (1986), "The Cultural Biography of Things: Commoditization as Process," in A. Appadurai (ed.), *The Social Life of Things: Commodities in Cultural Perspective*, 64–91, Cambridge: Cambridge University Press.

Bibliography

Korsmeyer, C. ed. (2005), *The Taste Culture Reader: Experiencing Food and Drink*, Oxford, New York: Berg.

Korsmeyer, C. and D. Sutton (2011), "The Sensory Experience of Food," *Food, Culture & Society*, 14, 4: 461–75.

Kummer, C. (2002), *The Pleasures of Slow Food: Celebrating Authentic Traditions, Flavors, and Recipes*, San Francisco: Chronicle Books.

Lamine, C. (2008), *Les AMAP: un nouveau pacte entre producteurs et consommateurs?*, Gap: Éditions Yves Michel.

Lefebvre, H. (1991), *The Production of Space*, Oxford: Basil Blackwell.

Leitch, A. (2003), "Slow Food and the Politics of Pork Fat: Italian Food and European Identity," *Ethnos*, 68 (4): 437–62.

Lien, M. E. (2004), "The Politics of Food: An Introduction," in M. E. Lien and B. Nerlich, (eds.), *The Politics of Food*, 1–17, Oxford: Berg.

Littaye, A. (2015), "The Role of the Ark of Taste in Promoting Pinole, a Mexican Heritage Food," *Journal of Rural Studies*, 42: 144–53.

London, J. (2020), *Grève générale*, Paris: Libertalia. [South of the Slot, 1909]

Lotti, A. (2010), "The Commoditization of Products and Taste: Slow Food and the Conservation of Agrobiodiversity," *Agriculture and Human Values*, 27: 71–83.

Low, S. M. (2016), *Spatializing Culture: The Ethnography of Space and Place*, New York: Routledge.

Low, S. M. and D. Lawrence-Zúñiga, eds. (2003), *The Anthropology of Space and Place: Locating Culture*, Oxford: Blackwell.

Luetchford, P. (2008), *Fair Trade and Global Commodity. Coffee in Costa Rica*, London: Pluto Press.

Lyon, S. and M. Moberg, eds. (2010), *Fair Trade and Social Justice: Global Ethnographies*, New York: New York University Press.

Mahmud, L. (2014), *The Brotherhood of Freemason Sisters: Gender, Secrecy, and Fraternity in Italian Masonic Lodges*, Chicago , London: The University of Chicago Press.

Marrone, G. (2016), *Semiotica del gusto. Linguaggi della cucina, del cibo, della tavola*, Milano: Mimesis.

Martinez Alvarez, B. (2019), "The Moral Price of Milk: Food Values and the Intersection of Moralities and Economies in Diary Family Farms in Galicia," in K. Harper and V. Siniscalchi (eds.), *Food Values in Europe*, 63–78, New York, London: Bloomsbury.

Mattioli, F. (2013), "The Property of Food Geographical Indication, Slow Food, Genuino Clandestino and the Politics of Property," *Ethnologia Europaea*, 43: 47–61.

Meneley, A. (2004), "Extra Virgin Olive Oil and Slow Food," *Anthropologica*, 46: 165–76.

Meneley, A. (2007), "Like an Extra Virgin," *American Anthropologist* 109 (4): 678–87.

Miele, M. and J. Murdoch (2002), "The Practical Aesthetics of Traditional Cuisines: Slow Food in Tuscany," *Sociologia Ruralis*, 42 (4): 313–38.

Migliorini P., C. Peano, R. Ponzio and C. Scaffidi (2010), "Slow Food Presidia: A Sustainable Agro-Food Systems?," 9th European IFSA Symposium, July 4–7, 2010, Vienna (Austria).

Mintz, S. W. (1986), *Sweetness and Power: The Place of Sugar in Modern History*, New York: Penguin.

Mintz, S. W. (1996), *Tasting Food, Tasting Freedom. Excursions into Eating, Culture and the Past*, Boston: Beacon Press.

Mintz, S. W. and C. M. Du Bois (2002), "The Anthropology of Food and Eating," *Annual Review of Anthropology*, 31: 99–119.

Molé, N. J. (2012), *Labor Disorders in Neoliberal Italy: Mobbing, Well-Being, and the Workplace*, Bloomington, IN: Indiana University Press.

Mollona, M., C. Papa, V. Redini and V. Siniscalchi, eds. (2021), *Antropologia delle imprese: Lavoro, Reti, Merci*, Roma: Carocci editore.

Bibliography

Müller, B. (2008), *La bataille des OGM: Combat vital ou d'arrière-garde?*, Paris: Editions Ellipses.

Murdoch, J. and M. Miele (2004), "A New Aesthetic of Food? Relational Reflexivity in the 'Alternative' Food Movement," in M. Harvey, A. McMeekin and A. Warde (eds.), *Qualities of Food*, 156–75, Manchester, New York: Manchester University Press.

Myers, J. (2012), "The Logic of the Gift: The Possibilities and Limitations of Carlo Petrini's Slow Food Alternative," *Agriculture and Human Values*, 30, 405–15.

Narotzky, S. (2012), "Alternatives to Expanded Accumulation and the Anthropological Imagination: Turning Necessity into a Challenge to Capitalism," in P. Gardiner Barber, B. Leach and W. Lem (eds.), *Confronting Capital: Critique and Engagement in Anthropology*, 239–52. London, New York: Routledge.

Narotzky, S. (2016), "Where Have All the Peasants Gone?," *Annual Review of Anthropology*, 45: 301–18.

Narotzky, S. and N. Besnier (2014), "Crisis, Value, and Hope: Rethinking the Economy," *Current Anthropology*, 55 (S9): 4–16.

Nash, J. (2005a), "Introduction: Social Movements and Global Process," in J. Nash (ed.), *Social Movements: An Anthropological Reader*, 1–26, Oxford: Blackwell.

Nash, J. ed. (2005b), *Social Movements: An Anthropological Reader*, Oxford: Blackwell.

Nonini, D. M., ed. (2007), *The Global Idea of "The Commons,"* Oxford: Berghahn.

Okely, J. (2012), *Anthropological Practice: Fieldwork and Ethnographic Method*, Oxford: Berg.

Orsini, A. (2009), *Anatomia delle Brigate Rosse: le radici ideologiche del terrorismo rivoluzionario*, Soveria Mannelli: Rubbettino.

Palomera, J. and T. Vetta (2016), "Moral Economy: Rethinking a Radical Concept," *Anthropological Theory*, 16 (4): 413–32.

Palumbo, B. (2021), *Lo Sguardo Inquieto: Etnografia Tra Scienza e Narrazione*, Bologna: Marietti.

Papa, C. (2002), "Il prodotto tipico come ossimoro: il caso dell'olio extravergine d'oliva umbro," in V. Siniscalchi (ed.), *Frammenti di economie. Ricerche di antropologia economica in Italia*, 159–91, Cosenza: Luigi Pellegrini Editore.

Papa Francesco, (2015), *Laudato sii. Enciclica sulla cura della casa comune. Guida alla lettura di C. Petrini*, Cinisello Balsamo: San Paolo Edizioni.

Parasecoli, F. (2003), "Postrevolutionary Chowhounds: Food, Globalization, and the Italian Left," *Gastronomica*, 3 (3): 29–39.

Parkins, W. and G. Craig (2006), *Slow Living*, Oxford: Berg.

Parkins, W. and G. Craig (2009), "Culture and the Politics of Alternative Food Networks," *Food Culture and Society*, 12 (1): 77–103.

Parry, J. and M. Bloch (1989), "Introduction: Money and the Morality of Exchange," in J. Parry and M. Bloch (eds.), *Money and the Morality of Exchange*, 1–32, Cambridge: Cambridge University Press.

Paxson, H. (2005), "Slow Food in a Fat Society: Satisfying Ethical Appetites," *Gastronomica*, 5 (1): 14–18.

Paxson, H. (2013), *The Life of Cheese: Crafting Food and Value in America*, Los Angeles, Berkeley: University of California Press.

Peace, A. (2006), "Barossa Slow: The Representation and the Rhetoric of Slow Food's Regional Cooking," *Gastronomica*, 61 (1): 51–9.

Peace, A. (2008), "Terra Madre 2006: Political Theater and Ritual Rhetoric in the Slow Food Movement," *Gastronomica*, 82 (2): 31–9.

Perullo, N. (2010), *Filosofia della gastronomia laica: il gusto come esperienza*, Roma: Meltemi.

Petrini, C. (2001), *Slow Food, le ragioni del gusto*, Bari: Laterza [English translation 2003, *Slow Food the Case for Taste*, New York: Columbia University Press].

Bibliography

Petrini, C. (2005), *Buono, pulito e giusto: Principi di nuova gastronomia*. Turin: Einaudi [English translation 2007, *Slow Food Nation: The Creation of a New Gastronomy*, New York: Rizzoli Ex Libris].

Petrini, C. (2009), *Terra Madre. Come non farci mangiare dal cibo*, Firenze, Bra: Giunti, Slow Food Editore [English translation 2010, *Terra Madre: Forging a New Global Network of Sustainable Food Communities*, White River Junction: Chelsea Green Pub].

Petrini, C. (2020), *Terrafutura: Dialoghi con Papa Francesco sull'ecologia integrale*, Firenze, Bra: Giunti, Slow Food Editore.

Petrini, C. and G. Padovani (2005), *Slow Food revolution: da Arcigola a Terra madre; una nuova cultura del cibo e della vita*, Milano: Rizzoli.

Petrini, C. and G. Padovani (2017), *Slow Food: storia di un'utopia possibile*, Firenze, Bra: Giunti, Slow Food Editore.

Petrini, C. and G. Piumatti (2010), "Prefazione," in *Slow Wine. Storie di vita, vigne, vini in Italia*, 7, Bra, Slow Food Editore.

Pietrykowski, B. (2004), "You Are What You Eat: The Social Economy of the Slow Food Movement," *Review of Social Economy*, LXII (3): 307–21.

Piron, F., ed. (2015), *Citoyennes de la terre*, Québec: Edition science et bien commun.

Portinari, F. (1987), "Manifesto dello Slow Food, Movimento per il diritto al piacere," *Gambero Rosso, Il Manifesto*, Roma.

Pratt, J. (2003), *Class, Nation and Identity: The Anthropology of Political Movements*, London: Pluto Press.

Pratt, J. (2007), "Food Values: The Local and the Authentic," *Critique of Anthropology*, 27 (3): 285–300.

Pratt, J. and P. Luetchford (2014), *Food for Change: The Politics and Values of Social Movements*, London: Pluto Press.

Quarta, A. and M. Spanò, eds. (2016), *Beni comuni 2.0. Contro-egemonia e nuove istituzioni*, Milano, Udine: Mimesis.

Rakopoulos, T. (2015), "Solidarity Economy in Contemporary Greece: 'Movementality,' Economic Democracy and Social Reproduction During Crisis," in K. Hart (ed.), *Economy for and Against Democracy*, 161–81, New York, Oxford: Berghahn.

Rakopoulos, T. (2019), "Seventy Percent Zapatista? Solidarity 'Ecosystems' and the Troubles of Valuing Labor in Food Cooperatives," in V. Siniscalchi and K. Harper (eds.), *Food Values in Europe*, 147–60, New York, London: Bloomsbury.

Ruffa, G. and P. Gho (1992), *Il piacere del vino. Manuale per imparare a bere meglio*, Bra: Slow Food Editore.

Ruffa, G. and A. Monchiero, eds. (2002), *Il Dizionario di Slow Food*, Bra: Slow Food Editore.

Sassatelli, R. and F. Davolio (2010), "Consumption, Pleasure and Politics: Slow Food and the Politico-Aesthetic Problematization of Food," *Journal of Consumer Culture*, 10 (2): 202–32.

Scaffidi, C. (2014), *Mangia come parli: com'è cambiato il vocabolario del cibo*, Bra: Slow Food Editore.

Schlosberg, D. and R. Coles (2016), "The New Environmentalism of Everyday Life: Sustainability, Material Flows and Movements," *Contemporary Political Theory*, 15 (2): 160–81.

Schneider, S. (2008), "Good, Clean, Fair: The Rhetoric of the Slow Food Movement," *College English*, 70 (4): 384–402.

Schurman, R. and W. A. Munro (2010), *Fighting for the Future of Food. Activists versus Agribusiness in the Struggle over Biotechnology*, Minneapolis, MN: University of Minnesota Press.

Scott, J. C. (1976), *The Moral Economy of the Peasant: Rebellion and Subsistence in Southeast Asia*, New Haven, CT: Yale.

Bibliography

Shore, C. and S. Wright, eds. (1997), *Anthropology of Policy: Critical Perspectives on Governance and Power*, New York: Routledge.

Shore, C., S. Wright and D. Però, eds. (2011), *Policy Worlds: Anthropology and the Analysis of Contemporary Power*, Oxford: Berghahn.

Siniscalchi, V. (1995), "Simmetria e asimmetria nel legame tra 'parsenali': relazioni e contratto in un rapporto agrario (San Marco dei Cavoti)," *L'Uomo*, VIII (2): 239–71.

Siniscalchi, V. (2000), "'Il dolce paese del torrone.' Economia e storia in un paese dell'Italia del Sud," *Meridiana. Rivista di storia e scienze sociali*, 38–39: 199–222.

Siniscalchi, V. (2010a), "Regimi di singolarità e politiche della ripetizione," *La Ricerca Folklorica*, 61: 125–34.

Siniscalchi, V. (2010b), "Appunti da un congresso," *Slow Food*, 47: 176–9.

Siniscalchi, V. (2012), "Au delà de l'opposition slow-fast. L'économie morale d'un mouvement/ Al di là dell'opposizione slow-fast. L'economia morale di un movimento," *Lo Squaderno*, 26: 67–74.

Siniscalchi, V. (2013a), "Environment, Regulation and the Moral Economy of Food in the Slow Food Movement," *Journal of Political Ecology*, 20: 295–305.

Siniscalchi, V. (2013b), "Pastori, attivisti e mercato. Pratiche economiche e logiche politiche nei Presidi Slow Food," *Voci. Annuale di Scienze Umane*, X: 173–82.

Siniscalchi, V. (2013c), "Slow versus Fast. Economie et écologie dans le mouvement Slow Food," *Terrain* 60: 132–47.

Siniscalchi, V. (2014a), "Slow Food Activism Between Politics and Economy," in C. Counihan and V. Siniscalchi (eds.), *Food Activism: Agency, Democracy and Economy*, 225–41, London, New York, London: Bloomsbury.

Siniscalchi, V. (2014b), "La politique dans l'assiette: restaurants et restaurateurs dans le mouvement Slow Food en Italie," *Ethnologie Française*, XLIV (1): 73–83.

Siniscalchi, V. (2015), "'Food activism' en Europe: changer de pratiques, changer de paradigmes," *Anthropology of Food*, S11. Available online: https://journals.openedition.org/aof/7920 (accessed April 28, 2022).

Siniscalchi, V. (2016), "Fairs and Festivals," in C. Donnelly (ed.), *The Oxford Companion to Cheese*, 259–61, Oxford: Oxford University Press.

Siniscalchi, V. (2017), "*Slow Food*: les politiques locales d'un mouvement international," in T. Grillot and S. Gacon (eds.), *Manger autrement*, 63–85, Paris: PUF.

Siniscalchi, V. (2018a), "Political Taste: Inclusion and Exclusion in the Slow Food Movement," in C. Counihan and S. Højlund (eds.), *Making Taste Public*, 185–97, New York, London: Bloomsbury.

Siniscalchi, V. (2018b), "Fieldwork and Changing Scales: The Analysis of Different Economic Spaces," *ANUAC*, 7 (2): 71–94.

Siniscalchi, V. (2019a), "Mobilisation, Activism and Economic Alternatives," in J. Carrier (ed.), *A Research Agenda for Economic Anthropology*, 105–18, Cheltenham: Edward Elgar Publishing.

Siniscalchi, V. (2019b), "Solidarity, Calculation, and the Economic Proximity Inside the 'Vegetable Basket' System in the South of France," in V. Siniscalchi and K. Harper (eds.), *Food Values in Europe*, 115–31, New York, London: Bloomsbury.

Siniscalchi, V. (2020), "Slow Food en France. Traductions et alliances locales d'un mouvement international," *Modern and Contemporary France*, 28 (2): 193–208.

Siniscalchi, V. (2021), "Il denaro invisibile. Circolazione, calcolo e valori negli spazi economici dell'attivismo", Cheiron, 1–2, 2019: 249–372.

Siniscalchi, V. and C. Counihan (2014), "Ethnography of Food Activism," in C. Counihan and V. Siniscalchi (eds.), *Food Activism: Agency, Democracy and Economy*, 3–12, New York, London: Bloomsbury.

Bibliography

Siniscalchi, V. and K. Harper, eds. (2019), *Food Values in Europe*, New York, London: Bloomsbury.

Siniscalchi, V. and F. Zecchin (2018), "Conservation et production de la valeur du *fiore sardo*. Les enjeux politiques et économiques de la typicité dans le mouvement Slow Food," *Techniques & Culture*, 69: 56–73.

Snow, A. (2005), *How Santa Really Works*, London: Simon & Schuster Childrens.

Stanziani, A. (2005), *Histoire de la qualité alimentaire. XIXe-XXe siècle*, Paris: Seuil.

Sutton, D. E. (2010), "Food and the Senses," *Annual Review of Anthropology*, 39: 209–23.

Sutton, D. E. (2017). "Synesthesia, Memory, and the Taste of Home," in C. Korsmeyer (ed.), *The Taste Culture Reader. Experiencing Food and Drink*, 303–14. London : Bloomsbury.

Teil, G. and A. Hennion (2004), "Discovering Quality or Performing Taste?," in M. Harvey, A. Mcmeekin and A. Warde (eds.), *Qualities of Food*, 19–37, Manchester: Manchester University Press.

Terrio, S. (2000), *Crafting the Culture and History of French Chocolate*, Berkeley, CA: University of California Press.

Thivet D. (2014), "Peasants' Transnational Mobilization for Food Sovereignty," in C. Counihan and V. Siniscalchi (eds.), *Food Activism: Agency, Democracy and Economy*, 193–209, New York, London: Bloomsbury.

Thivet, D. (2019), "'Small Farms, Better Food': Valuing Local Agri-Food System in Europe from the European Peasant Coordination to the Niélény European Forum for Food Sovereignty," in V. Siniscalchi and K. Harper (eds.), *Food Values in Europe*, 95–111, New York, London: Bloomsbury.

Thompson, E. P. (1971), "The Moral Economy of the English Crowd in the Eighteenth Century," *Past & Present*, 50: 76–136.

Tomasi di Lampedusa, G. (1958), Il Gattopardo, Milano: Feltrinelli.

Tonelli, A. (2012), *Falce e tortello: Storia politica e sociale delle feste dell'Unità (1945–2011)*, Bari: Laterza.

Tsing, A. (2005), *Frictions. An Ethnography of Global Connection*, Princeton, Oxford: Princeton University Press.

Tsing, A. (2015), *The Mushroom at the End of the World. On the Possibility of Life in Capitalism Ruins*, Princeton University Press.

Ulin, R. C. (1996), *Vintages and Traditions: An Ethnohistory of Southwest France Wine. Cooperatives*, Washington, London: Smithsonian Institution Press.

Ventura, A. (2010), *Per una storia del terrorismo italiano*, Roma: Donzelli.

Wallerstein, I. M. (1974), *The Modern World-System: Capitalist Agriculture and the Origins of the European World-Economy in the Sixteenth Century*, New York: Academic Press.

Wallman, S. (1979), "Introduction," in S. Wallmann (ed.), *Social Anthropology of Work*, Association of Social Anthropologists Monograph 19, 1–24, London: Academic Press.

Weber, M. (2005), *Economia e società. 1: Comunità*, trans. M. Palma, Roma: Donzelli.

Wedel, J. (2010), *Shadow Elite: How the World's New Power Brokers Undermine Democracy*, New York: Basic Books.

Weiss, B. (2016), *Real Pigs: Shifting Values in the Field of Local Pork*, Durham: Duke University Press.

West, H. G. and N. Domingos (2012), "Gourmandizing Poverty Food: The Serpa Cheese Slow Food Presidium," *Journal of Agrarian Change*, 12: 120–43.

Wilk, R. (2006a), *Home Cooking in the Global Village: Caribbean Food from Buccaneers to Ecotourists*, Oxford, New York: Berg.

Wilk, R. (2006b), "From Wild Weeds to Artisanal Cheese," in R. Wilk (ed.), *Fast Food/Slow Food. The Cultural Economy of the Global Food System*, 13–28, Lanham: Altamira Press.

Wilk, R. and L. Cliggett (2007), *Economies and Cultures: Foundations of Economic Anthropology*, (2nd ed), Boulder: Westview.

Bibliography

Wolf, E. R. (1990), "Distinguished Lecture: Facing Power—Old Insights, New Questions," *American Anthropologist*, 92 (3): 586–96.

Wolf, E. R. (2001), *Pathways of Power: Building an Anthropology of the Modern World*, Berkeley, CA: University of California Press.

Zerilli, F. M. (2010), "The Rule of Soft Law: An Introduction," *Focaal: Journal of Global and Historical Anthropology*, 56: 3–18.

Zerilli, F. and M. Pitzalis (2019), "From Milk Price to Milk Value: Sardinian Sheep Herders Facing Neoliberal Restructuring," in K. Harper and V. Siniscalchi (eds.), *Food Values in Europe*, 79–94, New York, London: Bloomsbury.

Filmography

Kitchen Stories (2003), [film] Dir. Bent Hamer, Norway and Sweden: BOB Film Sweden, Bulbul Films, Svenska Film institutet.

Slow Food Story (2013), [film] Dir. Stefano Sardo, Italy: Indigo Film, TICO Film.

Le conseguenze dell'amore (2004), [film] Dir. Paolo Sorrentino, Italy: Medusa Film, Fandango, Indigo Film.

INDEX

Abram, Simone   132
Alkon, Alison   18 n.4, 124
Alleanza Nazionale   43, 209 n.4
Anderson, Benedict   167, 198
Andrews, Geoff   5, 39 n.11
anni di piombo   22
Appadurai, Arjun   132, 140 n.3
Arcigola   21–5, 27, 29–32
Arcigolosi   21, 32
Ark of taste   123–4
Assmann, Stephanie   6
*Association pour le Maintien de l'Agriculture
   Paysanne* (AMAP)   40 n.16, 56 n.2, 150–1,
   199, 211
Associazione Ricreativa e Culturale Italiana
   (ARCI)   21–3, 29
Avanza, Martina   10–11

Banca del vino   183, 189 n.15
Bérard, Laurence   132
Beriss, David   172
Berlinguer, Enrico   72, 81 n.8
Berlusconi, Silvio   194, 195, 209 n.4
Bertinotti, Fausto   193
Besky, Sarah   132
Besso, Mercedes   194
Bistrò del Mondo   71, 81 n.5
Bitto   149
Black, Rachel   189 n.14
Bloch, Maurice   157–8, 212
Boccondivino   103, 172–5, 177
Bogliotti, Carlo   34
Boissevain, Jeremy   80
Bommel, Koen van   6
Bonilli, Stefano   24, 25
Borras, Saturnino Jr.   18 n.4
Bourdieu, Pierre   158
Bové, José   92, 96
Brillat-Savarin, Jean Anthelme   33, 88, 97
Brousse du Rove   149–51
Brundage, Dave   145
Buechler, Steven M.   4
Bukowski, Wolf   217

Caldwell, Melissa L.   211
Cante i'euve   23

Capatti, Alberto   171
Cappero Selargino   200
Cappone di Morozzo   148
Carlo Alberto di Savoia   18 n.3
Carrier, James G.   18 n.4, 189 n.8, 211
Cattani, Antonio David   200
Cavanaugh, Jillian R.   148
Cefaï, Daniel   4
Chee-Beng, Tan   157–9
Chiamparino, Sergio   194
chiocciola (snail)   173, 175, 184, 186, 188 n.4,
   189 n.9
Chrzan, Janet   6
Ciolos, Dacian   37, 194–5
circoli   22, 39 n.2
Classica cena (classic dinner)   55, 79–80, 160
Coles, Romand   125
Colombino, Annalisa   226 n.6
commensality   158
Communist Party (Italian)   22, 39 n.5, 72, 75,
   81 n.8
Community-Supported Agriculture   40 n.16
Condotta/e   2, 9, 17 n.1
   comitato (*di*)   53, 65, 77
Confédération paysanne   92, 199
conseil d'administration (Slow Food France)   83,
   88–91, 99 n.1, 128–9
consiglio di indirizzo   55–6
consiglio nazionale   53, 218
consom'acteur   40 n.16
convention (*wine*)   29, 35, 181
Convivium/convivia   2, 17 n.1, 94, 99
   Gap (convivium in)   89
Cooperativa I Tarocchi   23, 172
co-producer   34, 40 n.16, 45, 198
Corti, Michele   6, 149
Corvo, Paolo   6
Counihan, Carole   4, 17, 25, 33, 46, 119, 158, 160,
   168 n.1, 168 n.2, 188 n.8
Craig, Geoffrey   5, 199
Crozier, Michel   107–8
cultural intimacy   50, 160, 172

D'Alema Massimo   193
Davolio, Francesca   5, 6, 34
Deléage, Estelle   6

Index

Demeulenaere, Elise   199
democratization (process)   51–4, 59, 63, 75, 77, 118–19, 164, 221
Demossier, Marion   189 n.14
Domingos, Nuno   6, 133, 136
Douglas, Mary   157–8
Du Bois, Christine M.   157
Dubuisson-Quellier, Sophie   18 n.4, 125, 189 n.8
Dupuis, E. Melanie   98, 177
Durand, Stephane   45

Eataly   214, 217–18, 226 n.3
eco-gastronomy   3, 34
Edelman, Marc   4, 10, 18 n.4, 200, 211
Ente nazionale d'Assistenza Lavoratori   38 n.1
etichette narranti (narrative labels)   168 n.4
Evans-Pritchard, Edward Evan   107

fair trade   93, 126
Farinetti, Oscar   214, 217–18, 226 n.5
farmer's markets   32, 90, 150
Fassin, Didier   200
Ferguson, James   140 n.3
fiduciario/i   9, 26, 30, 44, 46
Fiore Sardo   138, 143, 146, 151–3, 167
Firth, Raymond   76
Fitting, Elisabeth   18 n.4, 154
flexian   37
Fo, Dario   39 n.7
foie gras   97–8
Fontefrancesco, Michele F.   6
food communities   32, 97, 164, 167, 193, 195, 197–200, 203, 207–8, 222
food project   4, 115
food sovereignty   73, 93, 202, 211
Foucault, Michel   64, 93, 148
Frattini, Franco   195, 209 n.4
Friedberg, Erhard   107–8
Friedmann, Harriet   6, 133

Gambero Rosso   24, 181–5
Garcia-Parpet, Marie-France   189 n.14
Garsten, Christina   47, 66–7
Gaytan, Marie Sarita   6
Geertz, Clifford   26
Genetically Modified Organism (GMO)   3, 109, 129, 145, 194, 217
Gho, Paola   215
gioco del piacere   80, 160–1
goliardata. See goliardia
goliardia   23, 27, 39 n.4
goliardico. See goliardia
good, clean, and fair   3, 16, 192, 200, 203, 216–18
   and cheese regulation   146, 151, 154

in France   92–3, 99
and gastronomic biodiversity   125–7, 133
and presidia   146
and restaurants   180
and taste   164, 167
and wine   182, 184
Goodman, David   98, 177
Gottlieb, Robert   126
governatori   27, 29, 53, 62, 77
   consiglio (dei)   53, 62, 67–9, 77, 185, 218
Graeber, David   4, 10, 132
grande tavola   53
Grasseni, Cristina   149
Green, Amanda   6
Greenpeace   124
Grimes, Kimberly M.   126
Gross, Joan E.   111, 125
Guccini, Francesco   39 n.7
Gudeman, Stephen   15, 203, 209 n.11
Gupta, Akhil   140 n.3
Guthman, Julie   18 n.4, 125

Hamer, Bent   10
Hann, Chris   209 n.11
Harper, Krista   4, 132
Hart, Keith   200, 209 n.8
Haute Qualité Alimentaire (HQA)   92–3
Hazard Analysis Control Critical Point (HACCP)   145, 154 n.1
Heller, Chaia   18 n.4, 92, 96, 199
Hennion, Antoine   163
Hermitte, Marie-Angèle   140 n.2
Herzfeld, Michael   107, 160, 172
Højlund, Susanne   17, 158, 168 n.1, 168 n.2
Holt-Giménez, Eric   18 n.4
Hsu, Eric L.   6

Illich, Ivan   33
intimacy (cultural). *See* cultural intimacy

Joshi, Anupama   126
Jung, Yuson   211
Juris, Jeffrey S.   4, 18

Karpik, Lucien   132
Kay, Cristobal   18 n.4
Khasnabish, Alex   4
Kilani, Mondher   18 n.6
Kitchen Stories   10
Kjaerulff, Jens   112
Klein, Jakob A.   211
Koensler, Alexander   4, 56 n.2
Kopytoff, Igor   132
Korsmeyer, Carolyn   157–8
Kummer, Corby   5

Index

laboratori del gusto   77, 81 n.5, 125, 140, 147, 163–5, 181, 202–5
La Campanara   173–4, 176–7
Lagorio, Gina   39 n.7
Lamine, Claire   40 n.16, 56 n.2, 199
lardo di Colonnata   5, 125, 139
Latouche, Serge   33, 96
Lavazza   204, 216, 217
La Via Campesina   4, 199
Laville, Jean Louis   200
Lawrence-Zúñiga, Denise   64, 140 n.3
Lefebvre, Henri   140 n.3
legality   14, 200
Legambiente   21, 39 n.7
Lega Nord (Northern League)   10–11, 43, 194
Leitch, Alison   5, 34, 133
Levi-Strauss, Claude   34
Libera e Benemerita Associazione degli Amici del Barolo   22, 168 n.3, 171
Lien, Marianne E.   154
Lingotto Fiere   30, 195, 202–3, 226 n.3
Littaye, Alexandra   6
London, Jack   11
Lotti, Ariane   6, 147
Low, Setha M.   64, 140 n.3
Luetchford, Peter   4, 18 n.4, 25, 126, 132, 189 n.8, 211
Lyon, Sarah   126

Maccagno cheese   166
McDonald   24, 32, 36, 92
mafia (and food)   200
Mahmud, Lilith   10
McNair, Amber   6, 133
Manifesto   39 n.8, 147, 182
   dei Vignerons d'Europa   181, 187–8
   dell'Arca   123–4
   dello Slow Food   24–5, 30, 34, 39 n.6, 85, 90, 159, 182, 189 n.14
   in difesa del formaggio a latte crudo   144
   Il Manifesto (newspaper)   24, 39 n.7
Marchenay, Philippe   132
Marinetti, Filippo Tommaso   25
Marrone, Gianfranco   39 n.6
Martinez Alvarez, Bibiana   211
Master of Food   62, 71, 81 n.5, 119, 162, 165, 205, 214, 219
Mattioli, Fabio   133
Meduni, Enrico   39 n.7
Meneley, Anne   6, 132
Mercati della Terra   71
methanol wine scandal   24, 181
Miele, Mara   5, 188 n.7
Migliorini, Paola   6
Milano Expo   226 n.5

Milano golosa   29, 40 n.14
Mintz, Sidney W.   132, 157, 158, 168 n.2
Moberg, Mark   126
Molé, Noelle J.   119, 120 n.2
Mollona, Massimiliano   112
Monchiero, Alessandro   34, 106, 130, 159, 171
Montanari, Massimo   33
moral economy   93, 166–7, 199–201, 206, 209 n.7, 211–12
Morin, Edgar   33, 96
Movimento Sociale Italiano   209 n.4
Müller, Birgit   154
Munro, William   18 n.4
Murdoch, Jonathan   5, 188 n.7
Myers, Justin Sean   6

Napolitano, Giorgio   193
Narotzky, Susana   4, 127, 199
Nash, June   4, 224–5
NGO   1, 46
Nonini, Donald M.   211
Nyqvist, Anette   47, 66–7

Obama, Barak   36
Okely, Judith   12
Opera Nazionale Dopolavoro   38 n.1
Orsini, Alessandro   22
Orti in Condotta   71
osteria/e   120 n.1, 159–60, 171–80

Padovani, Gigi   26
Palomera, Jaime   93, 209 n.7, 211
Palumbo, Berardino   18 n.6
Papa, Cristina   131, 132, 146
Papa Francesco (Pope Francis)   36–7, 167, 226
Parasecoli, Fabio   6
Parkins, Wendy   5, 199
Parlato, Valentino   39 n.7
Parmigiano Reggiano   149, 204, 216, 217
Parry, Jonathan   212
Partito della rifondazione comunista   193
Partito democratico di sinistra (Democratic Left Party)   193–4
Partito di unità proletaria (PDUP)   36
Patel, Raj   18 n.4
Paxson, Heather   6, 132, 134, 144, 168 n.2
Peace, Adrian   6, 194–5, 199
Però, Davide   129
Perullo, Nicola   6
Petrini, Carlo   35–8, 102
Pianetto (Galeata)   173
piccola tavola   53, 62, 64, 172
Pietrykowski, Bruce   6
Piron, Florence   121 n.6
Pitzalis, Marco   211

239

Index

Pollenzo   2, 17 n.2, 18 n.3, 33, 37, 59, 189 n.15, 226
Pompia   134, 136–8
Popolo della libertà   209 n.4
Porta, Antonio   39 n.7
Portinari, Folco   24–5, 159, 189 n.14
Pratt, Jeff   4, 6, 25, 132
Premio della biodiversità   125, 127, 130
Prince Charles   36, 37, 193
Protected Designation of Origin (PDO)   130, 134–6, 140 n.2, 146, 149–53

Quarta, Alessandra   211

Rabhi, Pierre   36, 96
Rakopoulos, Theodoros   76–7, 93, 211
Realacci, Ermete   39 n.7
Réseau semences paysannes   199
Resistenza casearia (Cheese Resistance)   143, 153
riflusso   22, 39 n.3
Rossi, Amalia   4, 56 n.2
Ruffa, Giovanni   34, 106, 130, 159, 171, 215

San Marco dei Cavoti   173, 188 n.5
Sardo, Stefano   39 n.9
Sassatelli, Roberta   5, 6, 34
Sassi, Gianni   39 n.7
Scaffidi, Cinzia   35
Schlosberg, David   125
Schneider, Stephen   6
Schurman, Rachel   18 n.5
Scott, James C.   200
segreteria nazionale   44, 55, 62, 64–78, 119, 162, 182–5, 213–19
sentinelle   129
Serpa Velho cheese   133, 136
Shiva, Vandana   36, 119–20, 121 n.6, 193
Shore, Cris   63–4, 67, 129
sinistra extraparlamentare   40 n.18
Slow Food Story [film]   39 n.9
Slow Wine   185
Snow, Alan   101–2
Sorrentino, Paolo   54
Spanò, Michele   211
Spicer, Andre   6

Staino, Sergio   39 n.7
Storico Ribelle. See Bitto
Sutton, David   158, 172

taste intimacy   167
Teil, Geneviève   163
Terra Madre   2, 26, 33, 39 n.10, 46, 57 n.4, 67, 71, 77, 97, 120, 123, 129, 191–209
   Terra Madre Day   71, 90–1
   Terra Madre Foundation   106
Terrio, Susan   132, 168 n.2
terroir (*produits de*)   131–2
Thivet, Delphine   18 n.4, 199, 211
Thompson, Edward P.   200
Tomasi di Lampedusa, Giuseppe   81 n.3
Tonelli, Anna   39 n.5
Tsing, Anna L.   132, 154, 155 n.9

Ulin, Robert C.   132, 189 n.14
U Magazzeo   173–4, 177, 188 n.5

Vacca Bianca Modenese   149
Vanoni, Ornella   27
Ventura, Angelo   22
Vetta, Theodora   93, 209 n.7, 211
Vignerons d'Europa   181, 183–4, 187
Vinitaly   181
volunteerism   76–7, 80, 112, 187

Waldren, Jacqueline   132
Wallerstein, Immanuel   222
Wallman, Sandra   103
Waters, Alice   119
Weber, Max   107
Wedel, Janine R.   37
Weiss, Brad   132
West, Harry G.   6, 133, 136
Wilk, Richard R.   4, 10, 15, 132
wine convention. See convention (*wine*)
Wolf, Eric   15, 108
Wright, Susan   63–4, 67, 129
WWF   67, 220

Zafferano di San Gavino   148–50
Zerilli, Filippo M.   148, 211